Richard Bosworth is Professor of History at the University of Western Australia. By background a WASP from Sydney's North Shore, he has previously published mainly in modern Italian history – for example, *Italy, the Least of the Great Powers* (1979), *Italy and the Approach of the First World War* (1983), with G. Cresciani (eds) *Altro polo: a volume of Italian studies* (1979) and with G. Rizzo (eds) *Altro polo: intellectuals and their ideas in contemporary Italy* (1983). Bosworth was Deputy Director of the F. May Foundation for Italian Studies (1978-86) and has not quite forgotten how to turn a ball down to fine leg.

Janis Wilton is currently Lecturer in Social Science at Armidale College of Advanced Education. Nurtured on a middle-class Australian education (at Fort Street and the University of Sydney) she has taught history at tertiary level and has spent time travelling. For the past eight years she worked in the area of Australian immigration with an emphasis on researching and recording the histories and experiences of Australians from non-English-speaking backgrounds. She was Consultant (1981-3) to the Oral Histories Project of the Ethnic Affairs Commission of NSW, and is General Editor of the *Oral History Association of Australia Journal*. She has edited *Internment: The Diaries of Harry Seidler* (1986). She cannot swim.

Old Worlds and New Australia

The post-war migrant experience

Janis Wilton and Richard Bosworth

Penguin Books

Penguin Books Australia Ltd,
487 Maroondah Highway, P.O. Box 257
Ringwood, Victoria, 3134, Australia
Penguin Books Ltd,
Harmondsworth, Middlesex, England
Penguin Books,
40 West 23rd Street, New York, N.Y. 10010, U.S.A.
Penguin Books Canada Limited,
2801 John Street, Markham, Ontario, Canada
Penguin Books (N.Z.) Ltd,
182-190 Wairau Road, Auckland 10, New Zealand

First published by Penguin Books Australia, 1984
Reprinted 1985, 1987
Copyright © Janis Wilton and Richard Bosworth, 1984

Typeset in Times and Italia by Dudley E. King
Melbourne Australia

Made and printed in Australia by
The Book Printer, Maryborough, Victoria

CIP

Wilton, Janis, 1951–.
Old worlds and new Australia.

Includes index.
ISBN 0 14 007017 6.

1. Europeans—Australia—Attitudes.
I. Bosworth, R. J. B. (Richard J. B.), 1943–. II. Title.

305.8'034'094

Acknowledgements

Many people have assisted in the production of this book; none of them can be held responsible for the way in which we have used their advice or adapted and interpreted their experiences. In particular, we wish to thank Lyle Allan, Michal Bosworth, Gianfranco Cresciani, Joe Eisenberg, Maurie Isaacs, Allan Martin, Ros Pesman, Geoffrey Sherington, Carla Taines, Graham White and Richard White for reading the manuscript. We also wish to thank the many people who remain unnamed but who, over the past six years, have willingly shared with us their experiences of coming to and settling in Australia. They did so in good faith and we trust that they are not disappointed in our use of their oral memoirs. The interpretations placed on these memoirs are, of course, our own.

For permission to use photographs and illustrations we thank:
p.4 Mrs E. Dedes
p.28 and p.148 the Department of Immigration and Ethnic Affairs
p.53 Mr J. Masszauer
p.70 The Gianoli family
p.84 Mr G. Galassi
p.101 Santina Rizzo and family
p.115 Mr A. Justin
p.119 Mrs E. van der Zwaag
p.159 Mr K. Entsief and the Macedonian Cultural and Educational Society for Australia
p.177 Mr Philip Luker

To the Unknown Migrant

Chapter ONE

The New Immigration Programme: attitudes and policy

In May 1945 Arthur Calwell used a homely metaphor to explain the importance of his soon to be approved new role as Australia's first minister of immigration: 'I wonder how many of us have ever thought how much we Australians are like the koalas. We both belong to dying races and both are well on the way to becoming museum pieces, along with the extinct moa and the great auk.'[1] Calwell's statement came as Australia, slowly and a little haphazardly, began to contemplate the previously unthinkable. In 1945, an insular nation of 7 million knew that it was 'very largely British. In blood, ... Australians boasted that they were the most British of all' and understood that 'such qualities as Australians have are ... only drawn from the British race'.[2] But a new immigration policy could not confine itself to British stock. Instead, it would have to allow into Australia previously abhorred 'foreigners' – 'Balts', Poles, Germans, Dutch, Italians, Yugoslavs, Greeks, and Lebanese, and, eventually, even Vietnamese, Filipinos, black Africans, and other Asians and Pacific Islanders.

Now, little more than a generation after the Second World War, many rhetoricians of multicultural Australia foreswear that old provincialism and racism. They exult in the fact that about one-quarter of the present population was born abroad (though about 45 per cent of these 'foreigners' are British) and that a further 20 per cent have at least one parent born overseas. They are proud that over a hundred languages and dialects are spoken in Australia and that Macedonian can be studied for the New South Wales Higher School Certificate. They even glory in the claim that, the Israelis apart, Australians are the most diverse people in the world.[3]

How did Australia come to change its attitudes and policies on immigration? To what extent is the change real and to what extent is it merely apparent? How has multiculturalism come about and what does it mean? Some of the answers to these questions lie in the years immediately after the Second World War, when Australia decided to implement a new and aggressive immigration policy but did so without first jettisoning old attitudes and assumptions.

Before 1945, if there was one area in which Australian politics were bipartisan it was the area of racial attitudes and policy. As Manning Clark, with his usual preference for biblical phrasing, has put it, the restrictionist, anti-coloured *Immigration Act* (1901) was the first 'tablet of the law' to be cut in Australia.[4] Any sense of special identity that Australians possessed had largely sprung from a belief – and fear – that they were the 'white guard' keeping the pass against a hostile world. As the radical, anti-war, Sydney historian George Arnold Wood explained in 1917: 'White Australia is not an opinion; it is the watchword or war cry of a tiny garrison which holds the long frontier of the white world in front of the multitudinous and expansive peoples of Asia.'[5]

Yet the theoretics of Australian racism were not posited merely on a dread of the 'yellow peril' and of those 'millions of brown men, ambitious, arrogant and poor' who were only waiting the moment to over-run Australia.[6] White Australia also scarcely approved the arrival of 'Afghans' or 'Syrians' or even Greeks and Italians. Before 1945, these last two nationalities and especially the Italians were the aliens that Australian public and political opinion deemed to be the chief infringers of British Australia. In fact, neither group had come to Australia in particularly large numbers and even fewer had stayed. Only about 7000 Italians and 2000 Greeks could be located in the census of 1911. And in each case the denomination of nationality covered an enormous diversity of peoples who, in Europe, had not yet been educated into their own nationality. Fifty years of an Italian state had not led more than 20 per cent of the Italian population confidently to speak the national language. The war-like and corrupt Greek state had not yet won Macedonia and the Epirus, and many other 'Greeks' lived in various parts of the Ottoman Empire.

Neither then nor later did British Australia pay much attention to such complexity. It is characteristic that, as late as 1947, Australian historians still could not get the name of 'Carboni Raffaello', the chronicler of the Eureka stockade and the most famous pre-1914 Italian immigrant, the right way round. And Barry Humphries seems not to have known that a certain Antonio Bazza was one of the heads of family at the utopian New Italy settlement near Lismore in the 1880s.

After the First World War, the rate both of Italian and Greek immigration did increase a little. It has been estimated that by 1947 about 12 500 Greeks lived in Australia, almost three times as many as in 1921. Italians came in still greater numbers. In 1927, the peak of what was still called a 'flood'[7] in 1947 was reached with over 7800 arrivals. By 1933, almost 27 000 Italians were listed as living in Australia (20 064 of them were male).

These newcomers were rarely much welcomed. *Smith's Weekly* led a viciously racist campaign against 'that greasy flood of Mediterranean scum that seeks to defile and debase Australia'.[8] Journalistic rhetoric could be seconded by the judiciary. In Queensland, the Ferry Commission was set up to investigate the foreign settlers. In 1925 it reported, with some uneasiness in geographical knowledge, that the migrants 'appear to be from the South, many of them being Sicilians'. Sicily, rumoured to be the home of the Mafia and the Black Hand, was an especially regrettable breeding ground for migrants since, as the Commissioners noted: 'The Southern Italian is more inclined to form groups and [thus is] less likely to be assimilated into the population of the State.'[9]

While judges pontificated, the populace sometimes acted. In 1919, 1928, 1930 and 1934, riots broke out at Kalgoorlie and Innisfail over the allegedly objectionable presence of Italians. Australian workers learned that Italians should best be defined as 'the Chinese of Europe'[10] and, given Australia's reception of the Chinese, the sobriquet was all the more menacing.

Participation in a war against Nazi and Fascist racism did little to shake Australians' views of Italians. During that war, the army did not mince words in its advice to Australian farmers about to receive the labour of Italian prisoners of war:

The Italian prisoner of war is a curious mixture, in that he can be made to give of excellent work if certain points are observed. 1. He cannot be driven, but he can be led. 2. Mentality is child-like; it is possible to gain his confidence by fairness and firmness. 3. Great care must be exercised from a disciplinary point of view for he can become sly and objectionable if badly handled.[11]

Nor did colour or geography map out distinct borders for Australian racism. Through many Australian minds ran a strand of anti-Semitism woven into the assumption that Jews would 'stick together', were 'not short of a quid' and were likely to be 'ikey moes'. The persecution launched against Jews by Nazism or by Polish nationalism only enhanced Australian fears. British Jews were bad enough; alien ones would be worse. On the eve of the Second World War, Sir Frank Clarke, the president of the Victorian Legislative Council, even stated that the refugees whom he saw in the streets of Melbourne were 'rat-faced men under 5 feet in height, and with a chest development of about 20 inches'.[12] Racism rarely was expressed so crudely or overtly, but perhaps most Australians knew what the young soldier Henry Gullett allegedly knew: 'Foreigners were confusing and we could see that for ourselves from our history books. Allies one day and enemies the next. Best not to become involved with them.'[13]

Behind these and similar ideas still lay the profound and even hegemonic influence exercised on Australia and on the wider world by

c.1920: White Rose Cafe, Uralla. One of the many country cafes established by Greeks in Australia before the Second World War.

nineteenth century racial theoretics as expressed by Arthur de Gobineau and his many successors. Most Australians were educated to believe that all non-Nordic or non-Aryan peoples were in some sense conditioned by an influx of inferior, probably coloured, blood. They could be crafty and sinister; they could be puerile and lazy; they were not and could never be genuine kith and kin.

Between the wars Australia had one special expert on 'race': Johannes Lyng whose *Non-Britishers in Australia* was published in 1927. Lyng was the Harbison-Higinbotham Scholar at the University of Melbourne, and his professor, Ernest Scott, wrote the foreword to his book. That same year, Scott had instituted the first tertiary courses in Australian history.

Lyng's book was a curious mixture of detail and bias. Using statistics from the 1891 census, Lyng was able to establish to his own satisfaction that 'racial characteristics are passed on from generation to generation', and that the Australian population was 98 per cent white, 1.3 per cent black, 0.45 per cent yellow, and 0.25 per cent brown. Of white racial stock, Lyng alleged 82 per cent belonged to the category of 'Nordics', 13 per cent were 'Mediterraneans' and 5 per cent 'Alpines'.

It was the 'Mediterranean' element that caused whites the most problems.

The Mediterranean temperament is emotional. Mediterraneans are passionate and excitable; loving and hating intensely. They are inclined to lack stability and tenacity and neither in politics nor in war do they possess a high sense of discipline. For this reason they have difficulty in holding their own, both against Nordics and Alpines. Strong magnetic leaders can do great things for them, but the personal element is necessary. They have a keen sense of beauty, form, colour and the joy of life, and particularly in the past have produced many remarkably clever men, but prone to be superficial.

In Australia, the Mediterranean peril exposed itself most blatantly in Queensland; no doubt because of its sizeable Italian immigration, its Nordic racial level was 4 per cent below the national average.

Lyng himself disapproved of too narrow an identification of race and nation and even tried to distinguish one Italian from another. Northerners, he said, could be readily enough assimilated; the problem lay with those Mediterraneans from the south. Unfortunately, he averred, few Australians possessed his knowledge or attention to detail: 'To them an Italian is an Italian – difficult to absorb and more likely than not to lower the social standard.'[14]

Lyng's ideas might be dismissed with derision as yet another example of belated imitation of that common tyranny of distance in Australian intellectual life. Yet what he said in 1927 was still almost universally believed in the Australia that, at the end of the Second World War, contemplated a difficult future. 'Inferior blood' could corrupt. Italians, for example, 'had the virtue of comparative docility and the ability to work in the hottest of weather', but their Mediterranean blood meant they were 'less reliable and less clean in their habits, more volatile and even having a strong tendency to form or join secret societies'.[15] Jews were deemed to possess similar deficiencies. Among the most vociferous opponents of the infiltration of Jewish immigrants was ex-Geelong Grammarian, ex-Oxonian, ex-Sorbonne pupil, newly elected Liberal member of the House of Representatives and now back from the war, Henry 'Jo' Gullett. In his view, not only had 'too many of this race, who had come to Australia before the war and since ... exploited labour, cornered the housing and avoided income tax' but they were also 'European neither by race, standard nor culture ... they are in fact an Eastern people.'[16] Italians and Jews, like other non-Aryans, could never be genuine members of the Australian family. As David Hunter, a New South Wales Liberal politician, explained in 1948:

Our policy should be to favour first, those of British stock and, secondly, those of Nordic stock – who are akin to us in outlook and background, and whose mainspring lies in a common fatherhood [sic] of centuries ago. Only in that way can we hope to preserve in Australia the principles and ideals which have made the British Empire such a great influence and force for good in the world, ... the only bulwark that can stand against those extremes in political life that would throw the world into a melting pot from which would emerge a totalitarianism such as we have not known since the days of Julius Caesar.[17]

In the best of all possible worlds, Italians, Jews and their kind should be excluded from this fair and British land. But, by 1948, Hunter and the many Australians who shared his sentiments or prejudices were beginning to sound like voices crying in the wilderness. It seemed that Australia might no longer reside in the best of all possible worlds. The implications of this change troubled Australian planners as they studied the requirements and implications of a new immigration policy.

In 1952, R. M. Crawford, who was at the time perhaps the most innovative historian in this country, declared: 'the history of Australia is a chapter in the history of migration'.[18] Few as yet understood the real implications of his statement, but Australian governments had for some time been trying to craft an ideal migration scheme. In 1926, Prime Minister S. M. Bruce had established the Commonwealth Development and Migration Commission. Its sometime chairman, Sir Herbert Gepp, a prominent businessman and eventual sponsor of the neo-conservative Institute of Public Affairs, knew, even in the midst of the Depression, that immigration was a necessary part of a process that had advanced and would advance Australia fair (and white and British). Through migration, 'a hardy young nation now flourishes on a part of the earth which not so long ago was the home of wandering aborigines'.[19] Prime Minister Lyons took up the argument and, in 1939, warned of 'a huge black cloud hiding what otherwise might be blue Australian skies'. Australia was under-populated and might not survive the approaching storm of war unless 'more shoulders' could be found 'to bear' the burden and thus pay off the 'gigantic bill for defence and development'.[20]

The experience of war and the nearness of a threat to Australia's own soil mightily reinforced the belief that Australia must expand its migration intake. As one Labor senator put it, 'but for the fact that we received help from outside, our population of 7 000 000 would ... have been swept off the face of the earth [during the war]. The lesson to be learnt from this fact is that we must increase our population as quickly as possible'.[21] Similarly bolstered by the experience of war was the idea that government should and could plan the new programme. Immigration became an essential element in reconstruction.

On 22 December 1942, Ben Chifley had been appointed minister for post-war reconstruction. Following a model established in Britain, where the Beveridge Committee had begun work some months before (it would report in February 1943), Chifley began to call on bureaucrats and experts to design a future Australia that would be fit for heroes. In late 1943 an inter-departmental committee was established to investigate and report specifically on immigration. It endorsed the need for a vigorous policy and emphasised that the vigour should be directed primarily at recruiting 'white British subjects' and, failing that, 'white aliens'. The finer details, about how many immigrants and from which countries they might come other than Britain, were left aside for the moment. Consensus might be hard to win on such questions. But it was agreed that something must be done about Australia's falling birth-rate. 'Our first task', said Arthur Calwell at this time, 'is to ennoble motherhood'. Australia must either 'populate the country or sooner or later be overrun by Asiatic peoples'.[22]

With little reference to the old debate about the carrying capacity of the Australian environment, politicians and their advisers began blithely to toss off the ideal figure – 25 million, 40 million, 50 million – that would ensure safety. Experts in demography consulted their charts and tables. At its present rate, they decided, the population would 'grow slowly to 8 250 000 at which stage ... the birth-line and death-line will meet.'[23] Australians alone, it seemed, could not procreate in a way that would fill up all those empty spaces.

In 1945, a curious novel entitled *Heed McGlarity* expressed some of the racial fears occasioned by this sad news. The author, a Hungarian migrant, Stephen Kelen, was introduced as a '"Dinkum Aussie" ... He can swear elegantly in about nine languages, and read and write in five or six.' The book tells of the various inhabitants of Ocean View, a guest house in Sydney. These include a Miss Eagleton, who rises to true virtue when she rejects a present of a diamond wristwatch from her United States army suitor and decides to settle down in Australia and breed. Miss Eagleton and the other characters are able to reform themselves because they follow the advice of the worthy professor, McGlarity, who also resides at Ocean View. McGlarity becomes the vehicle for much preaching about migration.

McGlarity is quite clear that Australia must populate or perish, no matter who has won the war. Currently, there is a disgraceful fall-off in the fertility of Australian women: 'While we're decreasing, the teeming masses of Asia, the coloured world, gains numbers.' In these circumstances we 'should greet every mother as a saviour of the nation'. Since mothers are still reluctant, however, Australia must turn to migration. Here, indeed, is the answer to all Australia's problems. Jews or Italians might seem to provide 'bad blood', but they could be 'controlled, harnessed and used like steam'. The Australian climate would inevitably help many to assimilate (and Australians themselves could assist the process by abandoning unnatural practices such as the eating of hot plum pudding at Christmas). But, for the Darwinian struggle in which Australia was involved, any new blood, be it that of the 'Chinese' of Asia or Europe, was good. It was up to Australia, McGlarity argued, to make the blood pump for Australia's benefit:

From the newcomers we require complete assimilation, their fecundity. The family from Southern Europe, which comes to Australia, under better conditions increases in number; but the children, or the second generation, adopt the customs of this country to such an extent that their reproductive capacity, or rather their willingness to have children, will be very much the same as that of native Australians ... all the same, in reproductive capacity they are going to have a good influence. Greater fecundity is needed. Therefore European races which still carry this capacity should be welcomed in every way. An unproductive body can be corrected with a serum. It is the same with nations. A reasonable influx of 'alien blood' might help us to regain our fertility, which is just as important as winning the war.[24]

Australian planners were less clinical in their prose than was Kelen, but all agreed that in a threatening world, Australia must populate or perish. The first motive behind the new immigration policy was thus that of defence.

Some have detected other motives. James Jupp, whose *Arrivals and Departures* (1966) was the earliest important analytical account of the new immigration policy, remarked that, rather than being engendered by defence requirements, the policy was little more than a 'coldly calculated drive ... to draft workers into Australia'.[25] Some Australian Marxists have underlined this aspect still more forcibly. They have argued that immigration is necessarily an exploitative process 'within the framework of world capitalism'. It both penalises poor and backward economies, in favour of rich and advanced ones, and divides and confuses the working classes, who start defining their interests in terms of ethnicity rather than of class.[26]

Unlike the western European model on which many Marxist analyses are based,[27] Australian policy emphasised a migration of settlement and generally spurned the notion of guest workers who could be thrown out once their usefulness was spent. Australia wanted to populate and develop. Australian policy makers, for the most part, also distrusted that variety of migrant which, because of its 'pre-political character', was welcomed in western Europe. The demographer W. D. Borrie warned in 1948 that arrivals would 'not be coming to an agricultural economy'. Therefore, he added simplistically, migrants from rural areas would not be wanted in an industrialising Australia: 'The peasant of Italy, Yugoslavia and other areas of south-east Europe, where rural population is likely to become redundant to home requirements as industrialisation proceeds, is not the person who can be absorbed in large numbers in Australia.'[28]

Indeed, even as Australia commenced its very partial industrialisation programme, the rhetoric of ruralism blossomed and flourished. In 1958, Russel Ward enunciated his Australian legend in which the bush became that place where the Australian working class preserved its innocence (and established its nationality) in a complex and corrupting world. Capitalist manufacturing industry was one snare in this world, and, for many romantic leftists, immigration was the great delusion.

In these circumstances, it is not surprising that many commentators, only partially weaned from their racist past, began to urge that the best way to turn new chums into Australians was to give them a sort of physical and intellectual sheep dip by requiring them to work for a time in the outback. Oddly, given socialism's internationalist pretensions, but predictably, given Australia's history, it was often the Australian Labor Party (ALP) that was the special home of this ruralist enthusiasm. In 1953, the New South Wales branch of the ALP formally moved that migrants be distributed across the country 'so that instead of a great influx to the eastern cities which strains the economy of the country, there will be a return to the country and Australia will again take her role as one of the greatest primary producing countries in the world'.[29] Calwell, too, had asserted during the war 'the continuing prosperity of the countryside is the only foundation upon which the prosperity of Australia can rest'. Even at the end of the war, he still pursued what he called artisans as the migrants most adaptable to the national scene. Among the experts, Borrie worried lest potential migrants were being given too urban an image of Australia by government officials. 'If they are introduced through films to Sydney and Melbourne', he asked, 'will they accept kindly a railway camp on the Nullarbor plains as their place of employment?'[30]

Even the *Sydney Morning Herald,* not normally averse to preaching the values and defending the interests of Australian manufacturing, editorialised its approval of primary producers getting first choice of any migrants. For, it proclaimed in 1952, 'since the post-war launching of the large-scale immigration scheme, far too high a proportion of New Australians have found their way into secondary industries'.[31]

In stressing the prime role of economic planning in creating the new immigration policy, some Australian commentators have asserted that immigration became the special plaything of Australian business (or of multinationals pressing their charms on a reluctant Australia). Yet by no stretch of the imagination did Australia possess a military-industrial complex in 1945. Racism, or the nebulous fear and comfort of isolation that lay behind it, kept Australia as homogeneous as it was until the Second World War. An adapted racism, built on what seemed ever more certain fears, defined and created the new immigration policy. If manufacturing industry was to expand, the first purpose of the process of industrialisation was to ensure that Australia remain Australian. Certainly then, and perhaps now, immigration was directed to the same end.

Another factor in the new immigration policy given some emphasis in the immediate post-war years was the humanitarian one. As David Hunter explained: 'Out of sheer decency we must give sanctuary to those who, in a topsy-turvy world have been turned out by their own nations; whose return would only end in political turmoil and economic chaos.'[32] And in 1961 the governor-general, Viscount Dunrossil, reminded the Twelfth Citizenship Convention that Australia's skill in recruiting and accepting immigrants was largely due to the generosity of Australians themselves who 'have been so long in the sun that its warmth and light have penetrated to their hearts with a pervasive sense of freedom and justice and the absence of prejudice and man-made barriers'.[33] Policy makers have also expressed a firm belief in the generosity and success of the immigration programme. As Calwell would maintain: 'no other country has done so much for its migrants in the post-war world as Australia has done'.[34]

Such naïve or self-congratulatory comments cannot be accepted at face value. Much of the little idealism or ideology that existed in the new immigration programme was imported from abroad. In the interwar period, even the best-disposed foreign analysts had occasionally grown irritated by Australian reluctance to seek out immigrants, and local commentators were driven to defensive explanations that Australians were the same as Britons but with some of their inhibitions 'melted by the sun'. Australian workers were not 'naturally hostile' to British migrants, although they might well be to Italian or Yugoslav ones.[35]

After the Second World War, many Australians were afraid that the foreign criticism of Australian racism would recur and would in turn unleash pressure from more insistent and more hostile and intransigent forces than those that had occasionally expressed themselves in London. Without rapid population increase, said Chifley, 'we will not be able to justify before the world our retention of such a great country'.[36]

After 1945, therefore, Australia was faced with a basic and agonising dilemma. A major increase in numbers was deemed a necessity. But that expansion could not come only from Britain. Calwell's most notorious comment while minister was probably his aphorism of 1947: 'Two wongs don't make a white'.[37] But, within Australia's racist traditions, for many Australians 'wongdom' began not in Asia but at Calais. In this regard, Australian immigration policy since 1945 is easy to recount: it is no more than a gradual, reluctant and partial contraction in the Australian mind of those once almost limitless borders of 'wongdom'.

The pain of such contraction was at first averted by frequent statements that no contraction was occurring, or that any perceived contraction was so small as to be insignificant. Calwell, plucking figures from the air, decided that 'every foreign migrant' would be out-matched by ten from Britain.[38] Another early expert explained 'We do not want anybody who looks, speaks or thinks very differently from ourselves. In fact ... we want people who are almost if not quite indistinguishable from ourselves or will rapidly become so'.[39]

If politicians and their advisers did their best to insist that nothing much was changing, the self-proclaimed knights-errant of Australian traditions were soon in the lists to defend a white and British Australia. Rumours that Egyptians or Italians could be let in were assailed by statements that such admission would be 'in defiance of the White Australia Policy'.[40] The thought of central European refugees was not much more pleasant to one spokesman of the Returned Servicemen's League: 'every Australian should hold his breath ... with indignation [and] fear of what Australia will eventually become ... it makes one wonder just to whom Mr Calwell feels he owes his loyalty – to the mother country or to foreigners of every other race'.[41]

Calwell and his aides thus trod carefully along the path to a new immigration policy. Formally appointed minister for immigration in July 1945, Calwell soon announced the formation of an Immigration Advisory Committee. To be chaired by ALP man Les Haylen, the committee included representatives of business, trade union and RSL interests. At its very inception, immigration was to be a bipartisan matter.

On 27 February 1946, the Committee reported its findings. As fishers of men, the members had gone first to London. But they found there problems as well as opportunities: 'The British Government and the press are wholly in accord with the principle of migration within the Empire, despite an expressed anxiety that key personnel might desire to go to Australia in such numbers as to be inimical to Britain's own policy of reconstruction.' A deferential acceptance of the reasonableness of these anxieties, or perhaps the unavailability of shipping, induced the Committee to turn to Europe. 'As the migration plan expands', it suggested, 'branch offices should be established in Switzerland, Holland, Norway and Denmark.' At least in one of those countries, a great prospect could await Australia:

There are thousands of first-rate migrants in Switzerland ready to come to Australia. They are intelligent, polite, keen and in the main, well-educated. They include doctors of medicine, university students, commercial men, mechanics, builders, dairy experts, farmers, technicians and at least one expert in boring for artesian water.

The image of a clean-cut, German-speaking mountaineer, Nestlés chocolate in back pocket, tapping away in search of water somewhere in the Australian interior, may have been pleasing but, in the event, fewer than 2000 Swiss would come to Australia in the first decade of the new immigration scheme. And many of them were Italian speakers from the Ticino. Nor did Norwegians or Danes make up a major part of Australia's migrant intake by 1956. Instead, Australia had been driven to cast its net in parts of Europe that its officials preferred not to mention in 1946.

Although they did not ponder what might happen to Australia if the Great British Wall be breached, the Committee members did contemplate the preparation of Australian public opinion for new knowledge about a difficult world. Haylen and his colleagues urged the commencement of a 'conditioning campaign amongst the Australian people'. Australians should learn of the 'necessity of migrants' and thus be 'in a mood to receive them as future Australians'.[42]

While he digested this advice, Calwell moved forward with circumspection. Early in 1946 he had agreed to provide entry permits for 2000 Jewish refugees as a 'mercy gesture', but their arrival provoked what was deemed a hostile public reaction – traditional anti-Semitism mixed readily with the popular cry that these aliens were taking shipping berths that should be used to bring our boys home. Calwell quickly withdrew his offer and, as well, imposed a 25 per cent quota on the number of Jews allowed on any ship coming to Australia.

In May 1947, Australia signed the Empire and Allied Ex-Servicemen's Agreement. Initially designed to attract United States, British Empire and some allied ex-servicemen not covered by an earlier treaty with the United Kingdom, the scheme was extended to include ex-servicemen from western European nations. A problem then arose over whether Australia could accept those emigrant Poles who had fought alongside and within the British Army and who, after the war, for political or economic reasons, did not want to return to a communist Poland. On the unofficial hierarchy of races, Poles, as eastern Europeans, occupied a lower place than did the British, Dutch, Belgians, French or Scandinavians already admitted under the scheme, and, indeed, below the ex-enemy Germans. But arguments were rapidly found to favour the blue-eyed, fair-haired, anti-communist, and socially upper-class Poles. Some of their forces had been engaged with the Australians in the heroic defence of Tobruk. Moreover, it was alleged that their experiences in England had accustomed them to the 'British way of life'. This, in turn, meant that 'they would make excellent Australian citizens, especially those who, after their escape from Poland, married English and Scottish lasses'. Calwell agreed, and he contended later that, 'a foreigner married to a British woman is probably halfway towards assimilation into the Australian community by virtue of his marriage'.[43]

Meanwhile, Calwell followed the Haylen Committee to Britain, the United States and Europe. There, as the political weather threatened Cold War, he called at the International Refugee Organisation's headquarters in Geneva and visited a displaced persons camp. The reason for this internationalism was simple. Before Calwell's renowned insistence that Britain provide both ships and immigrants, the British had stone-walled. Aliens, it seemed, were the only people available to become new Australians.

Before his own public opinion, Calwell was somewhat embarrassed by the open nature of this shift in racial preference. But, he said, the camps contained a 'choice sample'. As he would later explain in his memoirs:

When [the first displaced persons, mainly from the Baltic States . . .] arrived in Melbourne, I addressed them. Many of these new people spoke some English . . . There had been some doubt about the quality of these displaced persons who had the blood of a number of races in their veins. Many were red-headed and blue-eyed. There was also a number of platinum blondes of both sexes. The men were handsome and the women beautiful. It was not hard to sell immigration to the Australian people once the press published photographs of that group.[44]

And so they began to come, these so-called aliens. Between 1947 and 1951, over 460 000 immigrants reached Australia, more than 55 per cent of them from non-English-speaking backgrounds. No longer could white Australians boast that they were more British than the British.

Before this assault, the racial definitions of Australia trembled (though they did not yet fall). New justifications were sought to explain the acceptability of one 'sample' or another. Sometimes migrants were laudably anti-communist. Henry Strakosch, an Austrian Jewish convert to Catholicism, who had been forced to flee his country after the *Anschluss* and who, in Sydney, became a teacher of history, agreed with Stephen Kelen that the first purpose of immigration was to repel the yellow peril. But, he added, Australia had a duty to accept central and eastern Europeans in order to check Russia: 'To leave these potential soldiers of democracy to their fate would be an unpardonable sin on the part of the democracies.'[45]

Sometimes migrants from Europe were almost British. Zara Holt, wife of the Liberal who replaced Calwell as minister for immigration in 1949, knew that the Dutch (whether from Holland or the East Indies) were really very nice. In her memoirs, she recalls the occasion on which she was able to confide her appreciation to Queen Juliana.

Well, naturally, the Queen and Harry [Holt] sat at one side of the room and talked very seriously to each other about immigration and emigration, and the Queen was pouring the coffee, and it was all very friendly and easy together ...

Well, towards the end of the time we were with the Queen she was very polite and kind and suggested I came and sat and talked to her for a little while. I was delighted to do this because she is an interesting and charming woman. And she said to me: 'Tell me, Mrs Holt, have you met any of the Dutch migrants who have come to Australia.' And I said: 'Yes Ma'am, I have. Just before we left we had a Dutchman paint our house.' She looked very pleased at this and said: 'Oh, he must have done a wonderful job. I'm sure you were satisfied, because Dutch tradesmen are very painstaking and good.' And I said: 'Yes, he did do a wonderful job and we were very satisfied, but I was surprised because he was not really a house painter, he's a scientist.[46]

Sometimes historical accident made one lot of migrants attractive. Maltese had often before been defined as 'coloured' by Australians who believed that islanders from so far south must have an excessive Mediterranean content in their blood. In the 1930s the *Sydney Morning Herald* decreed that Maltese were 'the most troublesome class of immigrants that have come to Australia'. But in presenting his case for Australian acceptance of Maltese immigrants, an English official argued that Maltese who had experience in London 'would make excellent house servants' of especial value 'in the North and in the interior'.[47]

Despite such familiarly racist historical antecedents, by 1951 Australia had accepted almost 12 000 Maltese commencing the process which, in 1974, would permit the claim that Australia was then home to a Maltese population one-sixth the size of that of Malta. Maltese paid their own way, arrived as allied ex-servicemen, or came out under the Assisted Passage Agreement which was signed with the Maltese administration in May 1948. Behind this agreement lay an Australian acknowledgement that, whatever the (pseudo-) scientific findings of racial biology, Malta had shown itself worthy in playing the wartime part of David against the evil Axis Goliath.

Once an exception was made, it was hard to revert to the old policy. In January 1948, Australia declared that displaced person status could be extended to Polish refugees even if they had not joined the British Army. In July, Hungarians were given the same rights. August brought respectability to White Russians. In February 1949, widows, deserted wives and unmarried mothers from eastern Europe could be admitted along with their children, although it was suggested that Australian charity to erring women in the third category should not be publicised. In April 1949, south-eastern Europeans met Australian requirements. Bulgarians, Romanians and finally Albanians were formally deemed eligible for displaced persons status. A more exotic person than one who came from the hills above Tiranë or Shkodër could not yet be imagined in Canberra. But, in case the future bore still more surprises, Calwell advised his officials to exercise general discretion towards any other European 'racial groups' claiming to be refugees.

While the Cold War allowed one sort of ideological gloss to cover refugees, the Australian government had quickly moved on to search for 'economic migrants' from places previously despised. This new promiscuity produced occasional cries of outrage. Naturally enough, the entry of Italians excited particular alarm. Even Germans were better than they were. One correspondent of *Reveille*, the organ of the New South Wales branch of the RSL, asserted that 'broadly-speaking, ex-servicemen like to see coming here the type who had courage to stand up and fight for what they (like ourselves) considered just and right in their country, because, on the whole, they make good citizens.' Italians, unlike Germans, did not fit this category, he continued, since their military record was 'despicable and deplorable', since they were not 'good mixers' and since, indeed, many of them were 'communists'. A spokesman for the Victorian branch was more succinct, but he made the same point: 'The R.S.L., for defence, would rather have an Afrika Corps and some of its types, than some who have come here from Mediterranean ports.'[48]

The process, though, could not be stopped. With little public explanation or justification, the architects of Australia's immigration policy signed in 1951 an agreement with the Italian government offering some assisted passages to Australia. In the next year, it was the turn of the Greeks, Germans and Austrians; Spaniards (1958), Turks (1967) and Yugoslavs (1970) followed. Egyptians, Lebanese, Argentinians , Chileans and many more would come. Even the White Australia Policy would change, first in nomenclature and eventually, to some extent, in practice. A new Australia was in the making.

Through the new immigration programme, one of Australia's pretensions to uniqueness and justifications of insularity was collapsing. The wire of history was no longer only open to London (or Dublin).

Many old worlds had begun to erect a presence in the history of new Australia. As R. M. Crawford stated in a rather less remarked embellishment of his already noted thesis about the centrality of migration to Australian history: 'The seven seas may divide the migrant from his homeland, but he will never quite shake its dust from his feet.'[49] In the 1950s, while assimilation held absolute sway, such an idea was heretical. But Crawford expressed a heresy that would turn out to be true.

Chapter TWO

From Assimilationism to Multiculturalism: immigration policy 1949–83

In January 1952, Harold Holt addressed the Third Citizenship Convention, which was organised by the Good Neighbour Movement and funded by the Department of Immigration. His message was clear enough:

Australia, in accepting a balanced intake of other European people as well as British can still build a truly British nation on this side of the world. I feel that if the central tradition of a nation is strong this tradition will impose itself on [the various] groups of immigrants.[1]

Seventeen years later, the stress on Britain had weakened but the homogenising ambition remained the same. The then minister for immigration, Billy Snedden, who had been a selection officer for his department in Italy and England in 1952–54, gave his view of what Australia should be:

We must have a single culture – if immigration implied multi-culture activities within Australian society, then it was not the type Australia wanted. I am quite determined we should have a monoculture, with everyone living in the same way, understanding each other, and sharing the same aspirations. We don't want pluralism.[2]

Yet, in many senses, by 1969 the immigration programme created by Calwell and his successors had proved quite remarkably flexible. The ancient fortresses of racist Australia fell one by one, with scarcely a whimper of protest or regret from politicians, bureaucrats or public opinion. At one level, Australian flexibility and even humanitarianism seems very praiseworthy in contrast to the drastic nationalising of immigrants attempted, for example, in Israel, or the ruthless suppression of minority groups carried out in Greece.

But before Australians become too self-congratulatory about the achievements of the new immigration policy, it has to be admitted that, if some changes in attitudes and even in the character of Australia itself would eventually occur, both Australian decision makers and Australian opinion long denied that anything remarkable was happening. The mechanism that permitted this denial was the doctrine of assimilationism, the idea that migrants or their children or their children's children could meld into British Australia. Thus, Calwell was gratified to locate among the displaced persons 'people whose normal standards of living have been compatible with our own ... [and who] represent an ideal source of migrants who will fit smoothly into our way of life.'[3] And Holt could explain away recourse to Italy: 'There is a tendency to describe Italians ... as being too prone to use the knife ... [but] there need be no fear that we are introducing lawless elements into Australia.' Just in case there were such fears, Holt added that an immersion in the Australian way of life would soon cleanse even the most deeply ingrained pasts, so that 'second and third generation Australians of Italian descent ... are virtually indistinguishable from British stock.'[4]

The politicians were not the only Australians to trust that assimilation would preserve untouched the Australian way of life. The bureaucrats who, in Australia or Europe, laboured to make the new immigration policy effective, shared the assumption that immigrants should adapt themselves to Australian patterns rather than the reverse.

The first secretary of the Department of Immigration was the career public servant T. H. E. Heyes. According to a story printed on his retirement in 1961, Heyes had been surprised by the offer of such a job. 'I don't know anything about [immigration]', he remembered saying, 'but I'd be very keen to have a go at it.'

During the long years of his office, Heyes was careful not to flaunt his own authority or intellect. His academic training was modest and allegedly he rejoiced in the fact that his department was 'not full of Rhodes Scholars like External Affairs'. His ideas were conventional – immigrants should be grateful and should assimilate: 'The migrant should be encouraged to adopt our language and way of life and eventually to become an Australian citizen.' But lines still needed to be drawn. Heyes may have tolerated Mediterraneans, but he opposed abandoning the White Australia Policy. Characteristically, he advised Holt in 1951: 'unless we are "tough" we will get them [Asians] in thousands.'[5]

If there is little evidence that Heyes was an innovative planner of migration policy, he had at least been a most able warden of an expanding bureaucratic empire. When he was appointed in 1946, the department had seventy-four officers and assembled in the maternity ward of the old Canberra hospital. But under Heyes, the department soon showed a formidable ability to procreate, and in 1950, the staff peaked at 5725. There were then drastic cuts, as planning and processing lost their revolutionary aspects and became more humdrum, and by 1961 there were only 1684 employees. There were 2200 officers in Immigration by 1970 and, reflecting the pruning of the Labor years and cutbacks due to recession, 1964 by 1980. Expenditure on the department rose from $64,840 (1945) to $42,026,694 (1952), $68,708,307 (1969) and $73,918,087 (1980).

One early appointment was Noel Lamidey, an English migrant of the 1920s, who, in 1946, took up the post of chief migration officer at Australia House in London. He was another who gloried in the task of being a fisher of men: 'How to capture the best material available from the huge British manpower potential became at once an exciting and fascinating game' – all the more so because the British authorities sometimes displayed a stubborn proclivity to declare a closed season on Australian trawling for migrants.

Lamidey's memoirs tell of British stolidity, of the occasional puerility of Australian state officials unable to recognise a Canberra bureaucrat's intellect and seniority, and of attitudes endemic to his times and his career as an efficient bureaucrat. He noted that he was once able to expose cheating by some Jews who had professed to be Roman Catholic in order to avoid the regulation that then required that no more than 25 per cent of a ship's complement for Australia be Jewish refugees. Lamidey similarly voiced the spirit of his era when he regretted the failure to establish an effective child migration scheme: 'children would have been and still remain our best potential migrants who could be taught and grow up as Australians without any of the inhibitions which surround adult migrants from where-ever they may come'.

Lamidey returned to Australia in 1954 and served his remaining seven years in the public service as Assistant Secretary (Assimilation). His biases and innocence remained, and in 1970 he, like so many others, still saw Australia as the lucky country:

now as an Australian of many years standing I can faithfully claim, and stand steadfast in my belief, that Australia more than any other country has much to offer and much to give to those who may come here, and are not afraid. For here we have a fresh, virile and abiding country; still strong in the Christian faith of our forefathers who pioneered it. If we can continue on our way to the betterment of our people in advancing nationhood, without the scars and tragedies that have torn and mutilated the face and spirit of other less fortunate countries, then indeed I believe in the fullness of time we can have here in Australia a continent which might well become the envy as well as the admiration of the world.[6]

Heyes, Lamidey and other early bureaucrats of immigration were representative of certain aspects of the young Canberra. They were honest, honourable, and hard-working; blinkered, conservative, and prejudiced against the 'flashness' of the wider world. They were also often connected to the army and to the Australian secret service. Before his appointment, Heyes's chief claims to cosmopolitanism lay in his occupancy of the position of director of the Australian War Memorial in 1939–42 and his further work in the Defence Department in 1942–46. Lamidey had served the Aliens Classification and Advisory Committee in 1942–46.

When it became apparent that Australia would look beyond Britain for migrants, Heyes turned to the military for advice and action. In 1947, Australia opened its first office in Germany under the supervision of Brigadier General F. G. Galleghan. A career soldier who had been a prisoner-of-war at Changi in 1942–45, Galleghan had also been deputy director of the Commonwealth Investigation Service in Sydney in 1945–47. As the great powers began to recognise Australia's role in taking in anti-communist refugees and as the atmosphere of the Cold War grew more bleak, Galleghan was promoted to the executive of the International Refugee Organisation in 1948–49. In Australia, too, the military often operated in close collaboration with the Department of Immigration as they organised temporary transit camps or as, more furtively, they examined aliens' political or racial coloration.

Characteristic of certain antipathies still lingering in military minds was a long report drafted in 1951 by Raymond Huish, an English migrant who was president of the Queensland branch of the Returned Servicemen's League. In 1950 the federal executive of the League had recorded that 'objections at times have been raised by all State branches ... to the introduction of Southern Italians'. In reaction, Huish went on a fact-finding mission to Europe.

Like many a traveller, he found abroad the facts he had known before he left. A visit to Australian immigration offices in Rome persuaded him that 'the people I saw awaiting examination at the Rome office during my visit did not appear to be as clean, smart and intelligent as was the case in Holland and Germany.' Huish could remember, however, that some experts believed that there was a difference between northern and southern Italians.

Northern Italians are generally industrial and skilled types with higher living standards, better education and hygiene, with a lower unsuitability percentage, but a higher security risk ... [On the other hand,] Southern Italians and Sicilians are mainly agriculturalists with a lower standard of living, hygiene and education, with a higher unsuitability percentage based on Australian standards, but a lower security risk compared with the northern Italians.

These beliefs in turn brought Huish to what he regarded as practical suggestions. The Australian Immigration Office in Rome needed smartening up. It should stop employing Italian doctors who 'lacked objectivity'. Instead, an 'All-Australian team' should be dispatched to Rome and it should include both more medical staff (presumably for the 'southerners') and more security officials (for the 'northerners').[7] Huish only enunciated more crudely, stubbornly and vociferously what others, even sometimes those experts who were gradually appropriating a major advisory position in Australian immigration policy, believed.

Despite his impatience with intellectuals within his own department, Heyes had presided over the creation of a major network of expert, outside advisers. In 1949, he had recommended the establishment of the Immigration Planning Council under the businessman Sir John Storey. More importantly, Heyes and his department developed a close working relationship with demographers, social psychologists, and other social scientists at the Australian National University (ANU) and elsewhere.

Chief among them was W. D. Borrie, since 1957 professor of demography at ANU and now president of the Australian Academy of Social Sciences. Borrie began his career in New Zealand, whence he moved quickly through predictable imperial networks. Any student of post-war immigration is rapidly indebted both to the scientific purity of Borrie's statistical labours as a demographer and to the subjectivity of his changing explanations of what the product of those labours meant. An opponent during the war of Jewish settlement in the Kimberleys, after the war Borrie remained a resolute advocate of assimilationism who in 1949 suggested that migrant Italians had not in the past damaged Queensland too much: 'Here they were tolerated and even welcomed so long as they did not compete with white labour and white owners'.[8] Time, however, brought change and Borrie gradually metamorphosed into a more tolerant being. By 1958, he agreed that Australia must 'be prepared to take immigrants from sources from which they are available rather than the sources which we might consider ideally suited to our own economy and culture'.[9]

Borrie soldiered on into the multicultural 1970s and 1980s and has remained a major adviser to all governments. He has publicly endorsed what he prefers to call multiethnicity. But perhaps some of his old ideas have not altogether been surrendered. Unlike other multiculturalists, Borrie has underlined the fact that 'despite all that diversity ... *so far,* the post-war settlers from the British Isles have far out-numbered any other national group, and indeed have almost equalled all non-British settlers considered together'. Borrie seems happy that, although 'Anglo-Australianism is a myth ... Australia surely still has its roots firmly in its Anglo-Saxon past, whatever it may become in the future.'[10]

In much of his work, Borrie's chief lieutenant has been Charles Price, the son of A. Grenfell Price, himself a pillar of the Adelaide establishment. Grenfell Price had published a guide to the future through inspection of the past with the characteristic title, *Australia Comes of Age*. In its pages, he warned against the 'particularly alarming' decline of British immigration by contrast to the 'ominous' arrival of Italians especially to Queensland where they 'undercut the British whites and absorbed more and more farms'. North of the Alps, however, more worthy Europeans lived: 'Scandinavians and other Nordic migrants had in general proved satisfactory except where they were permitted to form hard racial cores.'[11] Following where his father led, Charles Price entered the field in 1945 with *German Settlers in South Australia*. He worried about the tardiness of the assimilation process in the Barossa valley. There, for a long time, he noted, it was as though 'a little piece of Silesia had suddenly taken wings and flown complete and undisturbed to a new land'. Fortunately, the passing years had gradually worn away much of the settlers' sense of German nationality but, in commencing a new immigration policy, Price advised, Australia should be careful not to allow too dense a settlement of early arrivals. They should rather be dispersed and Australia should concentrate on eliminating immigrants' old ideas, on destroying the old worlds in the interests of new Australia.[12]

In 1952, Price moved to Canberra. At ANU he has been the patron and sponsor of much important and often liberal-minded research. This research, however, has almost always carried the implication that, if assimilation has had to be abandoned for the first generation of migrants, then certainly it must be expected of the second and third. In 1968, Price expanded on these ideas at the Duke of Edinburgh's Third Commonwealth Study Conference. In his address Price remarked:

Taken by and large, however, the second generation are becoming assimilated to British-Australian ways, or rather to the new British-Australian way of life that is emerging under the impetus of modern technology and mass media and under the impact of so many new persons and influences ... British-Australians will not at present accept a Canadian type society, permanently divided between 'French' or 'British', still less an Indian type society divided by lines of caste and by lines of regional languages and cultures. They are now willing to let newcomers help develop Australia's economy and culture, and influence 'the Australian way of life' but they want all citizens to be in it together, not as 'German-Australians' or 'English-Australians' or 'Chinese-Australians' but as 'dinkum Australians'.

When Price was not engaging in such rousingly nationalist perorations, other old concepts could be located beneath the veneer of integrationism. Pressed in 1971 at an Australian Institute of Political Science summer school to give the ultimate justification for immigration, Price explained: 'I just feel in my bones that Australia will be better off in defence with a reasonably large population.'[13]

Though Borrie and Price are as Anglo-Australian in background as are the authors of this book, Jerzy 'George' Zubrzycki seems at first sight a more foreign figure, perhaps better representative of migrant ideas and traditions. Born in Cracow, Poland, Zubrzycki had served his intellectual and moral apprenticeship for Australia at the London School of Economics and in the British Foreign Office. There he absorbed the rightness of a process whereby immigrants adjusted to their new environment and slowly acquired its characteristics. In 1956, he took up a post at ANU, and by 1977 he had risen to become chairman of the Australian Ethnic Affairs Council and was included on many government committees.

In the 1950s and 1960s Zubrzycki argued that the ethnic press, ethnic associations, and old-world values had a place in new Australia during the first few years of settlement. By providing arrivals with familiar faces and words, migrant structures ensured a stable foundation on which a new Australian life could be built. But, once the need had passed and a migrant 'begins to notice some of the real advantages he may have gained through migration', the 'foreign' associations are no longer needed and fade away. Hence, in his *Settlers of the Latrobe Valley* (1964), Zubrzycki concluded that his 'overriding impression ... is of people who are doing their best to strike roots and contribute their share to the building of "Australia into a greater place to live in"'.

Zubrzycki's belief in the virtue of immigrant blending into Australia has not abated even as, in the 1970s, he has argued for the recognition of 'the primordial ties of ethnicity'. People may not forget their origins but, equally, they should not forget what it is to be an Australian and, for Zubrzycki, Australianness lies primarily in 'our freedom'. This is something which, he argues, exists in only a few other countries and which particularly does not exist in places like the Soviet Union.[14]

More aggressive in their ideology were those social psychologists who, by the 1960s, were active in the analysis of immigration and settlement policies. Typical was the work of Ronald Taft, after 1957 reader in psychology at the University of Western Australia. From a family that had fled Russian pogroms, Taft had been assimilated through an education at Scotch College and Melbourne University. He and his pupil Alan Richardson became the chief Australian experts on the proper psychological policy to be pursued towards immigrants. Yet, less than a generation later, the work of Taft and Richardson stands testimony to the hollowness of the scientific pretensions of such social scientists.

Among many possibilities, an example can be found in an article published by Taft in the *Australian Journal of Psychology* (1962). There, amid his jargon, Taft pondered 'opinion convergence in the assimilation of immigrants'. The jargon was not so necessary, since all a measurer needed was Taft's 28 point 'Scale of Australianism'. If a team of psychologists could catch any hapless immigrants, they had merely to hand out questionnaires. Did you think '1. Commercial broadcasting makes for better broadcasting'? Should you agree, and perhaps you must in Murdoch's Perth, you were showing healthy signs of Australianism. Other questions required a migrant to appraise the statements: 'One can hardly have more than one or two true friends in a lifetime' (an Australian would disagree); 'The Anglo-Saxon races owe their leading position in the world to their outstanding qualities' (agree); 'Mass-produced goods are better than hand-made goods' (agree); 'Good manners are more important than a lot of knowledge' (agree); 'A country is far more enjoyable to live in when the people come from a wide range of racial and national backgrounds' (disagree); 'Wine is a good drink to offer a friend who just drops in for a visit' (disagree); 'The use by foreigners of their language in public places is objectionable' (agree); 'The politician who truly has the good of the people at heart is very rare' (disagree); 'Social education of children is more important than intellectual education' (agree).[15]

A marvellous reflection of the prejudices of the moment, Taft's questionnaire has scarcely lasted well as a measure of what might make a good Australian (whatever that may be). Yet, Alan Richardson in 1971 was still arguing that his new scale could successfully predict which migrants would be 'satisfied' and able to 'control their own lives'.[16]

Hindsight reveals the insularity of many of the ideas of Borrie or Price, Taft or Richardson. Safe and unimaginative, their ideas were the ideas of their time: they were the academics of consensus and bipartisanship and, as such, they won recognition and respect and became the first counsellors of government.

What such academics were saying in the 1950s in turn reflected and reinforced public opinion. In this regard, the fundamental source expressing the world view of 1950s Australia remains J. P. O'Grady's (Nino Culotta) novel, *They're a Weird Mob* (1957). O'Grady was extraordinarily successful. By 1970, *They're a Weird Mob* had a claimed publication run of 520 000 and its spin-offs included a film, a catchy song, and all the other Nino books. Often very funny, O'Grady's books were scoured by sexism, the crudest political conservatism, and a rampant nationalism (which at times seems to border on racism). Despite or because of these attitudes, O'Grady was hailed by his contemporaries as a realist: 'It is O'Grady's intense preoccupation with setting down on paper an *exact* picture of certain types of contemporary Australians which has made him not only a most diverting writer but an important one as well.'[17] Today, it is hard to share such critical enthusiasm, but an emblematic writer of assimilationist Australia, O'Grady certainly was.

Assimilationism remains the ideology of the Nino books and no doubt helps to explain their critical and commercial success. O'Grady converted the unpleasantness and foreignness of immigration into an Australian heaven. When Nino, the purported (northern) Italian migrant, has run for long enough with the weird mob, at last he can see the Australian God:

Recently in the street, I heard a mother chastising her child in voluble Italian. And this small boy said to his mother, 'Gees mum, I dunno wot yer talkin' about.' I was very pleased. I told Kay. She said, 'It must be hard for the parents.' Of course it's hard. But the kids can do it. They do it by mixing with Australian kids, and listening. The adults can do it by mixing with Australian adults. All that is needed is the will to learn. Well, don't be bludgers. Hop in and learn. I've heard parents in shops talking to kids in their homeland language, and the kids translating into English, and making the purchases. This is disgraceful. Those parents should be bloody ashamed of themselves. They came to this country because their own is impossible and by their own laziness make this one impossible for themselves also. It makes me very irritable ...

So I will not think about it any more. I will stop writing now, and count my blessings. They are very numerous. I will stop worrying about these New Australians, and start wondering what I am going to do this afternoon. There are so many things I can do. I can work in my garden, or fix the electric iron which I should have fixed last week and which Kay will need to-morrow. Or I can take her and young Nino into the Domain and listen to the ratbags making speeches. Or we can all go down to Cronulla for a swim. Or we can visit Bob, and eat some of his oysters. Or go and talk to Joe about building, while Kay and Edie gossip as women do. There are hundreds of ways we could spend this sunny Sunday afternoon. Or we could just stay at home and do nothing, and perhaps that would be best of all. To rest on the seventh day. To thank God for letting us be here. To thank Him for letting me be an Australian. Sometimes I think that if I am ever fortunate enough to reach Heaven, I will know I am there when I hear Him say, 'Howyergoin' mate orright?'[18]

O'Grady's continuing success illustrates how profoundly assimilationism conditioned Australian opinion about immigration. Yet, even as O'Grady wrote, the more enlightened Australian politicians and their advisers were beginning to recognise both the sterility and cruelty of assimilationism and the impossibility of its application.

One of the inevitable effects of a mass immigration programme was a sort of osmotic penetration into some Australian minds of some internationalist ideas. Borrie, Price and other social scientists joined an international conference circuit which could assemble in Mexico or Switzerland. Back in 1950, Borrie's *Italians and Germans in Australia: a study of assimilation* was begun under encouragement from UNESCO. Borrie dutifully recorded that a demographers' meeting in Paris that summer had agreed on a definition: 'Assimilation is a psychological, socio-economic and cultural process resulting in the progressive attenuation of differences between the behaviour of immigrants within the social life of a given country.'[19] A less renowned sociologist put it in simpler terms: 'which of us takes the migrant home to dinner?'[20]

In time, the naivety of this remark gave way to the more cosmopolitan and reflective views of a new generation of social scientists, of whom Jean Martin and James Jupp were the most prominent. By the 1960s such researchers were no longer so simplistically ready to assume that all migrants were or should be truncated beings, that their foreign pasts were all bad and must be forgotten before they could discover the real pleasures and virtues of Australia. Assimilation became a term to be scorned; integration was the new word to define an ideal immigration policy.

No doubt some of the motivation behind this change came from inside Australia. But the concept of integration, of the toleration, at least verbally, of a greater pluralism was born elsewhere. In its attitudes and policies to migration, domestic models for 'the inventing of Australia' were borrowed no longer from England but instead from the United States.[21] Migrant power was only one of a number of movements – black power, women's liberation, gay liberation, and the rest – which, from the 1950s, planted seeds that would blossom in the Vietnam years when it still seemed possible to create a world that was heterogeneous, prosperous, and free.

Even in the gloomy days of McCarthyite xenophobia in the United States, Oscar Handlin carried the torch of liberalism in his classic study of migration, *The Uprooted* (1951). Although proudly patriotic, Handlin and his disciples continued to justify ethnicity and to urge governments to be kind to deprived migrant groups and not to hasten too aggressively towards their assimilation. In the 1960s, flushed with the excitement of the New Frontier, assimilationism in the United States weakened further. Book titles like *Beyond the Melting Pot* and *The Rise of the Unmeltable Ethnics* appeared, and the American metaphor even switched to the 'salad bowl'.

These concepts began to filter into Australia and to upset some prevailing ideas. After Heyes retired in 1961, some old prejudices began to fade. The new secretary of the Department of Immigration was the urbane Peter Heydon. Like many successful Sydney men of his generation, Heydon was an old Fort Street boy who rose through a career in politics and diplomacy.

In contrast to Heyes, Heydon was a bureaucratic innovator who believed that the future lay with the brightest and the technocratically best. In 1963, he was proud that his department introduced training courses for officers about to be sent overseas; in 1966, the duration of these courses was extended to four weeks. Heydon also highlighted the international side of a career in immigration. By 1968, 27 per cent of his staff were stationed overseas, prompting the acerbic Maximilian Walsh to observe that belt-tightening reform was unlikely: 'The Immigration Department has more than 2,000 career bureaucrats with a vested interest in the continuation of our immigration policy – they can be sent to "Peter Stuyvesant country" – London, Paris and Rome.'[22] By that time, the appearance of Australian immigration policy had drastically changed. The great issue in this change had become how and when to jettison the White Australia Policy.

The new liberal ideas entering from abroad had not triumphed at once. Until his retirement in 1963, Prime Minister Menzies proclaimed a British Australia which had rejected few of the values of the world before 1939. The meaning of the British connection was eternal:

[It means] a cottage in the wheat lands of the North-West of the State of Victoria, with the Bible and Henry Drummond and Jerome K. Jerome and *The Scottish Chiefs* and Burns on the shelves ... It means, at Canberra, at Wellington, at Ottawa, at Cape Town, the men of Parliament meeting as those met at Westminster seven hundred years ago, ... It means Hammond at Sydney, and Bradman at Lords, and McCabe at Trent Bridge, with the ghosts of Grace and Trumble looking on. It means a tang in the air; a touch of salt on the lips; a little pulse that beats and shall beat; a decent pride; the sense of a continuing city. It means the past ever rising in its strength to forge the future.[23]

In 1958, Menzies appointed Alexander Downer as minister for immigration. Another from the Adelaide establishment, Downer had moved through Geelong Grammar, Brasenose and the Inner Temple to Changi camp and to Liberal politics.

The year before, Downer's predecessor, Athol Townley (minister 1956-58), had announced the Bring out a Briton scheme to try to increase the number of Britons migrating to Australia. He had been especially pleased to record that £28,500,000 had been spent on Britons since 1946 against £9,500,000 'to bring nationals from 38 other countries'.[24] In these circumstances, the propaganda sheets of the Department of Immigration had been full of touching stories of, for example, well assimilated and financially successful Latvian ex-displaced persons sponsoring British workers. And the Labor opposition, through its leader, H. V. Evatt, duly joined in by deploring the 'dangerously low' level of the British intake and by asserting: 'Australia is basically and fundamentally a British community and must remain so'.

Downer seemed the ideal man to outflank this sort of criticism. Once in office, he quickly refurbished the propaganda base of the Bring out a Briton scheme. Another ten million, he said, needed to be added to the Australian population as soon as possible. 'Our own generation,' he

Make it easier . . .
help build Australia

BRING OUT A BRITON

To make Australia greater, richer, stronger, we must develop the country by expanding industry and primary production. By widening employment opportunities we raise the standards of living for all.

Part of the answer to a greater Australia is a greater population. We **must** have more people . . . more migrants who are

- **Skilled, for trades, industry and technical advancement.**
- **Semi-skilled, for occupations demanding workers.**
- **Unskilled, for labour on rugged projects.**

The Commonwealth Government has a major assisted-passages scheme to "Bring out a Briton" which requires the migrant to pay only £10 Sterling for his total fare. The scheme provides two main categories under which the Australian public can **actively** help to bring out more British migrants.

PERSONAL NOMINATION. Australians may nominate friends and relatives in Britain for assisted passages. The sponsor pays nothing, but he must provide initial living accommodation.

GROUP NOMINATION. Australian employers, including State instrumentalities, may nominate the type of workers they need. Most of these migrants are single men and women. The intending employer must provide living accommodation. The Commonwealth also operates its own scheme to bring out more British migrants. Make further detailed enquiries to-day!

Part of the publicity campaign in the late 1950s to entice more British immigrants to Australia. *Good Neighbour* (Department of Immigration Journal) 53, June 1958.

warned, 'may [thus] sacrifice a few material comforts, but we shall thereby hold a continent.' But, he regretted, 'good migrants with the skills we want are not just growing like cherries on the tree'. 'I concede to no one a greater admiration for our British tradition than I personally hold', yet Australia might have to search more pertinaciously beyond England. The Bring out a Briton campaign failed to take fire, and in July 1959 Downer opened a new drive for southern Europeans. 'In practice', he announced, 'Australian selection teams would operate mainly at Genoa, Trieste and Milan' where they could be expected to 'recruit Northern Italians'.[25]

If (northern) Italians were now deemed useful and valuable, others were voicing still more challenging thoughts. In January 1959, the governor-general, Sir William Slim, opened the annual Citizenship Convention with familiar phrases: 'The future of this land depends more upon the scale and success of immigration than upon any single factor ... And time is not on our side.' But another speaker was less predictable in his comments. He was Australia's most celebrated physician, Sir Macfarlane Burnet, who kept his language simple: 'Healthy parents of different race could produce healthy children, no matter how extreme the difference between [them].'[26]

Macfarlane Burnet's comment undermined a whole section of the labours of social scientists in the 1950s. Borrie, Price, and their followers had been accustomed to chart patterns of intermarriage, with the constant implication that marriage within an ethnic group was undesirable since 'racial clots' would block up the Australian system. Now so eminent a figure as Macfarlane Burnet pointed out that such a belief was rubbish. But there was a further implication as well. If 'healthy Mediterraneans' were acceptable, what was wrong with healthy Asians? Maybe the White Australia Policy, that fundamental canon in the ideology of Australian immigration policy, was practically out-moded and theoretically indefensible.

As the 1950s had proceeded, Australian commentators had gone on searching for that elusive moment when Australia would come of age. The *West Australian* of 10 December 1956 announced that the Melbourne Olympiad had persuaded 'people who once thought of Australia in terms of kangaroos ... that we are an advanced outpost of Western civilization'. In case an outpost still be deemed barbarous or provincial, men began to urge that Australia be more practical and realistic about the White Australia Policy. Pressure groups led by churchmen, such as the Methodist Alan Walker and the Anglican Bishop Moyes, and academics, such as Kenneth Rivett or J. A. C. Mackie, united in a series of Associations for Immigration Reform that demanded that Australian policy 'neither exclude nor appear to exclude people on the basis of their race and colour'. Such ideas were taken up by many university students and by several investigative journalists who were flexing the muscles that would be used more strenuously later. Even Charles Price began to say that '1,500 Asians' could be let in on a 'trial basis'.

Visitors from the United States reinforced this sense that times must change down under. In 1963, Robin W. Winks, a historian from Yale, appalled many worthies when he brashly announced that he 'would like to see 50,000 Negroes in Melbourne'. In the following years, similar views were expressed by a number of other visiting American liberals.[27]

But not all Australians had abandoned their traditional fears. Calwell, the architect of the new immigration policy, went on stating that 'no red-blooded Australian' would want to see 'a chocolate-coloured Australia'.[28] In 1970, Sir Henry Bolte, the Liberal premier of Victoria (1955-72), who was himself descended from German immigrants, still believed that American immigration was 'too dangerous. You say you want Americans and some big buck nigger gets up and says, "I'll go".'[29] Even in 1972, Charles E. Barnes, the Country Party minister for external territories, declared:

We in Australia have a particular problem. We are the outpost of Western civilisation in the western Pacific area ... We have millions of people of different cultures to the north of us. We can be friends with these people and can give them support but we can be taken over not by war but because of our immigration policies.[30]

Another factor prompting change was the growing assertion that Australia was part of Asia. Australian trade ties with Japan strengthened just as those with Britain and the European Economic Community (EEC) weakened; Australia had Asian allies in the South-East Asia Treaty Organization (SEATO). Asian politicians, such as Lee Kuan Yew, or a relatively free press, such as that in the Philippines of the 1960s, were not reticent in deploring racist practices among their southern neighbours.

It seems that Australian public opinion was nearer to that of Calwell, Bolte or Barnes than to the humanitarian pluralism of the reformers. Opinion polls show that views about who should be welcomed and who not had changed slowly since 1948 (see Table 1). Of listed ethnic, religious or colour groups, only the English, Irish or Germans were really popular, although overt anti-Semitism had lessened markedly by 1964.

Despite these surviving attitudes, policy, or the words in which it was expressed, had been subject to gradual reforms. In 1958, the Menzies government had abandoned the dictation test, which had been mainly used to exclude Asians. In 1956 and especially in 1966, racial restrictions were relaxed and a greater number of profession-ally qualified non-Europeans admitted. The status of non-Europeans

Table 1 Percentages approving immigration of particular groups[31]

	1948	1964
English	91	97
Irish	65	89
German	36	81
Chinese	31	20
Greek	26	50
Italian	21	47
Jews	17	68
Negro	10	18

already in Australia was also brought into line with that of other non-British residents. In 1966, it was officially announced that future immigrants would be evaluated according to 'their suitability as settlers, their ability to integrate readily, and their possession of qualifications which are in fact positively useful in Australia', though it was emphasised that this did not permit 'large scale admission of workers from Asia'.[32]

By 1966, the minister for immigration was the ex-cycling champion Hubert Opperman. During his period of office (1963-66), a number of embarrassing incidents came to public attention. Among the most prominent was the long-running Nancy Prasad case in which Australian immigration officials seemed determined to persecute an ill Fijian girl. Certainly both television and the press had a field day in reporting the events that led to the deportation of the Australian-born child (a departure which was briefly delayed when Nancy was sensationally abducted by sympathisers led by young Aboriginal activist Charles Perkins). Foreign journalists reported the story with relish, and some Australian diplomats were driven to admit that the White Australia Policy was 'an albatross around our necks'.[33]

Yet, much of the change in 1966 was more apparent than real. Now Asians could technically be admitted, but in practice they would not be. Opperman had done little more than achieve what Grenfell Price and Borrie had suggested back in 1945-49, change the 'somewhat unfortunate' name of the White Australia Policy and replace it with something nicer, like the 'Australian Immigration Policy'.[34]

The process started in the 1960s, however, has not been reversed. In the ALP, once the special redoubt of racism, the new humanitarianism, led by the South Australian premier, Don Dunstan, triumphed, in principle, at the Launceston Conference of 1971. In practice, however, the flood-gates did not open after Labor won power in 1972 since, as the economy rapidly turned down, Labor cut the overall immigration intake. It was only when the boat people began to steer their vessels into Darwin harbour that the White Australia Policy was really infringed. And then, given the extent of Australia's involvement in causing Vietnam's troubles, perhaps the reception awaiting Chinese, Vietnamese, and Cambodian refugees was scarcely as warm as it might have been.

By 1975–76, Australia had passed through the Whitlam era. The debate about the real achievements of that time of reform continues. But, as far as immigration is concerned, at least on the level of rhetoric, the early 1970s did represent a break with much of the past. By then, the voices of old Australia sounded tired and hackneyed, prejudiced and inadequate. A. J. Forbes, the last Liberal minister for immigration before the Whitlam years, lamented that Labor's immigration policy 'reduced the supply of good quality British migrants of European descent'. He wanted continued discrimination in their favour since 'What is wrong with treating differently people who are differently placed? What is wrong with discrimination when there are valid overwhelming reasons to discriminate?'[35]

Some social scientists became critical when they discovered that in twenty years the Australian government had spent 10 cents on publicity for each Greek attracted here, and $180 on each Swede; each German migrant had cost Australia twenty times as much as each Italian.[36] Although many still believed, as Billy Snedden put it in 1967, that 'the value of British migrants cannot be overstated ... They share our language, they share an orientation to our institutions and we have what might be described as a likeness',[37] it became unfashionable to say so out loud.

Into the placid and stagnating society of Liberal Australia, Whitlam seemed to propel a glittering new vehicle for pluralism and humanitarianism. Unlike his Liberal predecessors, Harold Holt or William McMahon, Whitlam comprehended the new words for a new age. When the president of Italy, Giuseppe Saragat, an old Cold War warrior, visited Australia in 1967 (the first head of state of a major non-British migrant country to do so), Whitlam referred to Raffaello Carboni. 'Eureka', explained Whitlam to a perhaps startled Saragat, was 'the Australian manifestation of the Risorgimento.'[38] But Whitlam could do better than merely echo newly fashionable historical myths. As prime minister, he did speak in genuinely new tones:

We do not want migrants to feel that they have to erase their own characteristics and imitate and adopt completely the behaviour of existing Australian society. We want to see that society enriched by cross fertilisation that will result from migrants retaining their own heritage.[39]

To some extent, these words were matched by deeds. The special agent of a new policy towards immigrants was Al Grassby, minister for immigration December 1972 – May 1974 and commissioner for community relations October 1975 – November 1982. Grassby's brief was to give substance to the claims that Whitlam's Australia was turning its back on a racist, discriminatory, and exclusively British past and building a future in which equality and diversity would go hand in hand.

Grassby was a complex and sometimes ambiguous figure. His mother was Irish; his father was an Australian who had wandered the world. Grassby's own life had taken him to Griffith in southern New South Wales in the capacity of information officer for the Commonwealth Scientific and Industrial Research Organization (CSIRO). Griffith was an unusual town, split between old Australians and migrants, mainly Italian, and split again because some of the Italians were Calabrians and some were from the province of Treviso in north-eastern Italy. Grassby's image of Griffith has been sentimental, although he has gradually expressed an overt preference for local migrant culture over the traditional Australian one. 'There were two worlds and I moved between the two, but in fact they never met.' The Anglo-Australian one was expressed in the 'soggy lettuce ... dehydrated meat ... and dreary speeches' of a local wedding; the Italian counterpart offered a 'dazzling smorgasbord of food and drink' and long hours of 'singing and dancing'.[40]

In addition to his job with the CSIRO, Grassby began to work on local radio, favouring separate broadcasts in English, Spanish, and Italian. Through this he constructed a political power-base. In 1965 he was elected to the New South Wales House of Assembly, and he claims that he quickly distinguished himself by introducing wine to the parliamentary bar, though he also carefully nurtured the interests of the farmers of his electorate and rarely said much about 'new Australia'. Four years later, he transferred to Canberra, and the rapidity of his political rise caused some to suggest that he had the potential to become prime minister.

In 1971, Grassby ousted Fred Daly, an old, inner-city, Irish boss as Labor spokesman on immigration. Grassby's triumph over so formidable a political manipulator as Daly (with his ancient credo 'You can have the arguments – give me the numbers')[41] signalled a drastic abandonment of Calwellian policies or rhetoric on migration. Grassby dressed for the part – flaired trousers, vivid ties, still more vivid jackets. He even offered visitors to his Canberra office *slivovitz* rather than whisky to drink. His public face, with its Calabro-Leichhardt paint, seemed almost deliberately designed to antagonise the heavy-bottomed paladins of the RSL and its kindred groups. For such Australians, Grassby has seemed a 'spiv', some sort of bastard Italian, Spaniard or Greek.

What such commentators did not see was that Grassby did not after all come from Calabro-Leichhardt. Grassby, the great spokesman of what was coming to be called ethnicity, was not an ethnic. The politician, who sometimes seemed the preacher of many nationalisms, belonged to none of them. No student of European nationalist leaders –

Napoleon, Garibaldi, Kossuth, Palacky, Parnell, Codreanu, Hitler, Stalin – should be surprised to find an antipodean outsider carrying the torch of those very nationalities to which he did not himself belong.

In any case, Grassby's political progress faltered. In 1974, he lost the seat of Riverina to the Country Party's Colonel John Sullivan, after a particularly nasty and personalised conservative campaign. Whitlam later said that, in the migration area, his minister had tried to move too far, too fast. Grassby's career was not over. Just before the downfall of the Whitlam government, Grassby was made commissioner for community relations, and so powerful was his image among migrants that the Fraser government waited until the end of his seven-year term in 1982 to replace him.

In the broadest sense, the Whitlam era symbolised the acceptance that multiculturalism had replaced assimilationism or even integrationism as the basis of a national immigration policy. For many, however, the conversion was partial at best. Racial hierarchies remained intact in many minds. In 1973, the Country Party's D. T. McVeigh still wanted Parliament to be aware that:

Based as we are on a predominantly British heritage it is reasonable to expect and to ask that other ethnic groups have to fulfil a longer term of residence to absorb our ethos, to grow accustomed to our customs and to do things in the Australian way.[42]

In 1980, Ian MacPhee (minister for immigration 1979–82) explained to a conference on multiculturalism: 'It is after all, the British heritage and tradition which enabled all present here tonight to meet on terms of complete equality, even though our origins are many.'[43]

Nor had old economic forces and old fears about defence requirements lost their power. After 1975, Australia rapidly expanded its migrant intake, while the *Australian* averred that it had been Labor's cut-back on immigration which had 'aggravated and prolonged the economic slump.'[44] The National Population Inquiry, instituted by Philip Lynch (minister for immigration 1969–71) rehearsed old phrases. Australia was headed for zero population growth. Industrial competitors with bigger markets threatened our manufacturers. Michael MacKellar, the minister for immigration (1975–9), took up the essentials of the report. Immigration was *the* essential part of a population strategy. 'Without being xenophobic', the minister pronounced, 'there is a question of whether we wish our continent to become the Great Southland in more than geographical size.'[45] Australia, it seemed, could still either perish, or populate and become that 'A1 nation' which Borrie had prophesied a generation earlier. Still more insouciantly (and more absurdly) many social scientists continued to use the categories 'northern', 'eastern' and 'southern' Europeans as they tried to probe migrant behaviour patterns through statistical analysis.

Yet not all was simple regression. Whether the conservatives had modernised or whether they were simply afraid of (the myth of) the migrant vote, they preserved a certain bipartisanship towards multiculturalism. They commissioned inquiries into the position of immigrants, and they endorsed sentiments similar to those endorsed by Labor. A Liberal Australia as much as a Labor Australia proclaimed:

all members of our society must have equal opportunity to realise their full potential and must have equal access to programs and services;
every person should be able to maintain his or her culture without prejudice or disadvantage and should be encouraged to understand and embrace other cultures.

And Malcolm Fraser, back on his farm, has listed the creation of a multicultural Australia as one of the major achievements of his government.[46]

The reality of 'multiculturalism' will be examined throughout this book. But these examples of surviving bipartisanship hint at another factor that has lain behind so much Australian immigration policy since 1945 – nationalism.

The most famous study of post-war Australia has been Donald Horne's *The Lucky Country* (1964). Its fame is justifiable because its thesis can be understood in optimistic or pessimistic direction. Maybe we are a farm or a mining town, a temporary settlement, to be closed down in drought or when our economic usefulness is outlived. Maybe we are the new America, the Great (White) Southland.

This unresolved search for a settled identity has characterised much Australian intellectual life since 1945. Whereas, after the Second World War in Europe, the age of nationality has seemed to many more and more absurd, the need to invent Australia and to find a distinctive, unifying, and justifying Australian nationality has become increasingly important.

The war showed that Australia could not survive as a (political) colony of England. More recent events have illustrated the danger of going all the way with the United States. The brooding and unmastered interior has gone on ominously mocking Australians as they play on the beaches or line up at their cities' international airports. In these circumstances, the way to adulthood, the way to overcome history and control the environment has seemed to be a new assertion of nationality, the crafting of an Australian legend to which we can all subscribe.

The immigration of an increasing number of aliens has been a major trigger to these ideas. First, there was a simple assimilationism when Australians in 1945 believed that they had only to shut their eyes and think of England. Then migrants just needed to be told how lucky they were:

'George', I say to myself, 'these men are Australians. They are the people who opened the doors of their homes for you, a man without a home to come in. And the only thing they ask you in exchange is to lend your hand in making this Australia still richer and more beautiful. So don't be shy boy! Raise your head! You're a free man here! Go to your task with joy!'[47]

By the 1960s, matters had become more complex. Imitating the nationalisation process of European countries one or two generations before, politicians began to unveil the sacraments of new Australia. A migrant could be justified by work: 'Mrs Turco who is very proud of her new home, said that her husband and brother had both worked hard to get their homes. "But in Australia you can get somewhere if you are prepared to work", she said.' For the inner man who could not survive on a nice home in the suburbs but who needed a sense of belonging, there was always citizenship: 'Naturalisation was like a marriage. When we marry, we pledge we will stay with each other for better or worse, for richer or poorer ... Australia has given us everything. It is up to us to make the bond work.'[48] By the 1970s, the Australian legend of mateship and meat pies seemed naive and dated. Yet the very arrival of multiculturalism coincided with a burst of new nationalism, with a new urgency in assertions of the uniqueness of Australia.

At first sight, immigration might seem to create new reasons not to believe that Australian history is detached from international influences or that Australian society is united in the one cause of the nation. But new nationalism has proved adaptable even before the fact of the disunity of classes or sexes, city or countryside, of one ethnicity or another. For Australians who either feared freedom, plurality, and ambiguity, or who wished to wrap themselves in a cocoon of our alleged uniqueness, multiculturalism began to seem an attractive mechanism by which unity could be preserved, even if only through diversity. So we became all the more proud to be Australian because we were polyethnic. So migrant historians were encouraged to detect that Julius Caesar, Alexander the Great, or a certain Duke of Courland had contemplated Australia, or that maybe Marco Polo or some French seaman or James Matra, whose Corsican origin if distorted enough could turn him into an Italian, was the real Father of Australia.[49] So schoolchildren were urged to construct an ethnic tree that displayed the flags of their own or their parents' countries of origin but which had that tree firmly planted in the Southern Cross and Union Jack of the Australian flag. The migrant presence, it was deemed, would make us all the more Australian.

History is always likely to become the servant of nationalism. Its practitioners in present-day Australia who seek out something new seem all the more slavishly anxious to make sure that the new is nationalist, that 'to be Australian' is more important than to be bourgeois or working class, male or female, left or right-handed, alive or dead.

Liturgy and ritual continue to play their part in proclaiming that religion of national unity in which a diversity of 'ethnic cultures' is significant and even pivotal. The opening spectacle of the 1982 Commonwealth Games in Brisbane provided a telling, if overblown, example. The red, white, and blue of the Australian flag fluttered in well-orchestrated patterns as 6000 Brisbane schoolchildren formed and re-formed in the middle of the arena to present images of the Australian flag, a map of Australia, and the logo of the games. Extra colour was provided by seventeen ethnic dance groups; beginning with Aborigines, the display moved speedily through Tongan, Italian, Filipino, German, Irish, Scottish, Welsh, Ukrainian and others. Here then, was multicultural Australia revealing and celebrating its diverse cultures. But diversity was not enough. The display went on to show how this diversity is bound together by the unity of Australian nationalism. The dance groups mingled, Tongan held the hand of Italian, Latin American of Welsh; the Brisbane schoolchildren enclosed the swaying multicultural mass in an outline of the map of Australia; and the strains of expatriate Peter Allen's 'I still call Australia home' seeped across the airwaves. Here was an embarrassing enactment of Al Grassby's much flaunted image of the Family of a Nation – differences exist and are good but their importance disappears under the all-embracing and inspiring knowledge that we are all Australians together, happy, triumphant, and moving towards an always better future.

But the history of migration really teaches a different lesson. It is a story more often of travail than of triumph, of confusion and chance rather than of planning. Many migrants pay more than they gain. Sometimes, however, there is something more than a tale of the crimes, follies, and tragedies of mankind. Sometimes, defying all the unifiers, migrants cling to what is small and beautiful – their village or neighbourhood, their culture, their dialect, their self-respect, their selves. Multicultural Australia pays lip service to this diversity of old worlds in its midst, yet many Australians remain sufficiently ignorant, naive or conservative to believe that there is such a thing as a 'commonly accepted way of life'[50] or that its creation is a national ideal. The spectre of assimilationism still stalks the land.

Chapter THREE

'Reffos' Old and New

Mrs Smithson* lives comfortably in a double garage home in one of the newer suburbs of Canberra. One afternoon in 1978 she settled back to recall the experiences that had led to her expulsion from her native Latvia and had set her trekking across the world until she ended up in the ordered and sparse Australian capital.

She had been born in the early 1930s and her family background was mixed. Her Baltic German father had disappeared into the ranks of the French Foreign Legion; her stepfather owned a hotel in the Latvian capital, Riga, and eventually served in the German army during the Second World War; her mother was a Latvian who, in order to keep the family from starvation during the First World War, had designed hats; and her grandfather was proudly Russian Orthodox and an ex-officer of the Tsar's army. He had fled west to Riga as the Tsarist regime had fallen to the revolutionaries of 1917. With this blending of ethnic, class, religious, and political backgrounds, family celebrations had been overburdened with friendly anti-German and anti-Russian banter bouncing off walls and across tables, and, as the 1930s dragged on, with endless debates about the direction of the approaching war and the threat it posed to a new and frailly independent Latvia.

Scarcely more than a decade old, Latvia was small and vulnerable. Its parliamentary system was uneasily structured, but, to many Latvians at least, their country was an outpost of culture, industry, and tolerance, beset by its two large and voracious neighbours, Germany and Russia. Mrs Smithson maintained that familial discussion turned on which of the two prospective invaders would be the more tolerable occupying force. Her family initially settled on the 'stupid Russians rather than the clever Germans'. Germans were too efficient; their war machinery and occupying forces would become too entrenched, and young Latvia would not be able to grow old.

*a pseudonym

But the family guessed wrongly, or, rather, did not see that there were no likely answers to their question. Russian, not German, occupation at length brought about their dispersal. By then Latvia had submitted to the embrace of each of its neighbours. Using the opportunity offered by the Russo-German Treaty of Non-Aggression (23 August 1939), Stalin's forces re-occupied the land which they still regarded as part of Russia. They were chased out in 1941 by German troops moving eastwards. When the Germans, in turn, fled west in 1944, the Russians were back, and, like their Tsarist predecessors, they would stay.

Mrs Smithson recalled that she had at first 'liked the Russians'. She was an adolescent and 'they treated children well'. Children could be educated into becoming the cadres of the revolution. But, for Mrs Smithson, the dream of revolution soon began to seem a nightmare. Communists, she learned, 'placed the state on a pedestal' and declared that 'even parents should be sacrificed to ideology'.

The family business, a picture theatre, was taken over by the state; the stepfather fled, pursued by the Russian police who knew of his part in the German war effort; and the apartment was forcibly let to a KGB officer. Mother and daughter stacked as much of the family silver as they could in a crate and dragged it with them to the coast. A hospital ship took them to Poland and, from there, they trudged on to Nazi Germany.

Life began to regain its order. Mrs Smithson attended a German state school and her mother managed to get some work as a waitress. Then Allied bombs started to fall. Mother and daughter took refuge in a bomb shelter in which they became trapped for 48 hours. When they emerged to a world deformed by high explosives, hopes of finding sanctuary in Germany died. With suitcases again in hand, they scrambled through the debris of buildings, swam across a bridgeless river, and climbed aboard the first train with open doors. They lurched off towards the Front and, when they realised what their destination was, panicked and lost each other. Mrs Smithson recollected that she wandered around for three or four days, desperately searching for her mother, and ran out of food. When mother and daughter were finally reunited, they boarded another train, exchanged suitcases for food, and were off-loaded at a male prisoner-of-war camp.

There, the German officers were very 'gentlemanly', at least to their Latvian guests, and expressed concern about leaving two women alone among freed prisoners of war, as they, the Aryan forces of law and order, retreated. So, before making their own escape, the gentlemen respectfully escorted the women through the woods, so that they would be safe from their 'racial inferiors'.

Deposited in a women's camp, the two refugees waited a little nervously for the triumphant American forces. United States style democracy was not necessarily perceived by the displaced Latvian of 1945 as bringing Utopia. Looking back, Mrs Smithson confided that, to her, the American troops proved to be less friendly and more officious than the Nazi Germans had been. But the American presence did mean that the future would be something more than a furtive search for shelter and endless, aimless wandering. The war had ended.

Mrs Smithson's mother was too broken to recognise the glimmer of hope now proffered. Her nerves gave way; she was hospitalised and, not long after, she died. Mrs Smithson, was left on her own. By some means she managed to complete her high school education through the system established in the displaced persons camps, and she then trained as a nurse. In 1949 she was accepted for emigration to Australia, a country about which she knew little, but which was far away from the turmoil of Europe.

Mrs Smithson's recollections are a mere fragment in the terrible mosaic of refugee oral histories. Jews and others who survived Hitler's concentration camps can recall in grisly detail the mutilated bodies, the emaciated faces, and the stench of death. South Americans remember the oiled moustaches and polished jackboots of the last dictator and his purchase of the latest electrode equipment guaranteed to quell the workers by Washington DC. White Zimbambweans bewail the interrupted cricket match, the servants turn nasty, and hint that a black Heart of Darkness will prove worse than a white. Vietnamese lament the false hopes built up by departing American forces, and the privations suffered on land and at sea as they strove to find sanctuary from the Marxist and nationalist discipline of the new regime.

The Australian press has often sold copy by relating the horror and pathos of such stories. In 1950–51, the newly established pictorial magazine *People* was studded with uplifting stories of refugees who were assimilating and making it in new Australia.

Characteristic was the 'Love Story' of Sava Spasojevic and Yelisaveta 'now Elisabeth' Brkic. Sava was described as a Mihailović supporter from Serbia who fell foul of the Germans and spent a good part of the war in German labour camps. Yelisaveta had lost her Hungarian father and brothers to a German firing squad and she, too, had bent her back in slave labour. These woebegone refugees met at Bathurst reception centre, where love soon blossomed under the gum trees. The past was forgotten.

People also introduced Hungarian-born Czech citizen Emil Koroscenko, a 'Man of Muscle'. At 15, he had squeezed a circus wrestling bear into submission and, with the outbreak of war, had made his prodigious strength available to the British army. In Sydney, he had successfully redirected his physical prowess into grinding coffee beans and stirring batter. He had established the Coffee Kup Inn in

Rushcutter's Bay to supply cakes and coffee to a 'European clientele'. More tranquil was the tale of a young Estonian girl who, triumphing over the perils of flight, had now been elected captain of her school in arcadian Goulburn. She had 'become as happily Australian as any of the smiling, sunburned playmates with whom she frolics on the red gravel playground'.

Gas chamber stories were also thought to appeal to *People*'s readership. Hanna Ungar had watched her mother and brother disappear into the ovens of Auschwitz, but she had managed to overcome the memories of two and a half years in German concentration camps and was now avidly studying medicine at Sydney University. Otto Schwarz had actually been gassed, but he had woken up to live again and somehow ended up in Australia. [1]

Three decades later, refugee stories still cross the pages of the press. In 1977, the *Bulletin* ran an account of some Vietnamese 'boat people'. Twenty-three Vietnamese were crammed into a 12 by 2 metre boat that had pushed off into unknown waters. Their food supply consisted of only 300 sheets of rice-paper and 3 kilograms of popped corn. Within 48 hours, the boat had sailed into a typhoon that raged for the next eight days. The boat was driven on like a cork; 'waves swamped . . . [it] at least thirty times'. The water supply ran out; some drank urine, others sea water. Friends and relatives began dying. Ships were sighted, but none stopped, perhaps luckily given the pirates who still roam those seas. When, after fourteen days, the boat by chance ran into Malaysian waters, nine of the original twenty-three were still alive. Two died soon after arrival. The other seven were left to wait in a refugee camp until some country decided to take them. [2]

It is hard, however, to maintain the credibility of horror stories. Perhaps part of the purpose and certainly part of the result of such telling of the refugee tale was to provoke cynical doubt and incredulity. As the *Daily Telegraph* warned about one group of boat people: 'The passengers and crew aboard . . . appear to be mainly fit and healthy young men who, at first sight, seem to be anything but desperate human beings crying out to be re-settled'. [3] In any case, reading such stories often only confirmed existing prejudices. Bruce Ruxton, president of the Victorian RSL, was worried about the effect of so much Asian immigration: 'I believe that the assimilation of races just does not work. Asian people are not the same as Caucasian people. In all the countries of the world where there are racial differences there is going to be racial strife.' [4]

The very notoriety and extent of the refugee waves that have flooded the world and overflowed into Australia since the Second World War have tended to disguise the fact that refugees, like the poor, have always been with us. They are not merely children of the political conflicts and technological terrors of the twentieth century's Age of

Violence. The past teems with individuals or families or nations that have been driven from hearth and home. The 'new history' of migrant groups in Australia is fond of locating figures who fled Poland after 1830 or 1863, Hungarians who left their country after the Russians repressed the revolution of 1848–49, or Germans whose religion or politics made them outcasts at home. Even Giuseppe Garibaldi, Hero of Two Worlds, touched an Australian shore in his wanderings in the 1850s. For Garibaldi, political recovery and triumph lay ahead; for others, the future offered only more 'painful settings out into the unknown'[5] and life in that place where past fame and status seemed to count as nothing. As Bertolt Brecht lamented:

> *Chased from my country now I have to see*
> *If there's some shop or bar that I can find*
> *Where I can sell the products of my mind.*
> *Again I tread the roads well known to me*
> *Worn smooth by those accustomed to defeat.*
> *I'm on my way but don't yet know to whom.*
> *Wherever I go they ask me: 'Spell your name!'*
> *And oh, that name was once accounted great.*[6]

Whether they were called expellees, exiles, or refugees, people have been displaced from their countries of origin throughout history. Yet, there is a distinction. Before the First World War, many victims of the latest round of Armenian massacres, Bulgarian horrors, or anti-Jewish pogroms just died. But the lucky few who escaped were then able to cross borders and oceans, and resettle without provoking much international expression of concern, assent or dissent. *Fin-de-siècle* Europe, for all its class struggles and ominous portents of worse international conflicts to come, was also the innocent world without passports (except in that land of ancient tyranny, Russia). People could travel across borders at will, and if the poor and the fleeing did, they would not do so in excessive numbers and, in any case, governments were weak and should not interfere too much. Even where some due forms were expected, bureaucrats were unprepared and ignorant. As one refugee who later took up residence in Brisbane recalled:

No visas were required to enter Australia, though as a formality an official who understood no Russian met every boat and demanded to be shown a passport. One of our company, an ex-soldier in the Russian Imperial Army who 'resigned' rather in a hurry, displayed a coloured theatre programme which fully satisfied the Australian official.[7]

Yet the world before 1914 was also changing. The state was becoming more intrusive; national rivalries were hardening. At home, each government was busily trying to educate its citizens into nationalism. Men of vision also proclaimed that international organisation brought benefits. Time was regularised. Nations began to agree about international postal systems, or began drafting international law. Experts on migration both in countries of origin and countries of reception started to think that migrants and refugees and their comings and goings needed to be controlled and guarded by government.

Both nationalism and internationalism expanded during the First World War and in the aftermath of the Russian Revolution. In 1917–18 Lenin offered international socialism to the world; Woodrow Wilson was the paladin of international liberal capitalism. At the same time, total war and total revolution further expanded the power and confidence of governments. All nations began to issue and demand passports.

In this new world, it was natural that international organisations should be constructed to systematise the handling of refugees. For the refugees were by then numerous. The political conflicts of the Russian Revolution and Civil War, and the foreign intervention in it, sent millions fleeing. The Graeco-Turkish war in Asia Minor, which culminated in the sack of Smyrna in September 1922, added yet more victims.

Given that one of the major ideological purposes of the League of Nations was to carry the standard of benevolent Wilsonian capitalism against Marxism-Leninism, it is not surprising that it was the League that became the agent of the 'new humanitarianism'. In 1919, it called on the Norwegian author and explorer Fridtjof Nansen to co-operate with the International Red Cross in dispersing and returning home unwanted aliens. Most were quickly and efficiently repatriated, but some Russians did not want to go back to their now communist controlled homeland. Other Russians, of similar political sympathies and past commitments, began joining their brothers in exile. By 1921 about 800 000 White Russians were scattered throughout Europe; others fled to Asia, establishing, for example, the community at Harbin in Manchuria.

Wherever they found refuge, they often had no passports and no citizenship. One woman, now an Australian, remembers living the first two decades of her life without identity papers or legal protection. Her father, an ex-Tsarist official, had thrown away his personal documents in fear of the consequences if he were caught. The Poland in which the family sought refuge allowed them only to live within a restricted area and, according to her recollections, refused the children any legal status until they came of age. The outbreak of the Second World War prevented her acquiring Polish citizenship and it was only when she became a naturalised Australian in the 1950s that, for the first time, she had an official and protected national identity and status.

Nansen appealed to the League of Nations to reduce such suffering and confusion, and, in 1921, an international agency (later known as the

League of Nations High Commission for Refugees), designed to regulate the movement of people between nations, came into existence. Nansen passports certified an official right to exist, and governments were petitioned to provide further assistance in the form of money or shelter. Groups other than the White Russians were soon included in the High Commissioner's mandate: Armenians again fleeing Turkish nationalism; Assyrians escaping from the social and political complications on the Russo-Turkish frontier and their repercussions in Iraq and Persia; and refugees from the French occupation of the Saar. Other refugees not officially recognised as such, and falling outside the protection of the Commissioner's office, also continued to seek a permanent haven. Among them were Jews who were putting an ever greater distance between themselves and the pogroms that had driven them from the Pale in the nineteenth century, and Italians who elected to join the ranks of the *fuorusciti,* those compatriots preferring to combat Fascism from a foreign shore.

Some of these wanderers eventually made their way to Australia. They came under normal immigrant requirements, unassisted, and as aliens without any special status, and they came to Australia partly because the golden door to America was now closed. One of these was Omero Schiassi, the self-consciously intellectual leader of the anti-Fascist cause and the scourge of Italian consular officials in interwar Australia. Schiassi, it was reported, 'had an amazing memory and could reel off whole cantos of the *Inferno,* always standing up to do so, and enhancing the effect of his voice by eloquent gestures. Although a socialist, he could dismiss airly an acquaintance with the remark: *E solamente un operaio'* ('He's just a worker').[8]

Among the Jews who arrived in the 1920s and 1930s, Polish-born Pinchas Goldhar was prominent. His short stories captured for his compatriots their loneliness and rootlessness in this strange land where a Jewish funeral could be conducted by an unshaven rabbi who was unable to speak Yiddish and where the hearse could be driven by a Gentile.[9] There was, too, the curious figure of Maurice Goldman. Competent in forty languages and fluent in fifteen, he liked to chant his prayers in Arabic at Zionist meetings.[10]

Pre-1930s refugees moved haphazardly, spilling across borders in rushes and trickles. They gained half-hearted international charity but were scattered and settled according more to the winds of fortune than to any seriously orchestrated international effort. Few finished in determinedly Anglo-Saxon Australia. But with the advent of Hitler, the term 'refugee' acquired a new and sinister meaning, as the age of democracy and of science turned into that of the technological control and extermination of the masses.

One Austrian Jewess who made her way to Australia in 1939 recollected the constant movement and the gathering ill-omen of the period. Born in a small Austrian town not long before the First World War, she studied photography in Vienna. She then lugged her camera through many of the grand cities of the defunct Habsburg Empire, snapping portraits of the wealthy and eccentric. In 1929 the bright lights and cabarets of Berlin beckoned. There she stayed for the next four years and watched, with slight interest, the rapid expansion of Nazism. No one took it seriously at first, she maintained. Then, began the hints, suggestions, and only half-credible tales of unpleasant experiences. Her Jewish employer lost his job and she was sacked soon after. Friends talked about going to Spain. One day she innocently wandered into a bookshop and, by chance, was grabbed in a police raid. After three weeks in prison, the arrest and subsequent release of her young man, and a further threatening inspection of her apartment block, out came the bicycles and it was time to say good-bye to Berlin. The couple pedalled off across France and into Catalonia.

In Barcelona, her skills were an asset and the municipal council employed her to photograph that part of the old city which still remained, the *barrio cino*. The proudly autonomist and progressive administration planned to pull it down in order to modernise the city but wanted first to create a permanent record for history. The photographs were taken and exhibited, but, in the event, the *barrio cino* stayed. The rebuilding programme had to be postponed. On 18 July 1936, the Spanish army rose in revolt against the Republic. The Spanish Civil War had begun.

From photographing crumbling buildings, the Austrian Jewess now turned to work on anti-Franco propaganda and publicity. But even such intellectual and artistic toil for the embattled Republic was not easy. Anarchist, Communist, Socialist or POUMist, autonomist Catalan, and centralist Spanish elements contended for supremacy. In 1937, a civil war within the civil war broke out in Barcelona and resulted in the massacre of the anti-Stalinist POUM elements. For a refugee, the main problem was stamps, many stamps, one for each party and each faction. She had most of them but, eventually, one, crucial that day, was missing. She was arrested and released.

Uncertainty, bombing, overcrowding, a closing border – all worked against a peaceful permanent refuge. She started moving again. Four months were spent in Paris as an *au pair,* but then her visa expired. Next it was off to Vienna to stay with an aunt. But that was in March 1938, a bad moment to visit. They were at the theatre when the Germans strode in and claimed Austria as part of the Greater Germany. A brief stay back in her home village, an unnerving encounter with Nazi officials on the Czech border and, finally, she arrived in England to work as a domestic. It was from there that she managed, in 1939, to gain passage to Australia.

There were others as fortunate. Some had left much earlier, many compelled by the closing of professions to Jews in Germany or Poland. During the early 1930s, entry to neighbouring countries, to England, and even to the United States had been relatively easy. The numbers were still small and the refugees were seen as desirable people who would bring skills, as had the Huguenots who had once fled Louis XIV's tyranny. Academics in England and America sought to sponsor fellow professionals. In 1938, for example, the American Psychological Association established a special committee that not only helped fellow German and Austrian psychologists to migrate to the United States, but also devoted itself to finding them professional posts. Earlier, action had come from a National Co-ordinating Committee designed to process scholars from central Europe into the American academic circuit. Into the United States rolled the great names of German arts, sciences, and professions, Albert Einstein, Leo Szilard, Theodor Adorno, Walter Gropius. Others, not so great but still distinguished, carried the numbers into the thousands.

In Great Britain there was a similar response. One organisation, the Society for the Protection of Science and Learning, had, by November 1938, placed 524 refugee scholars in permanent positions. Even in Australia, lagging well behind, a couple of institutions and individuals recognised the value of assisting established scholars. The vice chancellor of Melbourne University, Professor Raymond Priestley, arranged for a small number of professionals from Germany to join his staff. One of them has recalled that the university smoothed everything over for him, even to the extent of ensuring that naturalisation was effected in the shortest period of time and that he was accepted into the English Institute of Physics without British citizenship.

Religious aid organisations also sprang up in response to the plight of those rejected by Nazi doctrine as inferior. The Jewish community was particularly active. International organisations like the Hebrew International Aid Society and the American Joint Jewish Distribution Committee were galvanised into action and, in far off Australia, the recently established Australian Jewish Welfare Society and the German Emergency Committee began collecting funds. Assistance occasionally came from unexpected sources. One Austrian boy whose mother was Jewish was skilfully whisked away to England by the Quakers. They found a family to act as his sponsor for the long voyage to Australia.

By 1938, particularly after the *Anschluss,* and in the context of increasing anti-Semitic legislation in other European countries, notably in Poland, the numbers seeking sanctuary grew rapidly. Border controls and visa requirements became more strict; Nazi regulations allowed refugees to carry decreasing amounts of valuables with them; the American quota was almost full; and the British government imposed greater restrictions on those seeking to make their way to Palestine, then under British mandate. Shanghai became the only haven still open to visaless and fleeing Europeans.

Countries were reluctant to accept too many of the refugees who might be neither rich nor intellectual. The governor of Kenya was typical. His response to British representations that his colony might welcome a number of refugees was that only a 'carefully regulated influx of the right type – i.e. nordic from Germany or Austria' could be accommodated in Kenya, which must rather 'be developed on lines predominantly British'.[11]

Refugees had become a world-wide phenomenon, but it was one that most of the world preferred to ignore. The pattern was being set for the future. The horrors of expulsion or flight were not regarded as sufficient reason for accepting refugees. They still had to be selected and their flow controlled. International co-operation and responsibility offered one way out and was seized upon by United States president, F. D. Roosevelt. Bypassing the established League of Nations refugee organisations (in 1933 the League had created a special high commissioner for German refugees), the American president recommended an international conference. In July 1938, the representatives of thirty-five nations assembled at Evian on Lake Geneva. Cynics quickly dismissed much of the activity of the conference as mere posturing for domestic consumption and international respectability, and some gaily reversed its title, declaring 'naive' to be the more appropriate description of its intentions. Most government delegates muttered their concern for the situation of the refugees and found polite excuses for being unable to offer much assistance. The Australian delegate reported: 'As we have no real racial problem, we are not desirous of importing one.' The New Zealand delegate complained that the Conference was turning into a 'modern wailing wall'. Most delegates agreed that no financial commitment could be expected. But, good committee men all, they decided on the establishment of another international body geared to examining solutions to the refugee problem. The Intergovernmental Committee for Refugees was established and began slowly and properly to debate what could be done.[12]

One possibility was to locate a new, 'vacant' area in which Jews could be settled. Within the Nazi state, Adolf Eichmann and his bureaucrats, shuffling their papers while they plotted the twisted road to the Final Solution, favoured Madagascar. At the Evian Conference, Roosevelt had wondered if Mussolini might make newly conquered Ethiopia available. Others deemed Alaska a better possibility. The British Foreign Office meanwhile favoured the uplands of Guyana since, as one official noted, it was 'desirable ... to salve the conscience of His Majesty's Government in relation to European Jewry'.[13]

In these circumstances, thoughts also turned to the 'empty lands' of Australia. In the spring of 1939, two pillars of the dissenting tradition of the troublemakers, Norman Angell and Dorothy Buxton, wrote a Penguin Special entitled *You and the Refugee*. Amid emphasis on the economic advantages of immigration, the authors also declared that 'there are great empty spaces which cannot be made fruitful without large immigration in the Continent of Australasia ... In this vast undeveloped country ... Australia must surely offer unlimited scope for engineers, builders, trained mechanics, and skilled workers in all kinds of industry'. All in all, Angell and Buxton decided, a letter written to the *Times* had got it right: 'May it not be that in the long run Australia has the choice between the Jews and the Japs'. Pressure could, therefore, be applied to Australian governments so 'that an independent Dominion for the Jews might be established in north-west Australia'.[14]

Jewish groups themselves began to have similar, if more muted, ideas. Some had pointed out that Australia was ignoring an unparalleled opportunity to acquire 'first class scientists and artists'.[15] In 1939, I. N. Steinberg of the London-based Freeland League for Jewish Territorial Colonization came to Australia and made contact with J. C. Willcock, the Labor premier of Western Australia.

Steinberg visited the Kimberleys and was shown around by the powerful pastoral family of the Duracks. Like many a foreigner unaware of the caprice and cruelty of the Australian outback, Steinberg saw that 'the land is not dead nor even barren. It is only an empty land, a slumbering land. Just as in a fairy tale it needs only a magic wand to touch its sleeping treasures and to bring them to life.' Denying that independent Dominion status was necessary, Steinberg stated that the immigrants could 'become a new type of Jew – an *Australian* Jew'. Local poets, he said, would soon spring up and 'write Jewish poems about the kangaroo or the laughing kookaburra, the hot days and the cool evenings, the magic spell of the earth and the first steps of the wanderer pioneers'.

While Steinberg comforted his audiences, or himself, with such dreaming, the mills of bureaucratic preparation had begun to grind – slowly. In August 1939, Willcock signified his government's approval. The Australian Council of Trade Unions was contacted and in 1940 declared that they, too, would not oppose a Jewish settlement.

But no Jews landed at Derby. The Labor federal government procrastinated. Steinberg tirelessly sought out new supporters or sympathisers – Professors Alexander and Roberts, Archbishops Mannix and Mowll, the Labor premier of Tasmania (who thought that the south-west of his state might be a possible sanctuary for Jewish refugees). Others were less favourable – what if 'aliens' left the Kimberleys or the Franklin and flocked to the cities? By the end of

1941, it was plain that nothing would be done for the moment. W. D. Borrie soon offered an explanation: such an undiluted colony would have been 'an admission of failure [because] ... Successful immigration on any scale can only be considered on the basis of assimilation, not separation'.[16]

In the meantime, the publicity that had been stimulated at Evian and some further pressure from the existing Australian Jewish community led to another response from an Australian government justifiably wary of the return of Depression. In December 1938, it announced that 15 000 refugees could be accepted over the next three years provided that they could fulfil the normal immigration requirements and produce at least £200 in landing money or £50 and a sponsor who could guarantee accommodation and employment. Even the local Jewish community was unhappy about letting in all Jewish refugees. One member reflected in 1944: 'It must be admitted that many Australian Jews have maintained an aloof, patronizing, even hostile attitude towards the newer arrivals ... I am convinced many Australian Jews still look upon the new arrivals as aliens, not as fellow Jews.'[17] Some refugees (about 3300) had already come to Australia before the December 1938 decision. They were joined by just under 8000 more before the outbreak of the war.

Their stories were variations on a theme: the realisation that Europe was no longer safe; the first direct experiences of Nazi persecution; the denial of their livelihoods; the theft of their material wealth. They came to Australia because it was one of the few countries accepting refugees, even if the regulations were stringent. Looking back, many concurred with the recollections of one German-born Jew, now a successful doctor in Australia. He noted that the only other visas available were 'to a small state in Africa or a banana republic in South America'. Another who had fled racism but not altogether escaped it, chimed in: 'At least Australia was white'.

With the outbreak of war, the flow of refugees reaching Australia all but stopped. The one exception was the arrival of the *Dunera,* bringing among others Sol Encel, Henry Mayer and Felix Werder from internment in Britain to internment in Australia. Official records note that on board were 251 German and Austrian 'A' or 'hard core' Nazi internees, 200 Italians, and 1916 German and Austrian 'B' or 'C' internees. Lumped together on one ship designed to carry 1500, these internees arrived in Australia complaining bitterly of ill-treatment and harrassment at the hands of the British seamen and officers. Baggage had been pilfered, food rationed, men beaten with sticks until they agreed to scrub the floors. The commander of the ship was subsequently court martialled in England. His allegiance to theories of racial hierarchy seemed implicit in his reports to the military authorities in Melbourne. In one report he referred to the three categories of internee on board. The Nazi Germans, he admitted, were dangerous but, once he made plain to them their status as prisoners of war, 'their behaviour [was] ... exemplary ... They are of a fine type, honest and straightforward and extremely well disciplined'. By contrast, he found the Italians to be 'filthy in their habits, without a vestige of discipline, and ... cowards to a degree'. Finally, there were the Jews: 'subversive liars, demanding and arrogant'. They demanded and complained and, in order to gain their demands, would 'quote any person from a Prime Minister to the President of the United States as a personal reference'.

The reputation of the *Dunera* and its commander grew blacker as more details became public, as internees were released and returned to England or stayed to become famous in Australia. The voyage of the hell-ship *Dunera* is now seen as providing sordid evidence about Australian and British treatment of refugees. For the Zionist Benzion Patkin, the experience also demonstrated the failure of Australian Jewry to respond sympathetically to the plight of its brothers. In Australia's wartime history, the *Dunera* has become a symbolic concentration camp. But it is also eloquent testimony to Australia's cloistered outlook. What else but ignorance of the world beyond the Australian coastline could have influenced the official who, in investigating theft on board, noted sagely that the internees constantly mentioned Gannef as responsible for the trouble. Repeated efforts, he said, were being made to establish the identity of this character. The efforts were fruitless. A later pencilled comment on the report revealed: ' "*Gannef*" is the Yiddish for thief.'

Perhaps, too, the horrors experienced by those who endured the trip pale, when, in retrospect, they are compared with what was happening to relatives in Europe, if such comparison is possible. Even on the *Dunera,* Australians escaped the worst excesses of the 'rage of history'.[18]

In Europe, technology and ideology were already engaged in producing those death lists of 20 million Russians, 6 million Jews, 4 million Poles, and many more. Total war, defying semantics, changed its nature. In the Second World War, civilians were more at risk than were soldiers at the Front. But, even while the massacres continued, a few escaped. Sweden, Switzerland, Spain, and Persia and countries further east offered erratic and dangerous routes to exile. As the front moved in one direction or another, the European population, by car, train, boat, cart or on foot, began in their millions to move.

One Polish-born Australian Jew had the good fortune, after the outbreak of war, to punt on going east and on finding initial sanctuary in the Russian occupied part of Poland. There he was interned and, with his wife, was sent, ever eastwards, to work in the mines of the Urals. For the moment, Russia and Germany were allies. When their alliance ceased with the invasion of Russia in the summer of 1941, Jewish internees in the Ural area were released. From the Urals, the couple travelled south to Samarkand, by barge, train, boat, and on foot. It was another two and a half years before they left Samarkand and boarded a ship to carry them to Australia.

The Jews were not alone. Polish nationalists slipped across the Hungarian border to escape occupying German tanks; Dutch servicemen sailed across the English Channel to join the British forces; Danes and Norwegians crossed neighbouring borders to live beyond the horror of Nazi and quasi-Nazi occupation.

Then, as the war turned against the Axis powers, a new wave of refugees began to move. Latvians, Lithuanians, Estonians, and Ukrainians joined withdrawing German troops as the Russian liberators marched in. Other eastern Europeans (Hungarians, Poles, Czechs, Slovaks) joined the flight westwards as their countries fell to the Russian and communist liberating forces. Their reasons were similar: some were afraid because of what they had seen; some were afraid because of what they had done.

A Sydneysider, born in the Ukraine, recalled that the Russians had been appalling occupiers; they had mistreated and killed the local population. A Lithuanian-born Australian talked of the mutilated bodies and starving prisoners left behind when the Russians had retreated in 1941. In Hungary the liberating Red Army was described by an Australian-Hungarian woman, who had learned well central European myths about the evil that lay to the east, as 'full of Asiatics'. They were 'barefooted' and 'had never seen a watch'; they were like 'wild animals', although they refrained from harming children or old people and, instead, expended their barbarity on raping women. This particular woman avoided such a fate by having a doctor-friend encase both her legs in plaster.

In Yugoslavia, it was not a Russian incursion that impelled people to head towards Germany, but Tito's homegrown communism. Croatians, who actively or passively had supported Pavelić's cruel puppet Ustaša state, fled, as did more respectable citizens, like the now Australian Senator Misha Lajovic. His flight was provoked by a distaste for the philosophies and practices of Tito which, for a time, were the most hard-line in eastern Europe, and by the belief that a communist regime simply could not survive in Yugoslavia. His hopes were dashed and his distaste confirmed as months passed, particularly when his father was sentenced to ten years hard labour for being a monarchist and a capitalist. The family had owned a substantial plastics industry on the outskirts of the Slovenian capital, Llubljana.

In all, the war dislodged 60 million people, and, in 1945 many of these displaced persons still spilled across Europe. By September 1945 there were almost 7 million in the areas freed by British, American, and French forces, and a further 7 million were under Soviet rule. The spectre of starvation stalked vast tracts of Europe where it had not been known for centuries. In early 1946, it was reported that 100 million Europeans were making do on less than 1500 calories a day, half of what was deemed necessary for basic sustenance.[19]

Once the fighting ceased, some method had to be found to deal with this motley mass of homeless people. In western Europe military and bureaucratic structures sprang up to process people, structures that set a pattern for the future.

The first and most immediate problem was how to house and feed the refugees while they waited for decisions about their fate. Centralisation and organisation were the ready and perhaps necessary answers for civilian and military forces confronted with millions of displaced people. Under the auspices of the United Nations Relief and Rehabilitation Administration (UNRRA, established in November 1943) and its successor, the International Refugee Organisation (IRO, established in July 1947), ready-made venues were taken over. Army barracks became displaced persons camps, as did schools, factories, and even ex-concentration camps. Conditions varied. One Latvian woman, who arrived in Australia in her late teens and managed here to pick up the threads of a frayed education, recalled a succession of camps. The first was a converted school. It was quite comfortable with central heating and sportsfields. A later camp was a collection of fenced-in German private houses. Here the situation was more grim. Her recollections triggered deep-seated ethnic rivalries. The lack of furniture was lamented and was credited to previous occupation by the Poles: 'wherever they went they burnt the furniture for warmth'. They were, she said 'uncivilised by comparison with Latvians'.

Other Australians, when they recall their days in European refugee camps, tell of the shortage of food and of the devastated, hungry German towns in which they were housed. One man, who had done his service with the Czech forces in the British army, talked about bread made from sawdust, with rats' tails providing the texture. He maintained that the food rationed for four days was sufficient for one. Ingenuity and stealth had to become a way of life: the mayor's garden lost tobacco and the German police station yielded vegetables from its fertile plot.

Other memories of camp life tell of a 'black' unofficial economy, a 'black' political system, a 'black' social structure. Cigarettes became the great wonder-working currency. With them you could buy a lover or a tin of jam, a new nationality or a loaf of bread, a new religion or a new past.

Life in the camps was monotonous and frustrating. Even increased facilities and services – the provision of schooling, reading material,

February 1950: queuing at Bagnoli transit camp outside Naples, Italy. Most people assisted by the International Refugee Organisation were processed through Bagnoli before they boarded the ships which carried them to the new worlds.

sports, social activities – did not eradicate mental and physical alienation. Identity and existence seemed suspended while the inmates
waited for the Great Powers to open pathways back home, or to allow
resettlement in new and foreign lands. Antigone Kefala has recorded
her impressions of the endless, alienating waiting. With her Greek
parents, she had travelled from Romania and into Greece, before
moving to New Zealand and Australia. Of her period in the camp, she
has recalled:

> *We waited there two summers.*
> *Tall birds with upturned beaks*
> *picked us like grain.*
> *We moved in herds*
> *waited with patience to be fed*
> *drank at the water places*
> *between the walls our necks grew longer*
> *stretching for the night.* [20]

They waited, hoping and wondering, until, finally, the authorities
began to act. The priority was to repatriate as many refugees as
possible. By 1947, about 5 million people had been sent back to their
countries of origin. The remainder were unwilling to depart and the
creeping chill of the Cold War worked in their favour. The Allies,
readying themselves for McCarthyism, became reluctant enforcers of
repatriation to the east. The IRO took on the responsibility of
processing people out of Europe. Countries willing to take refugees
were sought. Australia was one. In December 1947 Calwell declared
that Australia would accept and house an initial 12 000 refugees from
the displaced persons camps, provided that they agreed to work for two
years at the government's behest.

Officials were sent to select suitable refugees. Kefala's poem takes up
the tale:

> *They came in the spring with the great winds*
> *the buyers*
> *walked through the gates in groups*
> *their marrow discoloured*
> *their eyes ashes*
> *gestures full of charity.*
>
> *Bidders, in markets for flesh*
> *untouched by the taste of coffee*
> *and the scent of the water*
> *on the hot stones.* [21]

Refugees rarely did the choosing. Instead they were chosen, though
speculation was rife. In her novel-memoir Cecile Kunrathy notes the

rumours that circulated about Brazil. There, it was alleged, migrants were used 'to clear the jungles', and 'monkeys helped the migrants to chop trees; they watched all day to see how the migrants did it, then by night they came down from the trees and continued chopping'.[22] Australia invited similar exaggerated and ill-informed descriptions. The eccentric, but prolific, Czech-born writer, V. L. Borin, recalled in his autobiographical novel, *The Uprooted Survive,* that the news that Australia would accept displaced persons 'electrified the minds of all the refugees in the camp'. But excitement dwindled into wonder as people asked: 'Where is it anyhow?'. One character 'was almost sure that in Australia there must be some European buildings, because there are many savage black people ... but also a few white people who went there from Europe to grow coconuts and dig for gold'.[23] Another refugee, a Ukrainian, later confessed his alarm when, on board ship, he was shown typical photographs of Australia – they were of Aborigines eating roast snake. Eventually, however, a Croatian found a securely assimilated metaphor to sum it all up: 'It was like a Sunday drive. You didn't mind where.'[24]

As the rumours circulated and the hopes became more vivid, the refugees tried to get to the countries they preferred. But selection criteria for all were similar. Health, family numbers, labouring ability, and previous political and national allegiances were always checked. Great Britain, Canada, the United States, the high preference countries, all wanted labourers, people able to work at the harsh activities of post-war reconstruction. Australia and New Zealand searched for similar skills. Doctors told the authorities that they were cleaners, lawyers became roadworkers, and genteel ladies, who had always had servants, vowed that they were trained domestics.

Receiving countries also had their national and political preferences. Ex-Axis supporters and servicemen were unwelcome, as were rabid communists. Pasts had to be shielded, forgotten or denied. There were reports of Germans masquerading as stateless persons. A Henri Cartier-Bresson photograph of the time catches the triumphant expression of a refugee who has accused a fellow camp inmate of being a Gestapo informer and not a genuine Displaced Person.[25] Russians said that they were Czechs, Ukrainians turned into Poles, and collaborators became resistance fighters.

By 1951, with the assistance of the IRO most of Europe's 1 million displaced persons who had refused repatriation had been located in new homes. Australia had accepted about 200 000, second only to the United States' 300 000. The somewhat reluctant pre-war recognition of the need to help solve the refugee problem had become an accepted international practice. In 1951, with the establishment of the United Nations High Commissioner for Refugees (UNHCR), IRO's successor, the arrangement was formalised. The status and legal rights

of refugees were discussed and defined. The agreed protocol declared
that a refugee was any person who

owing to well-founded fear of being persecuted for reasons of race, religion,
nationality, membership of a particular social group or political opinion, is
outside the country of his nationality and is unable or, owing to such fear, is
unwilling to avail himself of the protection of that country: or who, not having a
nationality and being outside the country of his former habitual residence is
unable or, owing to such fear, is unwilling to return to it.[26]

From being hapless individuals accorded reluctant assistance during
the interwar years, refugees had become a special category of migrants
requiring extra protection, extra care, and an extra supervisory
bureaucracy. And still the numbers did not dwindle.

In Europe, Soviet tanks crushed the Hungarian uprising in 1956 and
blighted the Prague spring in 1968. In 1984, many Poles and
Romanians plainly feared that they would be next on the list. Greeks
and Turks burned each others' villages in Cyprus. The Irish question
was never answered. As well, times of trouble occurred in China, India,
Israel, Egypt, Chile, Uganda, Vietnam, East Timor, Lebanon,
Afghanistan, El Salvador, and elsewhere. In 1969, it was estimated that
there were over 17 million refugees in the world. Since then, the total
has fluctuated (by 1980 it was said to be between 11 and 13 million),
but it has shown no sign of going away.

Since its acceptance of that first batch of displaced persons in 1947,
Australia has remained a party to international co-operation in
assisting and housing refugees. A signatory to the United Nations 1951
Convention, which defined refugee status, and also to its 1967 Protocol
which, as a symbol of the formal weakening of racism, extended this
definition to cover refugees in the world beyond Europe, Australia has
annually siphoned some money into the tasks of clothing and feeding
refugees in the camps and into moving them into new homes. The
contribution has not been over generous and has probably been
prompted more by self-interest than by humanitarianism, but, in the
world of international diplomacy and finance, it has not compared too
unfavourably with the amounts furnished by other, wealthier nations.
According to one analyst, Australia has 'in proportion to its population
... led the world in accepting refugees for settlement' and, in recognition of the Australian contribution, T. H. E. Heyes was awarded the
Nansen Medal in 1962.[27]

Predictably enough, racial hierarchies have conditioned Australian
charity, and over half the 400 000 or more refugees accepted since 1945
came from Europe and mainly from eastern Europe. The Budapest
uprising of 1956 sent 14 000 Hungarians here; the Prague spring of
1968 produced a small harvest of 5500 Czechoslovaks; and the Polish
winter of 1980–81 witnessed a new influx. Small numbers of refugees

from other eastern European countries have regularly slipped across borders and begged, borrowed, or bought their visas to Australia. Troubles in Cyprus in the 1970s expelled 4000 more Greeks to join their compatriots in Australia.

While Australia has been fairly solicitous of these refugees from Europe, until recently, we have chosen largely to ignore the plight of refugees in other parts of the world. Only a handful of Chileans, Ugandan Asians, and Timorese have been accepted. Since 1975, however, there has been a variation with the arrival of some 60 000 Indo-Chinese refugees. The reluctance and fear with which this change has been implemented is reflected in the guarded comments printed in government publications. There is concern that the Australian public will not meet this 'forceful challenge to the Australian community's traditional attitude towards people in need'. After all, 'Australia is accepting for resettlement as refugees a large number of people who come from very different racial and cultural groups and who, in the not too distant past, would not have been acceptable as settlers under any circumstances.'[28]

But it is not just numbers, composition, and Australian attitudes that matter. There are also the refugees themselves. Already during the Second World War, one refugee in Australia recorded: 'At best, Australians are kind to reffos as they are to animals. They want us to keep our place on the lowest rung of the social ladder.' Another has remembered, when he was interned as an alien, that the police who came to his house were bemused by what they found there:

'So many books', said one policeman in the other room.
'Why does he need so many?' asked the other ...
'No firearms, lady?' said the one in charge to the 'reffo's' wife.[29].

These comments echo through the refugee story. Refugees often have superior qualifications that Australians have disregarded as they have dispatched the new arrivals to the factory assembly lines or to the bush. Refugees are people who are able to understand at once that Australia is a place of low *kultur*. 'This is a country for labourers and business people.' 'Here, sports competition is encouraged, academic competition is unfashionable. In Vietnam, it was absolutely the opposite.'[30]

Perhaps, it is not only Australia that prompts such opinions or prejudice. Perhaps refugees have often clung to a lingering sense of superiority and not always believed in their clinging. As the great Russian memoirist Ilya Ehrenburg perceived in Paris:

Some émigrés sighed for the past, others lived for the future. But emigrés of different persuasions, different nationalities, different periods have one thing in common: a rejection of the foreign country where they find themselves through no will of their own, an acute nostalgia for their own country, the need to live in a narrow circle of their compatriots and the consequent, inevitable dissensions

... It is difficult to uproot fully grown plants; they become diseased and often
perish. In Russia now they practice winter transplanting: a tree is dug up while it
is in a dormant condition. In spring it comes back to life in a new place. A good
method especially as a tree has no memory.[31]

The refugees who reach Australia are often the lucky ones. They are
the ones who have survived, escaped, and found a new country.
Almost always the escape has not been a complete accident. Successful
refugee populations are likely to contain a high percentage of educated
and moneyed people of middle-class backgrounds. Their social or
intellectual status has often encouraged a new regime to punish them
and to produce their flight. At the same time, their status and traditions
have often provided the self-control, wealth, and imagination that
have made the flight successful, and that habit of getting what they
want which has often allowed rapid upward social mobility in
Australia.

In the 1950s and 1960s, as the sociology of ethnic groups began to be
studied, it used to be the fashion to collect statistics that demonstrated
that Jews or 'Balts' or Polish Catholics, central or eastern Europeans,
did better educationally or in status than Greek or Italian southerners.
These statistics in turn could engender semi-racist pondering about
what distinguished refugees from those who still had to escape the
'moral basis of a backward society'.[32] But what such commentators
often ignored was the simple point of class. For the individual
concerned, it is a terrible and a tragic tale to be a refugee, to flee your
home for political reasons. But much about that flight, and a refugee's
subsequent behaviour in a new country is conditioned by class, and not
so much by the class position gained in Australia as by class and status
in the place of origin.

Australians, at first, paid little attention to such complexities. All
'aliens' were alien, although they were not necessarily absolutely to be
avoided. Indeed, in the 1950s, 'reffos' and 'Balts' achieved a place
among the most famous new sights of Australia. One, who settled in
rural Victoria near Seymour, has recounted in her memoirs the
reaction of her neighbour, Madge, to the newcomers who

made her sick, not only because they came shooting at weekends and left gates
open, but because they were trying to take over the country ... they all worked
too hard and made money too fast, then they bought better houses than decent
Australians had. The way they gabbled got on her nerves; they should have been
made to learn English before they arrived.

But the same memoirist, a Polish Jewess who had endured the most
horrific experiences during the Second World War, continued, 'in
practice, despite her rhetoric, Madge couldn't do enough for me'.[33] In
1984, students of migration to Australia are likely to react in an

opposite but similar manner. 'Refugee' conjures up the names of famous contributors to Australian culture or economy: Felix Werder, Antigone Kefala, Judy Cassab, Louis Kahan, Alexander Barton, Sir Paul Strasser, Harry Seidler, Claudio Alcorso, Ernest Bramsted. But just as it is important not to be too harsh on Madge, not to see her racism and miss her charity, so it is important not to assume that all refugees are intellectuals of the quality of Freud or Toscanini, or that they all make it. In our history of migrant work, migrant politics, and migrant society, refugees will often be found as the self-conscious intellectual leaders of their communities. Some will be fearful of their pasts and want to forget or obscure them; some will have assimilated, have become as ocker as Sir Henry Bolte and deny they ever had a past; some will be rich; some will be poor; but all will remain, somewhere in their hearts, children of an old world and will have borne some of its wealth, achievement, and belief in its own superiority, and some of its tragedy to the new Australia.

Chapter FOUR
Emigrants and their Odysseys

In one summer [on the plain], you can get five times what Abdi Agha [the landlord] gives in a year. There's a city there, Adana, all of clear glass. It sparkles day and night, just like the sun. You walk in the alleys between the houses, they call them streets, and it's all glass. It's as clear as can be. Trains come and go. On the sea, ships as big as villages go to the other end of the world. Everything shines like the sun, bathed in light. If you look at it just once, you can't take your eyes away.

So the Turkish novelist Yashar Kemal, in *Mehmed, my Hawk* (1961), sketches the emigrant dream for some mountain villagers of Anatolia. For them, Kemal explains, emigration opened a path to paradise out of that old 'world by itself, with its own laws and customs. The people ... know next to nothing of the worlds beyond ... Very few have ever ventured beyond the limits of the plateau.' The prospect of Adana might seem celestial; the reality was not. A villager who does go off to the plain labours for six years so that, if all goes well, he can come back home sufficiently rich 'to bring a woman in to the house and [buy] a pair of oxen and a warm coat for my mother.'[1]

Yashar Kemal's story reveals that life for many men (if not for many women) has not been a sedentary and static matter of village, house, work, and family. Mountaineers, starving in bad seasons, have sought the plain; shepherds, in summer, have carried their flocks from the plain to mountain pastures; seamen have stayed away from home for months or years at a time in pursuit of whales or pearls or sponges. Bandits have roamed the hill country far from their village, and soldiers have chased bandits still farther afield. The formal, hierarchical and static 'world we have lost' nourished also the myths of emigrants, of Joseph and Mary departed from Nazareth, of Ulysses far from Ithaca while Penelope waited back home.

Most often, the straying was meant to be temporary. Anthropologists have argued that, for peasants, time was often understood not as linear but as cyclical, the wheel of the seasons that turned 'upon itself beyond human control'. Peasants in this flux of time clung to their village, but really to their history, to the past. The past became 'a path, the only possible path, away from the misery surrounding them'. Since 'the structure of the past was static, while its content remained dynamic', a peasant or an emigrant could use the past 'to conquer time itself'. Away among incomprehensible and dangerous foreigners, a man could save his identity through his recollections of his village past, and know, too, that the wheel of fortune and of time one day would carry him home.[2]

But in the nineteenth century, industrialisation began to undermine these age-old *mentalités* just as it began to speed up and formalise the rhythms of work, of play, and of time itself. In the world that technology was reducing in size, more men began to travel more often and to go geographically and spiritually farther and farther afield. They flocked to the cities, drastically altering the traditional balance between urban centre and countryside. They fled the old worlds of Europe or Asia for new worlds in the Americas or Australia.

The United States became the especially favoured destination. Swedes left their rocky, infertile, and small landholdings to find new land, new farms, and new lives on the American frontier; the Chinese packed their ghosts and tales, bought cheap passages, and slipped into American cities to grow vegetables and to launder clothes; Italians petitioned their families for the entrance fee to an earthly *paradiso*. *'Mamma mia dammi cento lire che nell'America io voglio andar'* (Dear mother give me a hundred *lire* so that I may go to America).[3]

The figures were staggering. Of the estimated 51 million people who left Europe between 1846 and 1939, 38 million passed through the American 'golden door' and most had done so before the First World War. Argentina in the mid nineteenth century consisted of little apart from the port of Buenos Aires, but from 1869 to 1960, the Argentinian population increased from 1.7 million to 20 million, much of it through immigration.[4]

A world away, Australia saw little of what one American historian, with infelicitous but characteristic metaphor, termed 'the swarming of the peoples'.[5] To 1945, the Australian population grew more slowly than that of North or South America. The only immigrants to be cherished were British, and even they could not expect much of a welcome if they arrived in a time of drought or depression.

Multicultural Australia has tried to make amends for traditional xenophobia by seeking out any ancestors of modern ethnic communities who managed to penetrate colonial Australia. 'Ethnic historians' have unearthed some strange and not very convincing fathers of ethno-Australia. For the historian of the Hungarian community, the arrival in Australia of Baron Cézár Mednyánszky, ex-chaplain-general of the revolutionary army of 1848–49, can seem significant. Less underlined is the fact that Mednyánszky did not remain long in Australia and ended by poisoning himself in 1857 on the French Riviera after some unsuccessful love affairs.[6] The historian of the French community has been delighted to locate a scion of the Bourbon family, Gabriel Louis Marie Huon de Kerillian, in the Sydney of the 1790s. This aristocrat was engaged in the task of *chercher la femme*. Once he had found his woman, Huon de Kerillian did have enough time to act as a sort of symbol for the later role of the French language in the Australian education system by becoming a tutor to the children of John Macarthur.[7] Perhaps more bizarre is the listing of Jan Jerzy Forster among the ancestors of Australia's Poles. Presented as a Polish university professor, albeit of Scottish descent, his status as an Australian pioneer rests on his participation in James Cook's journey to New Zealand.[8]

More numerous migrant groups have also been pleased to locate their first Australian ancestors. The Italians (like the Jews and the French) have detected an ethnic presence among the convicts of the first fleet.[9] Greek historians have to delay the first recorded arrival of their country-men to 1829 when seven 'Greeks' arrived on a British ship. Their position as convicts tried for piracy under British law in Malta and the rapid re-emigration of four of the seven does not deflect proud claims to their role as the founders of the Greek communities in Australia.[10]

This quest for legitimation through history is absurd, if predictable. But the ethnic historians have done some useful work in indicating that colonial white Australia was not after all completely British. There were some Greeks and Italians; some Scandinavians jumped ship here or in New Zealand; and Germans began to farm the Barossa after 1838. The gold rushes had attracted 17 000 Chinese to Victoria by 1855, although the goldfields commissioner remarked that 'even if the Chinese are considered desirable colonists, they are unaccompanied by their wives and families under which circumstances no immigration can prove of real advantage to any society'.[11]

Racism would soon harden Australian hearts against further Asiatic migration, but Europeans did continue to slip in. In particular, the 1920s brought a fresh increase after the United States had barred its doors through restrictive legislation in 1921 and 1924. By the 1933 census, over 26 500 Italians, 8000 Greeks and 3500 Yugoslavs were registered here. Most had arrived in the previous ten years.

Perhaps to term these migrants Italians or Greeks or Yugoslavs is to falsify history, anachronistically to nationalise them before they had participated in that great process of the 'nationalisation of the masses'.[12] Modern Italian scholars have developed the useful term 'the Italies' to define these unnationalised societies within the borders of their country. To the Italies can be added the Greeces, the Polands, the Chinas, the Turkeys, the Lebanons and all the others.

To the cafes, market-gardens or canefields of Australia they came, these men of Ithaca, Kythera, Kastellorizo and Lesbos, the Lipari Islands, Messina, Molfetta, Reggio Calabria and the Abruzzi, Macedonia or the islands off the Dalmatian coast. Who were they, these forerunners of Australia's mass non-British immigration? They were and they remained what Italians call *paesani,* villagers, although, especially in the south, a 'village' or 'agro-town' may have 30 000 inhabitants. Even as they journeyed to a new world, they lived in an old world which, in the cities of Europe, had already disappeared. It was a narrow world: 'Wife and children from your own village'; 'Whoever doesn't have fellow-villagers also lacks good fortune in any of his affairs'; and a cruel one: 'Only a Neapolitan would steal from a poor bastard worse off than he, but it is a lesson: trust no-one'; or, as a Greek Cypriot saying assessed the fate of the poor man: 'When the rock falls on the egg, alas for the egg. When the egg falls on the rock, alas for the egg.'[13]

Present day films such as *L'Albero degli zoccoli (The Tree of Wooden Clogs)* or *I tre fratelli (Three Brothers)* are inclined to romanticise peasant society. It probably does not deserve such romanticisation. Rather, the peasant world was the violent one of *padre, padrone, padreterno,*[14] a world of hatreds, within the family and especially of the neighbours, of those who these days are pushed together in Australia as belonging to a single ethnic group. In Sicily, during the 1950s, poor youth were reported not to know what 'Italy', 'America' or 'the Pope' meant.[15] By contrast, the inhabitants of one agro-town did know who lived in the surrounding five towns. These rival *paesi,* they reported to a visiting anthropologist, were 'respectively, (1) struck by evil spirits, (2) mentally retarded, (3) filled with cuckolds, (4) perfumed, and (5) a haven for gangsters'.[16]

Why did they come, these *paesani* of the 1920s? The question has traditional answers. There had been an earthquake in Messina (1908) or in the Abruzzi (1915); Kastellorizo was governed by Turks or Italians; a harvest would fail or threaten to fail; the sponge-fishing industry was in crisis. In retrospect, many of these early arrivals dwell on the hardships that propelled them to leave: 'I couldn't see anything in the future. I was only sixteen but I couldn't see that I could live in that country [Greece] – there was no money. I went out to work digging the grapevines and I got one drachma a day – ten pence. Just imagine! So how could you come up a man and bring up a family?'

How did they know where to come? Some were pioneers but most followed a migrant chain along which they could move physically, though perhaps not spiritually. As one Greek-Australian has observed of his parents who fled Greek Asia Minor after the Turkish sack of Smyrna in 1922:

They just followed the path of many people who came out around that time. They had a choice to go to America or Australia. Or they could go back to Greece. They didn't have any close ties with anyone in Greece ... many selected to migrate. A majority of them, particularly Kastellorizans went to America and Australia ...

My uncle had come out prior to my parents ... They sent the brother out first, which was the traditional thing to do, he came out here and he worked and made enough money to send the fare to bring them over. I understand the fare was approximately twelve pounds. Apparently it was a reasonable amount of money then.

What did they know of their destination? Very few of the Australian-born understand just how savage is the tyranny of distance, especially in the mind. Even educated Europeans had only the vaguest information about Australia. Some celebrated it as the realm of King Workingman.[17] Others deplored the selfishness of the inhabitants of its empty lands and argued that a population of up to 200 million could be accommodated here. An Italian journalist, based in Japanese-occupied Singapore during the Second World War, dreamed of what the Axis could do to Australia:

In reality, Australian soil is neither bitter nor sterile. All those who have travelled over it and studied the matter seriously are agreed that, both in the interior and along the coast, Australia could become a sort of Europe of everlasting Springtime ... [Australia] could become [anew] the Mediterranean world of the Eclogues and Georgics, while remaining at the same time, the tropical world of [Rousseau's] Paul and Virginia.[18]

Most ordinary migrants probably did not even possess this sort of mis-information. They came to Australia because in a way they were not coming, because their Australia would be one defined by other (male) members of their family or community, and because one day, a ship would take their body or at least their photo or their ashes back to the village that their soul had never left.

From an Australian point of view, they were not, in any case, so numerous. Only 2 per cent of the recorded Australian population in 1939 claimed origins in continental Europe or Asia. Though W. K. Hancock had announced that some Australians 'would welcome a few Latin plums in the solid lump of Anglo-Saxon dough',[19] non-British migrants at that time had made a minimal public impact on Australia, and, generally speaking, Australia had made a minimal private impact on them.

Then came war. It devastated Europe. In 1945 and for years thereafter, in much of Europe, both the civilisation and the economy of the old world seemed irreparable.

In Italy, Fascism had kept down the working classes so effectively that real wages in 1938 were no greater than they had been in 1913. The war further struck at the fragile national economic base. In 1947 the wholesale price index had increased by 5500 per cent compared to 1939. Most consumer goods were unobtainable except on the black market and, with unemployment rampant, many Italians were reduced to surviving on their wits alone. Of all disaster areas in the peninsula, Naples was the most spectacular and degraded, remaining long after the war in a nightmarish world depicted so graphically by the emblematic proverb used to begin a major study of post-war Naples: '*Quando un cavallo caca, cento passeri fanno il loro desinare* (When a horse shits, a thousand sparrows dine).'[20]

Much of industrial Europe, in the Rhineland or the low countries, also lay in ruins. German coal production in 1947 stood at 50 per cent of its pre-war level. In the Netherlands, economic conditions were worsened by the government's futile attempt until 1949 to save the Dutch empire in the East Indies. In England, in 1948 the meat ration stood at 13 ounces a week.

As in the Depression, agrarian Europe suffered even more than industrial Europe. Poland, apart from bearing the psychological scars caused by the moral abandonment of all civilisation at Auschwitz, had lost in the war 60 per cent of its cattle, 75 per cent of its pigs, and 68 per cent of all its buildings had been destroyed or badly damaged. In the Greece of 1947 the cost of living was 176 times higher than it had been ten years before. Throughout Europe, agricultural production in 1946 stood at less than two-thirds of the 1938 level. In these circumstances, the United States secretary of agriculture was certainly brutal, but perhaps realistic, when he remarked on the European scene: 'Some people are going to have to starve ... We're in a position of a family that owns a litter of puppies; we've got to decide which ones to drown.'[21]

Economic collapse was accompanied by political dislocation. Administrations in Scandinavia, the low countries and France began enthusiastic de-Nazification processes, but most soon decided that it was best to conceal the 'sorrow and the pity' of wartime collaboration and resistance.

The Cold War descended on Europe and its effect was especially harsh in Yugoslavia, where Tito's zealous Stalinism turned unexpectedly into an equally zealous 'third way' in 1948. Similarly, in Greece, the effects of Cold War great power politics on the ordinary population were drastic and disagreeable. In 1952, the conservative administration in Athens admitted to 12 000 political prisoners languishing in its gaols. Greek governments then and later viewed with especial disfavour elements in the country whose first language was not Greek – Macedonians, Albanians and Vlachs. A Hellenisation campaign that combined nationalism with the most reactionary political, social, and religious values was commenced and has scarcely been halted even by the Papandreou socialist government which, since 1981, has finally begun to bind up some of the wounds left by the Civil War.

In all these circumstances, political, social and physical, many a European mind began to turn to that ancient nostrum for hard times, emigration. Already the political and economic troubles of the 1930s had increased the number of Europeans living outside their birthplace from 75 to 150 million. New worlds beckoned where men and women did not have to starve and where perhaps they could be free. In the Netherlands, a rash of publications and radio programmes depicted the better life available outside overpopulated Holland. One headline proclaimed of Canada: 'Two or Three Years of Poverty, Then Success already Dawns'.[22] In Italy, Alcide de Gasperi, the Christian Democrat prime minister, gave the population of the south of his country a terse message: *'Imparate le lingue e andate all 'estero'* (Learn some languages and go abroad)'.[23]

And so emigrants began to depart – to the United States, to Canada, to South America, and, as gates were hesitantly opened, to Australia. Between 1945 and 1983, over 400 000 Italians came here as 'permanent and long term arrivals'; there were also over 230 000 Greeks, 190 000 Lebanese, 30 000 Turks, 18 000 Chinese and, amid many others (for example 559 Albanians), there were just under 59 000 officially recorded as stateless.[24]

What was the process of their emigration like? Experiences were so different for each emigrant that generalisation is hardly possible. Nonetheless, oral evidence can give some impression of what it meant to be added to Australia's immigration statistics.

A Maltese–Australian who arrived in 1949 could only remember the bleakness of his life back home. Although born in Malta, he had grown up in Tunisia. His family was poor. His father died when young and he was placed in a French orphanage where heads were regularly shaved to keep down the lice population, and where discipline and punishment included denial of meals and forced employment in white-washing the school walls. A pencil of his own was a great and cherished possession. Having been trained as a carpenter, he set off in the summer of 1939 to visit members of his family remaining in Malta. He was trapped there by the outbreak of war and discovered that enlistment in the army provided three meals a day and a pile of clothing, even if it was only army issue. Service in north Africa, an arranged marriage with an illiterate Maltese woman, a further five years in the regular army after the war, five children, a low income, and the prospect of only sporadic employment once he left the army augured ill for a comfortable future. When the opportunity to emigrate was offered, he grabbed it.

When the migration opened, I was very interested because, although Malta is my original country, I only suffered in Malta. I never seen anything good and I wanted to get out, even before the war ... I had in mind to go to Canada and I also put in for Australia but [the offer from] Australia came first ...

A Dutch woman, who emigrated with her husband and their three children in the immediate post-war years, could recall a reasonably pleasant and well-off existence in Holland. Born in 1922, she had grown up in a small town near the German border. Her memories of life there abound in descriptions of the games played as children, of the sumptuous food prepared for festivities, of her work as a shop assistant, and of the restrictions and fun of courtship. She married in 1939, but her husband, who was in the reserve of the Dutch army, was soon captured by the Germans and sent to a prisoner-of-war camp. It was a tough war. The first child was born, her husband was missing, and German planes kept flying overhead like 'a swarm of birds migrating'. Her husband was eventually released and returned ravaged by the treatment he had received. Danger could originate anywhere, and in September 1942 Allied planes struck the town. Then she saw 'all blankets and blood everywhere. And the city burnt for days, the sky was red and all the smoke, it was shocking'. But neither the traumas of war nor poverty provided the trigger to emigration. Rather, she and her husband left because business after the war was bad, because her husband was restless, and because there was so much talk about the opportunities awaiting those who emigrated from the old world.

You went because you thought you could do better. He wanted his own business and wanted something different. I think we went through a war and things didn't go our way, and we were just in that age group [who were emigrating] ... We stopped going to Indonesia because I didn't like it and then I had to give in to something.

Members of an eastern Sicilian village who emigrated in the late 1950s gave various reasons for their departure. They talked about the war and how it had made life even more difficult; they referred to earlier times when other villagers had gone to America and had come back able to build bigger and better houses; they remembered the stories they had heard about life in Australia or America where 'there was money to be dug up'; and they discussed the simple desire of the young to travel and to see a bit of the world. The constant theme, however, was the wish to get on and to acquire a life-style that did not seem obtainable in their own village. A number of *paesani* had already gone to the United States and to Argentina when, in the late 1950s, one villager decided to try his luck in Australia. Others quickly followed. First the males and then wives and children came. Life began anew; a fresh version of that small Sicilian village was created on the other side of the world.[25]

Political factors, poverty or the fear of it, the age-old dream of the Gold Mountain, the restlessness of youth – all could explain emigration. But in 1945, emigrants confronted a world that was changing. Emigrants must be counted and guarded, and their destinations must be defined not by their own will but by that of a watchful bureaucrat. The international organisations which had sprung up to deal with the refugee problem turned their attention to the issue of general emigration. In 1951 a new body, the Inter-governmental Committee for European Migration (ICEM) was established to complement the services already offered by IRO or UNHCR, and to extend them to non-refugees. Transport, language, and re-orientation programmes, even selection of suitable migrants, came within the organisation's ambit. Over the next thirty years and with a fluctuating membership (Australia was a founding member but withdrew temporarily during the Labor government of 1972–75), ICEM processed over 2 million emigrants. Of these, about 400 000 non-refugees and 130 000 refugees came to Australia.

ICEM's interest, however, was not just in facilitating the movement of people and in preparing them a little for their new environment. The organisation also evaluated the needs of migrants themselves as well as the requirements of the old and new countries. Initially, the main concern was to move excess population out of Europe and into countries that wanted more inhabitants and workers. The organ-isation's journal published articles on population and economic problems and on how these could be solved through migration. Borrie, Price, and Zubrzycki were among those employed to assess Australian interests and achievements. Glowing pictures emerged of the success of the whole scheme. An editorial in 1971 observed that ICEM's migrants 'have all been moved with consideration being given to the labour problems of their country of origin *vis-à-vis* opportunities for fruitful advancement abroad – to their individual benefit, as well as to that of the receiving countries themselves'.[26]

This image of successful international control and protection of migrants' movements and rights pales a little, however, even from a reading of ICEM's own reports. By the 1970s the organisation was holding seminars on the 'adaptation and integration of immigrants' at which concern was expressed about their general lack of political rights, or social mobility, and the incidence and effect of return migration. An international body could only make recommendations and international co-operation, regulation and assistance readily faltered before the immediate power of national governments.

Italy, source of Australia's most numerous non-Anglo-Saxon migrant group, provides a major example of this developing bureau-cratic interest in emigration. Since unification in 1861, successive governments have sought to make emigration conform to their ideologies. The new Italy preached liberalism, and this liberalism defined the first reaction to emigration. In 1875 Sidney Sonnino, who became the most important new conservative in pre-1914 Italy and was twice prime minister, declared that emigration would bring 'redemption' to Italy. A man who had emigrated, he said, would 'return as a real man, conscious of his own dignity of work. He has seen other climes, other agricultural methods, other civilisations; he no more lives in the old medieval atmosphere and has the courage to complain and to call upon justice if wrong is done to him.'[27]

Such a splendid belief in progress and man's innate goodness was soon countered by other factors. One of the most publicised was a perplexed solicitude for the emigrants' well-being. Emigration, it began to seem, was not necessarily the path to freedom and prosperity, rather it might lead to deprivation and discrimination. Commentators soon began to note that emigrants were exploited: entrepreneurs, contractors, and government officials within Italy who sold them boat passages or hired them for later employment might be venal, self-interested and prone to engage in false advertising. Matters might be still worse in the country to which migrants went. American capitalists might turn out to be not idealists but 'the most ferocious exploiters of human beings yet seen on the face of the earth'.[28] Migrants might be the new and most oppressed social class.

The history of Italian emigration was soon stained by incidents of murder and looting in which newly arrived Italians were punished for their poverty and their alleged racial inferiority. In 1891, there were killings of Italians in New Orleans, and in 1893 at Aigues Mortes in Southern France. In Australia, too, at about that time, anti-Italian prejudice increased. So, despite the liberalism inherited from unification, Italian authorities were soon claiming that it was 'a national duty' to offer 'a powerful defence, a genuine course of mercy for all those who leave the homeland'.[29]

Building on previous legislation, the Italian government in 1901 passed a law which, through the Commissariato Generale dell'Emigrazione, established a bureaucracy to survey and process emigrants and which also pledged that Italian diplomatic and consular agents would continue to watch over emigrants wherever they were.

In a sense, all subsequent Italian policy, however ambiguous and uncertain has been much of its implementation, was posited on the 1901 law. After 1922, the Fascist regime was initially anxious to pursue continuity in emigration matters. When, in May 1924, an International Migration Conference assembled in Rome, Mussolini gave a statesman-like vindication of emigration as one of the major channels for 'the development of human civilisation'. The world 'economic order', he told Anglo-Saxon observers, would always benefit from a 'free exchange of the energies of work between the nations'.[30] But in the aftermath

late 1940s: the parents left behind in Italy and the photo kept as a memento of their son and daughter-in-law in Australia.

of the failure of this conference and a second held in 1926, to which the future ALP leader, H. V. Evatt, was an Australian delegate, Fascism began to look with more suspicion on emigration. In 1927, a government circular proclaimed:

For each emigrant who departs from Italy for ever, the country loses economically everything which has been spent on feeding him and making of him a productive element. Militarily [Italy loses] a soldier; demographically [Italy] loses a strong youth who will make fertile foreign fields and give sons to foreign lands.[31]

Dino Grandi, the under-secretary for foreign affairs, with the sort of grand and superficial gesture of which Fascism was so fond, declared that, henceforth, the word 'emigrant' would be rooted out of the Italian language,[32] and, with some success, attempts were made to restrict emigration.

As well as trying to prevent more Italians leaving their homeland, the Fascist administration campaigned to hold the loyalty of its emigrants. Extremist Fascist vice consuls showed up in places such as Detroit or Perth, although the usual ideology of the Italian government towards its emigrants remained nationalist more than anything else. It also remained vaguely paternalist, hoping to remind at least the electorate at home that emigration was a painful business and that Italian emigrants were often the victims of the racist sense of superiority that existed in what Fascism condemned as the 'plutocratic states'.

Although emigration was discouraged in the 1930s, it did not altogether cease. Particularly within Italy, Fascist rhetoric about how much better off a man was down on the farm was passively resisted by many in the population. A stream, which in the 1950s and 1960s would become a flood, began to take *paesani* from the south or from mountain regions to the Northern cities.

The fall of Fascism and the creation of the Republic after 1946 coincided with the re-opening of borders and, therefore, with a recommencement of emigration. In 1948, over 300 000 Italians emigrated, the highest number since 1924. In 1957, a peak figure of almost 400 000 was reached.

It did not take post-war Republican governments long to review their concern that their citizens not be victimised in the process of emigration. After the experience of totalitarian control under Fascism, there was at first a certain belief or expectation that *laissez-faire* should be revived. In the short term, this mingled with the view that, given Italy's calamitous economic condition, any place in the new world would have to offer a better life than did Italy. As Mariano Rumor, a young Christian Democrat, remarked in 1949, Australia, in contrast to Italy, was 'a country rich in energy, natural resources and [possessed] a very strong will to develop', and it was a place that would 'swiftly overcome her [traditional] racial and religious prejudices'.[33] But, as these last clauses perhaps hinted, many Italians were uneasy about an uncontrolled revival of emigration. In particular, the left, in Italy as elsewhere, rapidly became the partisan of welfare legislation directed at emigrants. The Warsaw Pact countries, where it was known that both Marx and Lenin had deplored the capitalist conspiracy behind emigration, generally forbade emigration as something as damaging to the individual as it was to the state. In Italy, as early as 1948, Antonio Giolitti, then a member of the Italian Communist Party (PCI), demanded the creation of international structures to defend the emigrant worker from the capitalist. This sort of government intervention was, he explained, the reverse of Fascism, since that ideology had only advocated the defence of the Italian from the foreign. By 1958, a socialist was proclaiming that one of the fundamental rights for all Italians should be that of being able to live at home: 'Emigration is not only a tragic affair from the human point of view but it is essentially antisocial and economically damaging.'[34]

In Italy, the left has failed to impose this pessimistic viewpoint. Popes John XXIII and Paul VI both publicly defended emigration. According to the latter, a man had a right both to his *patria* and to be an emigrant so long as he was permitted to keep 'his own language, his own culture and his own religion'.[35] But, given national traditions, the constant criticism from the left, governments' enhanced sense of their own powers and duties, and common social justice, Italy since 1945 has sometimes been a watchful and stubborn warden of its emigrants. Much of the diplomatic dealing between Australia and Italy since the beginning of mass migration has been caused by Italian attempts to pressure Australia into being more solicitous of Italo-Australians. In 1961, for example, an Italian government under the Christian Democrat Amintore Fanfani refused to renew its migration agreement with Australia until more guarantees were provided for assistance with passage costs, settlement benefits, and employment opportunities for Italians equal to those granted to British immigrants.

Both in general and because of the specific size of its emigration to Australia, Italy provides an important example in the growth of a bureaucracy of emigration. But it is by no means exceptional. Even the feeble Chinese imperial government of the nineteenth century made some attempt at first to control its emigration flow – the death penalty was prescribed for Chinese who settled abroad. Once they had left their home country, however, these early Chinese emigrants were forgotten by their governments. It was only in the twentieth century that moves were made to protect Chinese living overseas and that political parties competed for the support of compatriots living outside China. The Kuomintang mounted a campaign to bring them into the party fold and, after 1949, the new communist government also realised the political and economic potential of the overseas Chinese and established an extensive administrative machine to record, oversee, and offer protection to expatriates and to their relatives still in China.[36]

The stridently nationalist governments of post-war Greece have also often seen reason to interfere and thus preserve the nationality, religion and anti-communist purity of Greek emigrants. Similarly, Dutch governments and Dutch churches in the immediate post-war years, while they strove to assist as many of their number as possible to emigrate, aimed to retain emigrant loyalties. As one Orthodox Calvinist wrote in 1951 an emigrant 'must remain grateful to the Netherlands for all it did to help bring him up, and he must prove his gratitude by maintaining his relations with our country and by impressing this point of view also on his progeny'. And it was not only the emigrant who would benefit, since 'if the Netherlands faithfully fulfills its calling with respect to emigration, the Netherlands will also realise profits from it'. The writer was referring not to profits of the spirit but of the purse: 'Many of the business connections that the Netherlands has today with foreign countries began with the contacts that Dutch emigrants made'.[37]

As this last statement indicates, governments and society in old worlds were often prompted into a stern guardianship of their emigrants by financial reward, by those remittances that emigrants traditionally sent from their new country. Before 1914, the industrialising Italian economy relied on emigrant remittances to cover half of the considerable balance of payments deficit. In the years since the Second World War, the trend has continued. In the early 1960s over $US520 million were remitted annually to Italy by its emigrants, and this figure did not include the presumably large amounts passed through unofficial migrant networks. Other emigrant countries also received their share. By 1973, for example, Spanish workers abroad were sending back over $US750 million, Greeks $US570 million and Turks $US740 million each year to their respective countries of origin.[38]

Despite the impetus given by financial self-interest, governments have often become most involved with their overseas brethren just as emigration stopped being such a serious matter. In Italy, emigration fell away drastically after 1962 and by 1975 was less then 100 000 a year. Of those, only about 2000 came to Australia. Greek emigration to Australia peaked at around 18 500 in 1965 but in 1979–80 had declined to little over 1000. In these and other cases from the Mediterranean world, emigration to Australia had usually been only a small part of the national total, especially when, with economic recovery by the late 1950s, Italian, Greek, Yugoslav, and Turkish migrants successively flocked as 'guest workers' to Germany, France, Switzerland, Scandinavia, or the low countries.

Even as governments became more solicitous and demanding, so individuals thought up new ways to function independently of officialdom. As though staffing an alternative bureaucracy with branches throughout the world, migrants have helped each other to slip past the scrutiny of beady official eyes. A survey of one Calabrian town at the height of Italian emigration to western Europe showed that, of those who left between 1961 and 1963, fifty had official migrant passports and one hundred and sixty had tourist visas. Similarly, the records of a Turkish village, which lost 135 of its inhabitants to emigration between 1967 and 1975, indicated that at least 80 of the departures left as tourists.[39] These illegal and uncounted emigrants then functioned in their new country in the way so wittily portrayed in films such as *Bread and Chocolates* (Italians in Switzerland) or *Montenegro* (Yugoslavs in Sweden). Distant Australia has probably experienced less of this problem of illegal immigration, despite an occasional moralising hue and cry against it.

For both legal and illegal emigrants, informal networks have developed. Recent anthropological work on Calabria has demonstrated that these networks have changed in character as society has changed. Before emigration, 'the authority and prestige of [the head of the family] were limitless'. In all classes, sons, no matter how old, were expected to use the very formal word *vussuria* rather than the intimate *tu* when they addressed their fathers. The godfather could be even more dominating. 'The *compare* [godfather] remains *compare*, even if you do not come back for fifty years.' Women were absolutely subordinate; the purpose of marriage for a male was to widen or reinforce contracts.

Particularly after 1950, emigration became the mechanism by which the modern industrialised world has entered Calabria, but the ancient systems of the family or of patron–client relationships have not disappeared; rather they have adapted themselves to new times. If anything, the networks have become still more ruthlessly self-interested than they were in the past:

every successfully arranged marriage represents a new stitch in the fabric of family bonds which link ... [the *paesani*] to the world through a chain of reciprocal obligations which distance can sometimes break but which, more often, distance, suitably manipulated, simply reinforces.[40]

In this regard, emigrants not only resist and exploit their governments' attempts to control and define their well-being, they may also resist and divert the attempts by old or new bureaucracies to nationalise them. Many major emigrant breeding grounds have been in border regions or mountain areas, distant from the capital, where nationalisation proceeded slowly and doubtfully or could be resisted. Friulians or Sicilians, Calabrians or Abruzzesi, different in so many other respects, share this inheritance of 'the Italies' rather than that of modern, national Italy. Greek emigrants have left Aegean islands, far from Athens and highly suspicious of it, or they have come from frontiers on which much of the population may not be Greek. Even in the 1960s, Macedonia and Thrace, where much of the population was Slav, had high emigration rates, while in the Peloponnisos, the heartland of the modern Greek state, emigration rates were relatively low.

In trying to assess the emigrant experience, even the pinpointing of a region of origin or of a suppressed nationality is often insufficient. Just as peasants from one village are unlikely to revere peasants from the next village, so patterns of political or social behaviour can vary drastically from one settlement to the next. A recent English language study on two *paesi* in the Fucino basin of the Abruzzi has found that the political conservatism of one and the radicalism of the other have survived for at least four centuries. Migration from the villages (for example to Australia and back) had very little effect on this diversity.[41]

Although Italy is the most renowned for its regional variations, other countries show the same patterns. In a recent study of Turkey, villagers explained departure from their settlement but not from neighbouring ones because the richest village was full of 'capitalists' who had all they needed and whose wealth had made them 'slothful'; the inhabitants of the poorest village were 'exceptionally uncivil and backward' so much so that they ' do not even know what Europe is'; and a third village was dismissed because its residents were suspected of 'gypsy descent' and, hence, were quite backward and incapable of showing 'initiative'.[42]

Nor are more industrialised countries by any means simple and united places with a 'commonly accepted way of life'. A 1976 study of Switzerland unveils an extraordinary diversity within the formidable patriotic unity and economic comfort of that state.[43]

In both industrialised and agrarian states, the completed process of the 'nationalisation of the masses' sometimes has engendered a resistance which emphasises a stubborn retention or re-invention of localism. 'Brittany' may mean as much as 'France', 'Belluno' as 'Italy', 'Rhodes' as 'Greece'. Even politics is acknowledging this retreat from nationality. Italy has already devolved considerable authority (for example, in cultural matters) to local administrations, and Greece, France, and Spain are contemplating similar concessions. Unless economic performance and welfare provisions improve, it is unlikely that Australia will draw many more migrants from such sophisticated European societies. It is possible that those who do come may well want to defend their ethnicity, not just in its national but also in its local sense. And so may those ethnic Australians who are best informed about the most positive recent developments in their country of origin.

To hope that Australian bureaucrats, experts or the general public will either comprehend or favour such endless diversity is perhaps utopian. But it must be admitted that the process of emigration is extraordinarily varied. Different countries, different regions within a country, different villages within a region, different individuals within a village will engage in emigration at different times. Emigrants will also be conditioned by class and by the extent to which they have yielded to the hegemony of modern nationalism.

At the same time, some generalisation is possible. Most emigrants will not be the first of the personal network to reach a new country; most will neither be the poorest nor the richest in their society; many will be enterprising and adventurous; and almost all will hope somewhere in their hearts not to have lost the old world.

Most, too, in one way or another, will find aspects of the new society to be bewildering or forbidding. The society left behind may well have been one of violence and tyranny, but at least it was familiar. In the new country, bosses or fellow villagers who have emigrated earlier, government officials, landlords, or employers may all threaten and attack, as those with power are always expected to do, but they will do so in new, unlearned, and inexplicable ways. And worse, in the new country it is not just those with power who cannot be trusted. A husband and wife may also now not trust each other, or their children, or the fields, or the weather, or even time itself. A person's identity may disappear; an emigrant may be cast into a limbo that has no sense, no end, and no escape. Emigration may be another of the unending, unrewarded and pointless labours demanded by a cruel God.

Even America, to the peasants, has a dual nature. It is a land where a man goes to work, where he toils and sweats for his daily bread, where he lays aside a little money only at the cost of endless hardship and privation, where he can die and no one will remember him. At the same time, and with no contradiction in terms, it is an earthly paradise and the promised land ...

As a place to work, it is indifferent to them; they live there as they would live anywhere else, like animals harnessed to a wagon, heedless of the street where they must pull it. But as an earthly paradise, Jerusalem the golden, it is so sacred as to be untouchable; a man can only gaze at it, even when he is there on the spot, with no hope of attainment. The peasants who emigrate to America remain just what they always were; many stay there and their children become Americans, but the rest, those who come back twenty years later, are just the same as when they went away.[44]

Traditionally emigration has had another limitation. It has been a matter of arrival and departure, something short-term. In their hearts, a man or woman, no matter how bleak the present aspect, could always craft comforting words:

I am returning
I am tired of going
Dying of fields and of churches
Carrying you in my heart

I am returning
The scent of my own country
Will cure me.[45]

By 1940, of the 20 million Italians who had left their villages since unification, only 7.7 million, less than 40 per cent, remained abroad; of the over 190 000 Yugoslavs who had emigrated overseas between 1918 and 1937, just under 111 000 had returned.[46]

Australian immigration policy, unlike that of western Europe, has always played down this aspect of the emigrant experience and asserted instead that this country is a place of permanent settlement. Since Australia needed to populate, its immigrants must stay; as Borrie characteristically phrased it in 1944, given that Australia was failing to 'rehabilitate the family as [the] fundamental unit' of fertility, immigration would provide 'another reproductive unit to replace it'.[47] And, comfortingly for Borrie or Price, Australian retention rates have long remained high compared with those of other immigrant countries.

But, with the 1960s and 1970s, as the Australian economy drifted into crisis and as political stagnation allowed Australia socially to lag behind many of the welfare states of Europe, return migration increased. In the 1950s, it used to be the fashion to note how readily Dutch migrants 'assimilated'. But already in the 1960s, the Dutch departure rate had reached 40 per cent and in the 1970s, Australia was experiencing an absolute loss in Dutch settlers.

More recently, there have been signs of a similar development among Italians. S. L. Thompson has estimated that 33.5 per cent of all Italians who came here in the 1960s have gone back home. For those from the more developed (or developing) regions of Italy, the departure rates were much higher (for example, 77.5 per cent for Friuli-Venezia Giulia, 72.3 per cent for Lombardy, 67.9 per cent for Tuscany, as against 14.1 per cent for Calabria and 9.4 per cent for the Basilicata).[48]

Greeks also began returning home in the late 1960s, and, by 1972–73, with the fall off in the number of arrivals, more Greeks left than arrived in Australia. Indeed, return rates from Australia could even be higher than they were among guest workers in Europe.[49]

The increased rates did worry Australian officialdom. Inquiries were implemented in the late 1960s and early 1970s, but, reassuringly, they claimed that, generally, Australia still retained a higher percentage of its immigrant population than did equivalent countries and that, anyway, those who returned were the failures, the ones who could not grasp the nettle in this land of opportunity. A 1976 government committee observed: 'The majority, about three in four migrants, get along well; the remainder, because they failed, leave Australia'.[50]

Many analysts disagree. Those who returned are not so much the failures as those who have reached their objective and can go home or who go home because family, soil or language call them. A Dutch–Australian who had come out in the 1950s and who had prospered materially in Australia, went back, he said, because it was '*his* place, *his* accent and dialect, *his* Brabant'.[51] Moreover, many of those who have not been able to depart physically have remained absent from Australia in their minds as they polish and repolish myths of the idyllic world left behind.

> *Send me a crust of warm bread, and send with it*
> *Some of our pure Sicilian olive oil,*
> *Because this bread has neither taste nor odour*
> *and foreign bread is never satisfying!*
>
> ...
>
> *Send me, besides, if you are able to do so,*
> *A reflection of this sun, of our own sun,*
> *To make me warm and to keep me company*
> *Because I feel alone and feel cold and lost.*[52]

One commentator cynically – or despairingly – remarked in 1980 that emigration is no more than 'an unnatural act between consenting adults'.[53] Certainly, it is hard to imagine an action that offers more of a threat to an individual's sense of identity:

When I stepped on that ship, I tell you my brains were working more than I can imagine. I thought, 'What are you doing. You don't even know where you're going, what you'll find. You're leaving everything behind you, your relatives, your securities. Everything.' I only had my children with me. Because I was a believer, I left it in God's hands which made me quite calm about it, otherwise I would never have left Holland.

I was so lonely I couldn't communicate. I couldn't tell you my feeling really, it was a terrible feeling my personal feeling. The country made me very lonely. There was open space, but people couldn't communicate. The Australians were selfish and very nationalistic at that time. They didn't want Dagos. They used bad words. You couldn't say that you were from another nation.

Total shock! I found everything, including the Barossa valley, which my aunt had described in her letters in the most glowing colours, as unspeakably ugly, our sponsors as go-getters who wanted to please the church and get the most from our situation ... The people were so behind the times that I thought I had been trapped in a time-warp.

Assimilationist Australia had little awareness of the pathos or tragedy of the emigration story. Rather, it was a very simple world, as *Good Neighbour* proclaimed through the words of an allegedly German migrant: 'After my first week in Australia, I already had a higher standard of living than in Germany. I can only recommend to everybody to leave Europe.'[54]

A generation later, the economic irony of these phrases seems almost macabre, yet multicultural Australia often still flies the flag of a land of opportunity and still showers new arrivals with promises of work, wealth, and happiness. It also promises, as assimilationist Australia did not, a land in which past, present, and future immigrants may preserve their ties to old worlds and may nurture their nostalgia, their language, and their pasts.

Justification by Work

On 28 January 1950, the USAT *General Blatchford* set out from Naples harbour with its cargo of 1800 passengers, all migrants bound for Australia. Typical of other ships in this fleet bringing Australia's first wave of new immigrants, the *General Blatchford* was a troop-carrier which had been hurriedly and inadequately converted to passenger service. There were separate dormitories for males and females, and, in the evenings, husbands and wives would meet secretively on deck. One passenger, a White Russian who had grown up in 'democratic' Estonia, recalled that the officials on board were concerned about the 'mischief' in which idle and frustrated couples might indulge. To avoid this, everyone was kept busy: 'A police force was formed, whoever could paint had to paint, any nurses were sent to the ship's doctor'. Refugee passengers on other IRO ships remember similar patterns of constant employment: a Polish woman was set the task of keeping the purser's office in order; a Hungarian man avidly checked and rechecked the lists of names of those on board; another Hungarian became a member of his ship's 'police force'; others were assigned to cleaning brigades. Free time was devoted to English lessons, singing competitions, and the production of a newsletter. It was a fitting introduction to Australia – keep busy, work hard, and all will be well.

The lesson was reinforced in print. Passengers were presented with pamphlets with titles such as *Your introduction to Australia: hints and help on knowing your new homeland* or just *Know Australia.* By perusing these publications, migrants learned that, in Australia, 'there are jobs for tens of thousands of newcomers', and that 'the freedom-loving people of Australia' were bidding them welcome 'to help make this young land richer'. Although, they were reminded, 'as a new Australian you will have to work for your living' just as 'the Australian people do'.[1]

And this is what migrants did on landing. The plans of bureaucrats succeeded well, though perhaps too well for some Australians. Old clichés have constantly resurfaced. Migrants, it is said, 'work too hard', live too cheaply, and have elbowed their way past old Australians even to the extent of taking their jobs. They have taken over the rag trade or the fish and chip shop circuit through unreasonable exertion or artful deception; they have studied hard so that every Hungarian–Jewish boy grows up to become a brain surgeon or a real estate operator and every other second generation Greek a professional.

Though such resentful murmurings have continued, work and economic development gradually replaced defence as the ultimate justifications of an immigration programme. Economists in Australia and elsewhere rapidly became the experts who could judge precisely whether or not migration was a good thing. One Greek economist by 1969 was claiming that a simple application of the formula:

$$v(c)j = \sum_{j=1}^{\hat{n}} (Wj - Cj) \, P_j^n \frac{1}{(1+r)^{n-j}} \quad \cdot \cdot \quad \cdot \cdot \quad \cdot \cdot \quad 1$$

would at once show that emigration was bad for Greece.[2]

In Australia, economists were also pressing their cause, usually arguing that immigration was good for Australia. Until recently, only Marxists have doubted the conventional wisdom which has equated immigrant work with rising profits and continued development.

Economists nearer to the government have tended to deprecate any claim that the cost of immigration outweighs the benefit as being regrettably and irresponsibly conditioned by political bias. But sometimes the more orthodox economic experts have also disclosed a certain political bias of their own. In 1971, a time of political promise and uncertainty when the national economy was showing signs of ill-health, delegates to the Australian Institute of Political Science Summer School heard spokesmen for Blue Metal Industries and Colonial Sugar Refineries (CSR) question whether immigration really did help Australia. As R. W. Harvey of CSR explained it:

The economics of this issue are not complicated. There may be all sorts of difficult side-issues, admittedly; but the basic economics are perfectly simple. We have capital resources in Australia which are shared among a certain number of people. If more people share them there are less to go round and our standard of living, relying on these resources, is reduced accordingly.

The slow growth of the gross national product in Australia, he said, could be attributed to our immigration policy.

It was not difficult to find experts to contest this sort of pessimism. The celebrated agricultural economist Colin Clark was peremptory with any of the doubting Thomases:

When I hear proposals for halting the population growth of Australia I can only understand them as the death wish – a state of mind which can only be analysed by psychologists. In the world of the coming century Australia could not have a hope of survival without continued immigration.

R. T. Appleyard, a good committee man often near to Taft, Borrie or Price, and then professor of economic history at the University of Western Australia, said mathematically speaking, that the 'effects of immigration are almost impossible to measure', although he did add that well-financed research programmes might unlock some secrets. In any case, the economic case for migration was 'in no small measure an act of faith', and furthermore migrants 'have made my country a much better, more exciting and more mature place in which to raise my children'.[3]

In recent times, dominant among those measurers of immigration who find a negative result has been the sociologist Robert Birrell. His cause has as often been advanced by what he regards as conclusive statistics as it has been obscured by his convoluted prose. Politically looking to the middle ground, he has been particularly anxious to show that the Australian environment is the casualty of immigration. Rather than 'populate *or* perish' the slogan has been adapted to 'populate *and* perish'.[4] Sometimes, elements suggestive of the old hierarchy of preferred immigrant groups have shown through Birrell's analysis. He has complained that 'by the early 1970s Australia was left with a legacy of large numbers of low-skilled, non-English speaking migrants from Southern and Eastern Europe, who were difficult to integrate'. These, he contrasts with the less 'problematic' newcomers received from 'the United Kindom [*sic*], South Africa, New Zealand, North America and Western Europe'.[5]

Whether because of attitudes such as these or because of the power and achievement of the more optimistic and conventional experts, Birrell, until recently, has seemed to be an unhonoured prophet in his own country. Bipartisan optimism was still the dominant theme of a conference on the economics of immigration organised by the Department of Immigration and Ethnic Affairs in February 1982. But from the travail came only an agreement that there was no agreement except that the effects of immigration were not yet accurately measured. Subsequently, a $500,000 research programme was launched. With official backing it would be conducted jointly by academic economists and business interests. Yet, even as research was getting under way, the government endorsed an interim increase in the immigrant intake, and a figure of 180 000 a year was apparently contemplated.[6]

But the economic disorders and calamities of the present have brought new opportunities to Birrell and the pessimists. By the end of 1982, the last Liberal minister of immigration, John Hodges, was sufficiently embarrassed to declare that 'far less' than 130 000 would arrive in 1982–83, although he had not yet engaged in a full-scale haggle with Birrell, who was stubbornly asserting that 50 000 would be an appropriate figure.[7] Hodges's relative optimism was bolstered by a

Sydney Morning Herald editorial which pointed out that immigration could 'not be turned on and off like a garden hose' and that, 'after 1985', a recovering Australian economy would need to be geared to 'the importation of specific labour skills ... still necessary to ensure economic growth'.[8]

The economists will undoubtedly continue to disagree about the economic costs and benefits of migration, and governments will continue to alter or preserve their immigration policies according to the advice of chosen experts. But whichever side is supported, it is plain that, since 1945, immigrants have occupied a major position in whatever development of the Australian economy and workforce that has occurred. Immigrants have constituted about half the increase in the total workforce, which grew from 2.6 million in 1947 to just under 6 million twenty-eight years later. And they played an undeniable part in assisting secondary industry to outstrip its rural counterpart in output by the late 1950s.

Specific examples abound. The Snowy Mountains Scheme depended on immigrant labour. Harold Holt bluntly admitted that fact. Without immigrant labour, he declared, work there 'could not go on'.[9] At the height of its construction, about 60 per cent of the Scheme's workforce were new arrivals. All accounts of the Scheme repeat, often unwittingly, the old tale of immigrants brought in to do the hard labour, which otherwise would not get done. Even a children's book set in the early 1950s cast its characters accordingly: there is blustering Italian-born Mario, who drives the bulldozers and snow ploughs, plays his accordion, and can work hard for long hours; there is Hungarian refugee, Uncle Kovash, from a peasant background, and suited only to dig with pick or shovel; there are the two labourers, Polish Jan and German Willie, who jeopardise their jobs by constantly fighting over their pasts; there is Connor Mahoney, the Irish storekeeper; and there is Australian-born Mr Hendricks who is the chief engineer.[10]

Such stereotypes did reflect something of the Scheme's reality. One Croatian-born member of the workforce recalled his years as catering manager and relieving employment officer. He spoke a number of languages and was quickly called on to do some interpreting. He met a number of migrant engineers then employed as labourers, and he presented their case to the management. Why keep on importing German or British engineers when there were already trained staff at hand, who were less likely to complain or to leave?

A Russian woman who also served an apprenticeship on the Snowy has remembered that her husband was already working there when she managed to gain employment in one of the administrative offices. Her reception at Cooma was frosty. She was a 'foreigner' and the foreign women who worked on the Scheme were occupied cleaning and cooking. What was she doing in an office and at a typewriter?

The Snowy Mountains Scheme: one of the many imported labourers at work, and friends and brothers from Italy relaxing in between shifts.

Other major projects similarly became dependent on post-war immigrant labour. Already in 1953, about one-fifth of the labourers in the steel industry were immigrants; in 1956, one in five railwaymen in Victoria had come from Europe; and between the end of the Second World War and 1961, the percentage of the La Trobe Valley population who came from non-British backgrounds rose from 8 to 25. The same saga could be told for the heavy industrial complexes of Wollongong, Whyalla and Geelong which have expanded at a faster rate than the rest of the country in the post-war years.[11] It is to developments such as these that supporters of immigration point as evidence of the economic benefits of immigration.

Such optimistic assessments of the role of immigration in Australia's economic growth have often been accompanied by self-congratulation over the manner in which Australia has greeted its immigrants. Characteristic was an article published in 1953 by N. R. Wills, an economist working for BHP (in 1961 he would become the foundation professor of business administration at the University of New South Wales). Wills began by praising business growth since 1945: 'Of the many developments of the recent past, none has been more spectacular than the expansion of manufacturing industry in Australia'. Then after commending the success of the immigration programme, Wills addressed himself to more practical questions about the deployment of migrants to Port Kembla where, he said, Europeans made up 17 per cent of the workforce. At first, he noted, there had been a small issue about language: 'To help with the problem, multilingual notices have been used liberally around the plants and interpreters have been quick to come forward. With the passing of time, however, the difficulty has tended to decline and it is now of a minor character.'[12]

Perhaps a genuine but innocent incomprehension of complex foreign societies is the most reasonable conclusion to draw from Wills's article. After all, Sir John Storey, a businessman from the Immigration Planning Council, displayed a similar stance. In his official capacity, Storey had experienced a 'pleasant surprise' on a trip to Italy. In *Good Neighbour* he confessed 'with some shame', 'like many other Australians' he had held views about Italians 'which immediately associated them with fruit shopkeepers'. The problem was that, in the past, Australia had not received a fair cross-section of Italians but rather had taken 'agriculturalists from the poorer districts'. Now, he learned, there were in the north some of the 'most brilliant industrialists in the world'.[13]

In the following years, official Australia continued to enthuse about the opportunity given immigrants to work. Migrants, it was assumed, came from poverty-stricken backgrounds where both work and simple survival were a life-draining struggle; refugees were unwanted by their countries of origin and unable to be gainfully employed in other parts of the world. To these people, battered by their individual struggles for existence, Australia proclaimed a utopia: 'there shall be opportunity for all ... If you have the ability, the determination and the readiness to work, there are no boundaries to your advancement. Australia has been proud to be called the land of the "fair go".'[14] Even in the 1980s, such clichés can still be heard. Some still claim that the record of achievement is simple and straightforward. Men emigrate, work and then become rich, powerful, and famous.[15]

Many immigrants themselves agree. A Maltese-born Australian asserted proudly in an interview that not only had he managed to get a job in his trade on the day after he stepped off his ship in 1951, but that, in 1981, 'there's still plenty here [in Australia] if you want to work'.

Since 1945, journalists and other commentators have been fond of underlining the success stories of those who have made it in Australia. Ever since colonial days, the self-made man has been depicted as being dear to the egalitarian Australian heart. These are the men or women next door who are able to 'get on' and 'make a buck', and migrants take their place among them. The story of Gennaro 'Jim' Abignano, reported in the *Sun* in August 1981 is typical. Under the catchline 'Road to riches? – Hard work', the tale unfolds. Twenty years ago, when Jim took his first job as a contractor, 'he couldn't even afford a wheelbarrow so he carried rocks until his hands bled'. This baptism in work contrasts starkly with the ten million dollar business he now directs. Reflecting on his life, he said: 'We all worked hard – it didn't come easy'. But the chance was still there for anyone: 'There are many more opportunities today than in those days [when I arrived], but you have to be prepared to take responsibility.'[16]

Similar success stories are narrated from time to time about other immigrants who now play an important part in Australian commerce or culture, finance or sport. Sometimes, success has been automatic. There are the Japanese, Swiss, or Italian businessmen who arrive to take up executive positions and then decide to stay on. They bring out families; their children go to private schools; and they reside in upper middle class suburbs. Theirs is not a story of direct hardship or struggle. The tale of one such migrant was reported glowingly early in 1983. Sixteen years ago Renato Maffei was a senior executive with the General Confederation of Italian Industry. He left his job and his country, he claimed, because 'nothing moves there'. He wanted to escape 'a stale system'. He had no job lined up in Australia but, soon after arrival, his executive credentials gained him employment with the ANZ Bank. Then, the Italian business networks of Olivetti and EPT (Electric Power Transmission) took over. The 'Italianness' of Maffei's subsequent employment passed unnoticed by the journalist but, as with so many imported executives, it is their 'ethnic' or national networks in business that provided protective cover and lucrative employment. Olivetti and EPT were followed by Maffei's new, and current, career in the burgeoning 'ethnic' industry. He began as an 'ethnic' public relations officer for Medibank and is now in a management position with the Special Broadcasting Service.

A product of the multicultural 1970s, Maffei's employment pattern (and his material success) reflects that of many of his fellow managers in ethnic affairs. They have come from executive positions in private industry and commerce to equivalent positions in the ethnic industry. And Maffei and his family say and do the right things. They have *tortellini* and turkey for Christmas dinner; they are proudly Roman (and not from the still suspect south or the industrialised north); they regularly return to Rome but always, after four or five weeks, yearn to return to the garden and sunshine of their Vaucluse backyard. They are happy and comfortable in Australia but, as Maffei's concluding remarks confirmed, it is not easy to be a migrant: 'Sometimes it can be painfully hard to move within the system even if you like it, even if you accept it, even if you want it ... I think for any migrant you can say in sports terms you are permanently playing away.'[17]

Such successes have usually been the exception and not the rule. But official Australia kept preaching that work either now or later brought freedom. Characteristic was a letter written to *Good Neighbour* in 1951 by a Byelorussian, its prose echoing her new master's voice:

even if many New Australians may find their lives hard for a start in their new homeland, what of the people who were first to reach Australia [i.e. in 1788] and who gave the foundation to such a prosperous country of today, starting from and with nothing. Knowing and realising that, we ought to work and wait patiently and we'll go more into Australia's happy and joyful life.

In case the message was obscure, *Good Neighbour* intervened editorially to praise these dutiful sentiments as an example of 'realism and commonsense'.[18]

But it did not take long for some immigrants to grow tired of waiting. First to organise their criticism were tradesmen and professionals among the displaced persons. As early as 1950 the issue of the recognition of overseas qualifications was raised at the initial Citizenship Convention, and debate began about appropriate policies to be applied towards highly skilled immigrants. It became apparent that experience and qualifications frequently were denied or unrecognised, and that there were many cases of toil at unfamiliar and unprofitable tasks, of re-acquiring in English of skills already known in another language, and of passing and failing in examinations which migrants had triumphantly passed and sometimes even set in a former life.

In many professions, the world of learning, as far as Australians were concerned, stopped short at the borders of the British Commonwealth. Doctors from Vienna or Budapest, engineers from Rome or Berlin, lawyers from Athens or Warsaw, did not have an English degree and, therefore, could not know medicine, engineering, or law.

These assumptions surfaced as soon as the displaced persons reached their camps. The refugees had willingly signed their agreement to do two years work, any sort of work, at the behest of the Australian government. A short-term sacrifice of skill and status was tolerable in order to reach the new world in the Pacific. But, it was hoped and expected, the sacrifice would be temporary. An engineer, who has worked with the Department of Works in Canberra for the past twenty years and who gained his training in his native Latvia and in the displaced persons camps in Germany, has recalled that the over-riding attraction of Australia was the prospect that, after two years labour, you were free to pursue your own career. This, he contrasted with Canada, where only long-term labourers were wanted, and to the United States where he risked becoming dependent on his sponsors, the Lutheran Church. Refugees in the know, he said, queued to get into Australia on such terms.

In a world that was temporarily upside-down, many a displaced person believed that it was better for old skills to be kept hidden. One refugee, trained as an accountant, entered Australia by officially stating that he was a *sanitaire,* a medical orderly. His hopes of a soft job were high. It was with some consternation that he found, on arrival at Bonegilla, that he was expected to work in the amenities block. The camp commandant, whose French must have been somewhat rusty, thought that he had acquired that unusual being, a self-declared sanitary worker.

Although statistics about them are unreliable, at least 10 per cent of the displaced persons had tertiary or professional training. For many, winning some recognition of these qualifications has been a difficult task. Not surprisingly, the conservative and hierarchical medical profession has been particularly suspicious of migrant doctors. Beginning in the 1930s, when Jewish refugees, excluded from their professions in Germany, began arriving in Australia, the then Australian section of the British Medical Association (which became the Australian Medical Association in 1962) and the various university medical schools imposed stringent regulations on foreign doctors. All newcomers from outside the British Commonwealth were required to re-study at least three years of medicine (in Victoria it was five years) at their own expense. Australia's doctors have long bolstered their social eminence and their wealth with rhetoric about the austerity and dedication demanded in their profession. Foreign qualified doctors, they proclaimed, might not meet their standards. It was even rumoured that continental doctors advertised their wares, and legally could use their own names to do so. In 1939, a medical practitioner of Sydney asked fearfully where it might all end.

I believe I know the technique of these alien people. One will be introduced by a friend 'on a friendly visit', and will forthwith insinuate himself into a home and a family's confidence. Is this playing the game? Decidedly not – at least in the light of British standards. Why, then, this urge to introduce alien practitioners who every knowledgeable person knows full well are possessed of what may be termed eastern European standards of ethics?[19]

Behind the door of the doctors' closed shop, foreign qualifications, foreign experience, foreign names, foreign languages were regarded with suspicion and distaste. One Sydney doctor, who was born in Poland, fled anti-Semitic legislation in his homeland in order to study medicine at the University of Bratislava in the Czechoslavakia of the 1930s. During the war, he worked as a doctor and was placed in charge of large hospital complexes in Russia. Despite the extent of his training, once in Australia, he acknowledged that he must go back to formal medical studies. He spent three years at Sydney University while his wife scrubbed floors and took in washing in order to support the family. With examinations successfully passed, there was one further obstacle: the University of Sydney, using what elsewhere might have been termed a *numerus clausus*, had established a regulation that allowed only eight 'foreign' doctors to register each year. In his year, twelve possessed the appropriate qualification. Optimism about the subsequent lottery proved unwarranted and this doctor had to wait a further year before he could resume his profession. In 1983 he was still running a successful medical practice in one of Sydney's inner western suburbs, and, in his spare time, had taught himself Greek and Lebanese so that he could more readily assist his many patients from those migrant groups.

Although medicine is an extreme case, other professions have not been much more yielding. The staffs of Australian universities are packed with British, New Zealand, South African and North American immigrants. Sometimes Anglo-Saxons have continued to dominate in what seem the most inappropriate places. At Sydney in 1961, the head of the Italian Department was attacked in the Italo-Australian press as one who in 'twenty-five years had never published one word of research, criticism, comment or study', who positively discouraged students from continuing their studies, and whose own Italian was open to question.[20] The new professor of Italian, in 1963, was Freddie May, who became famous through saying 'fuck' on the ABC and through teaching the best and most innovative English courses in the university. But he was an Englishman, and it was rumoured that not all of his fourth year students had yet mastered Italian. On his death in 1976, only one permanent member of his department was a native Italian speaker.

It is unfair to single out individual subjects or universities, because the story can be repeated throughout Australia, in most of the professions, and in those very areas of technical competence where it might be assumed, as cliché has it, that 'the language of science is universal'. Even in engineering, acclaimed among the most lenient and receptive of the Australian professions towards overseas qualifications, resumption of past careers has not necessarily been simple. The story of Egon Stern provides an example.

Now recognised as an expert in aviation navigational systems, Stern began his career in Vienna, where he obtained a diploma in electrical engineering at the technical college, and where he worked as a design and production engineer with manufacturers of electrical equipment. He arrived in Australia on the eve of the Second World War. His Viennese qualifications were not automatically recognised, and to gain registration he was required to sit for an examination set by the Australian Institute of Engineers. He decided not to try. Language and the need for an income militated against successful cramming for such a test. So he began working for EMI. In his own words, he started by 'sweeping the floors' and, slowly, as war work was converted into regular peacetime activities, more opportunities became available. From EMI Stern moved on to the Department of Civil Aviation. There, to continue his progress up the ladder, he had to have some qualifications, or be treated as a 'special case', always a risky business in a bureaucracy. Stern opted for obtaining a qualification. The alternatives were either to commence a completely new course in Australia or to sit for the institute's registration exam. With a decade of experience in Australia behind him, Stern chose the examination and passed with flying colours. Stern has not complained about his treatment at the hands of his co-professionals. After all, he claimed, he had first to become familiar with a different language, a new environment, and even different electrical circuits. And, despite the long delay in having his qualifications recognised, he had only good things to say about his experience in Australia. He had made it.

Such examples of Australia's 'successful immigrants' are varied and numerous. Yet, they must be offset by the greater number of immigrants who have not managed to resume former careers, to regain professional status, or to redirect their talents successfully. Among the 370 medical doctors in the displaced persons intake, only about 100 males and 55 females managed to resume their professions.[21] The remainder either re-migrated, died before their qualifications were recognised, failed the exams, or simply were unable to face the re-processing that promised eventually to admit their European training and expertise.

Even today, there is still some evidence that the situation in the medical profession has not changed much, despite the toning down of the AMA's edicts, the overseeing by the federal government's Committee on Overseas Professional Qualifications, and the relucant acceptance by the medical authorities that immigrant doctors may have useful qualifications and indeed that their ability to speak a language other than English is perhaps the most useful of all. Yet, in multicultural Australia, as once in assimilationist Australia, spokesmen for the medical profession still express concern about a glut of foreign-trained doctors. In 1978 the South Australian president of the AMA, Dr Pickering, wrote to the *Age* with a familiar message: 'The immediate solution is to stop foreign-trained doctors coming into this country with the exception of those from the United Kingdom and New Zealand.'[22] In 1980, in the aftermath of Timor, the Portuguese-language press in Australia reported that about fifty non-registered foreign doctors were meeting to discuss the possibility of organising a medical language course to facilitate their registration. At about the same time, the Universities of Sydney and New South Wales did establish programmes to assist graduates with overseas qualifications to prepare for the Australian Medical Examining Council and, in 1982, the example was followed by Newcastle University. Despite such innovations, it was reported that only about 17 per cent of those who sat for the exam in 1981 passed it.[23]

Immigrants who confront such narrowness and prejudice from their Australian colleagues, and some who do not, can become bitter about Australia. It may be that they echo the ancient refugee cry that culture only exists at home: 'For intellectuals, [and] artists, Australia has nothing to give except food, accommodation and a place as a labourer.'[24] It may be that previous class and status is simply not sufficiently recognised anymore: 'There are the wealthy people and the poor people in Australia. Australians think of immigrants as all the same. They are all grouped with the poor people. And so the rich have nothing to do with them.'[25] It may be that Australia has not offered the expected opportunity for gain (or that the opportunity somehow has been missed): 'We feel only tolerated slaves here in Australia. We are good enough to do the manual dirty work, but to rise , give us a "Fair go" would be too much to ask.'[26]

Not only refugees or professionals can be led to such barren pessimism. One Italian who had returned to the Abruzzi was glad to have left behind a 100 hour week and inadequate pay and social services: 'Australians exploit us', he remembered, 'they give us the hardest work and they do not pay us enough.'[27]

Not only Australians do the exploiting. In the United States and South America many tales can be told of earlier migrants steadily increasing their wealth and power through their control over new arrivals from their own region or village. One man recalled how his father, sponsored by a cousin to come to Australia from their home on one of the Dodecanese islands, arrived here in 1951 only to discover that he was obliged to work for 16 hours a day, six days a week, cleaning and scraping fish, and doing other menial tasks in his cousin's shop. His income was £8 per week. After a few weeks he met a compatriot from his own island who pointed out that he could work the same hours at similarly unpleasant labours in a glass factory but earn three times the salary.

Factories, however, have far from necessarily offered an escape from abuse. Migrant women are especially vulnerable. Economic circumstances and the desire to educate the children force them into jobs in small factories where government inspectors are not welcome, or into doing out-work at piece rates. The traditions carried from their place of origin scarcely encourage objection to any behaviour from their male employers. Migrant working women are especially unlikely to be aware of the advance of women's rights and the feminist movements either in their country of origin or in Australia. They remain isolated from the help available through social services, trade unions or women's groups, and they become easily buried at the bottom of the heap, vulnerable to corruption, exploitation, long hours, harsh conditions, and sexual harrassment.

One woman, who came to Australia from Spain in 1962, recalled a series of job experiences that ranged from the mildly unpleasant to the horrifying. She had been a dressmaker in Spain, but, in Australia, she was criticised for being too slow as she machine stitched clothes. Work in a salami factory made her vomit and the boss's advances towards the females disgusted her: 'sometimes I see the big boss pass around some girls and touch them, on the bosom and backside, like they were street girls, and they laughed. I think that outside the factory they would never allow anyone to touch them.' More militant than most of her migrant colleagues, this woman did, at one stage, go on strike, but it only resulted in her being hounded from her job as a nurse's aide.[28] What, then, was the point of speaking out? For many migrant women the answer to this question was obvious if depressing: it was best to stomach the degradation and poor conditions.

Many reasons have been adduced to explain the unpleasantness of much migrant work and the failure of many migrants to escape from it. Are some migrants simply restless and rootless, doomed to 'fail', with the same social and personal instability as the lumpenproletariat or the criminal classes? Or is it the very harshness and strangeness of migration which, like an angry god, inevitably demands some human sacrifice? Can those who fall victim in the migration process be found not only in Australia but in many places and at many times? Or have Australians, personally or institutionally, been particularly insouciant, ill-equipped by their Anglo-Saxon traditions, to comprehend migrants from so many diverse backgrounds?

Some facts do stand out. Every census reveals that, after Aborigines, migrants, as a group, are worse off in terms of occupational mobility, working conditions and unemployment (and, probably, knowledge and usage of social security). Social scientists have spent much time refining census results and they have carried out some useful work by breaking down the figures by nation of origin, or by those categories of 'northern', 'eastern' and 'southern' Europeans. It has been demonstrated that particular sections of the migrant workforce have filled the lowliest and dirtiest occupations. There has been some change over time, but the general statement can be made that the worst jobs go to the newest arrivals and to those of lowest ranking in Australian racial preference. Hence, in the 1966 census, the 'national' groups with the greatest percentage in the categories of semi-skilled and unskilled manual workers were the Greeks. Then came Maltese, Italians, and Yugoslavs. By 1971, with the influx of Yugoslavs during the late 1960s, this particular group of southern Europeans was more heavily clustered at the bottom of the socio-economic scale. In the two subsequent censuses, southern Europeans were replaced by the more recently arrived immigrants from the Middle East.

To some extent, these results might have been predicted. In this context what becomes important in the migrant story is not so much class in Australia or ethnicity, but rather class in the country of origin. Until the 1970s, migrants from Greece, Italy or Yugoslavia were likely to be unskilled, to have grown up in a village, and to have belonged to some section of the peasantry. Their literacy in their language or dialect of origin was doubtful at best and they had seldom stayed long at school. In the period 1947–69, for example, 76 per cent of Greek male migrants and 50 per cent of Italians were formally deemed unskilled on their arrival in Australia.[29]

Such migrants reached Australia and here were greeted by a strange language, a different living standard, and an often alienating urban and industrial environment. They were shunted into unskilled work in areas that became accepted by Australians as permanently occupied by migrant labour, such as the motor vehicle industry of the 1950s and 1960s. Foreign-owned, amorphous, and bitterly competitive, its continued expansion and profitability were built on migrants passively manning the assembly lines. As one Italian recalled of the GMH factory in Melbourne in the late 1950s: '99 per cent of the workers in the foundry were immigrants—Italians, Greeks, some Poland people. One per cent is Australians, foremen.'[30]

Statistical analyses have confirmed that this pattern can be found elsewhere. Particular jobs have fallen to particular migrant groups. In Melbourne, by 1966, 49 per cent of Italian men in the workforce were in jobs which, in comparison, employed only 9 per cent of Australian-born males. The percentage for Greeks was even higher: 58 to 7. A similar result emerges from the 1982 figures, in which about 64 per cent of Yugoslavs, 52 per cent of Italians, 50 per cent of Greeks, and

49 per cent of Lebanese in the workforce were categorised as tradesmen and process workers. This contrasted to the 26 per cent of the Australian-born and the 31 per cent of the United Kingdom born in the same occupational classification.[31]

Statistics and surveys also reveal that most non-British and non-northern European first generation immigrants do not change their occupational status. They take on first jobs in unskilled or semi-skilled areas and stay there. A report of the Ethnic Affairs Commission of New South Wales asserted that, in 1973, of household heads surveyed, 47 per cent had remained in the same occupational category since their arrival, 22 per cent had gone down, and only 31 per cent up the occupational ladder.[32]

Associated with the apparent lack of upward immigrant mobility is unemployment, which has almost always been greater among immigrants as a group than among the population at large. In 1972, 3.2 per cent of overseas born were out of a job, against 2.1 per cent of the Australian-born. In the 1980s while unemployment spiralled ever higher, the aggregate figures on overseas-born out of work were still greater than those for the Australian-born; although, if the statistics are regrouped into ethnic, age and sex categories, some groups fare better and some much worse than their Australian-born counterparts. Hence, older Italian males (but not females) who had been in Australia for some time had fewer unemployed, while the more recently arrived Turks (men and women) had an unemployment rate which, by 1981, was 49 per cent higher than that for the Australian-born.[33] British migrants do better than southern Europeans; southern Europeans do better than those from the Middle East; established groups do better than new arrivals; men do better than women.

Why are so many migrants so blatantly disadvantaged? 'The capitalist conspiracy', cry some Marxists: international migration works to the advantage of western capitalism, it is part of the 'international proletarianisation of the subaltern [lower] classes'.[34] Western European countries have often encouraged both immigration and emigration depending on the moment of the cycle of economic growth. Immigrants, more often as guest workers than as permanent settlers, are imported to take the places at the bottom of the socio-economic ladder and to complete the tasks which members of the established native working class refuse to do. Immigrants are thus conscripted into the reserve army of international, multinational capital. Moreover, it is said, a migrant presence divides the working class. The indigenous working class can be prompted to form a labour aristocracy and may well become vulnerable to the appeal of reformism and reject revolution. The immigrants are outsiders; they will have no politics, or they will be manipulable and can be harnessed for conservative causes in the style of a lumpenproletariat. They can be used as black-legs and strike-breakers. No one will mind, either, if they are expended. They are the ones whose presence is to be emphasised in times of economic hardship as a menace to the jobs of the locals. They will exist outside the trade union system, and thus, locking it in a vicious cycle, they will both weaken it and ensure its always greater labour aristocratic exclusiveness.

There is some substance to this argument. At least until the 1970s, it was easy to find employers who callously manipulated their workers. There are the countless stories of people called from the factory floor to interpret and explain to newcomers their jobs. The fact that the new employees were Greek, for example, and the old hand Maltese was irrelevant. They all spoke 'foreign'. Even the relatively alert Snowy Mountains Authority, with its high percentage of non-English-speaking employees, expected miracles. Migrants were required to learn sufficient English within six months in order to prevent injury to themselves and others. If, by the end of that time, their English language ability was not adequate, they risked losing their jobs. They simply had to know or to pretend to know what the safety notices and regulations said. In assimilationist Australia it did not often occur to management that a surer method was to have those rules and signs printed in as many languages as possible, though even that may not have been much help to a migrant who was illiterate or who understood only a local dialect. In any case, the main objective was merely to get migrant workers to turn screws and fit the parts in the right way. Communication about conditions or rights was regarded as unimportant, and smoothing the relations between Australian workers and their 'foreign' counterparts was of little concern to employers.

Even when, in the 1970s, more recognition was given to the need to introduce immigrants from non-English-speaking backgrounds to the language and ways of Australian factories, it remained doubtful that the nature of immigrant backgrounds and needs was recognised. In 1978 a social worker commented on steps taken by Leyland Australia to introduce new immigrant workers to the plant and to their jobs. He noted that 'Leylands were considered leaders in the field of welfare work', but that even their record was weak. The introduction and safety courses were held in English: 'The safety officer ... was quite convinced that he was getting his message across by speaking in a mildly accented voice.' There was no counselling about the types of jobs available and training 'consisted of an exercise performed by whatever worker happened to be standing next to him'. No consideration was given to different cultural values. The example cited was of a Turkish woman who was required to work lying underneath the chassis of the motor vehicles. Her workmate was male. Two days after she had started the job she collapsed out of anxiety. The report observed: 'No one understood that she had done so because she had violated an essential Turkish taboo: Turkish women aren't allowed to be alone with a man unaccompanied by their husbands.'[35]

If employers have rarely gone out of their way to be sympathetic towards their migrant workers, Australian-born workers have been more directly suspicious of the newcomers. Before 1945, Australian labour had a long tradition of regarding immigration as an employers' conspiracy, and such opinions did not die overnight, despite the consensus of Labor and Liberal politicians that Australia must both industrialise and populate. Even an English immigrant in 1948 had sensed that 'the average Australian worker looks upon every newcomer ... as a potential competitor'.[36] Since then, moments of economic downturn have always produced comments from the shop floor condemning migrants.

In 1952, in the wake of mild economic recession, the Clothing Trades Union proposed that it should fix a quota of 25 per cent in any one factory for 'new Australians' who had been in the country for less than five years.[37] The same reluctance to accept immigrants as fully fledged members of the workforce lies behind many of the hostile motions about immigration brought before the ACTU Congresses between 1945 and 1975. At least thirty-one times concern was expressed about the connection between immigration and unemployment. On fourteen further occasions, the adverse effect of immigration on living standards and wages was raised. Ten motions touched on the difficulty of organising immigrants in trade unions; four criticised official overplaying of the availability of jobs in Australia; two noted the inadequacy of immigrant trade qualifications; and six referred to the political attitudes of immigrants.[38] The migrant presence, when it was noticed, was seen as a problem. And the tension between styles and rates of work has never been resolved. As an Italian put it in 1978: 'Australians don't like you to work hard – they lay six bricks, you lay ten and they tell you to go slower because you are making them work harder.'[39]

At first, the views of the Australian trade union leadership on migration were scarcely distinguishable from those held by others in the political elite. A. E. Monk, the president of the ACTU from 1949 to 1969, was a member of both Labor and Liberal commissions investigating migration. And his comments carried the same optimistic superficiality that characterised most assimilationism. In 1954, he asserted: 'We have been astounded by the facility of assimilation of New and Old Australian Labour in almost every category of employment.'[40]

Sometimes, too, unions were not very solicitous of their migrant comrades. Migrant workers could be hustled into union membership in order to make up the numbers, but little attempt would be made to explain how their union could help them. The Australian Railway

Workers Union in 1952 agreed with employers in New South Wales to deduct union dues automatically from new Australian pay packets. The same system was not extended to old Australians until ten years later. At about the same time the State Council of the New South Wales Nurses Association expressed disapproval of displaced persons training as nurses. There was a shortage of expert personnel, yet they were unwilling to employ 'foreigners' to fill the gap.[41]

Often, too, the Australian union system posed a structural problem to migrants. In their countries of origin, the defeat of fascism had generally reinforced the tradition of big political unions. From West Germany, Sweden, the Netherlands, and Italy, news has filtered through of continual gains being made by these large unions in relations between workers and bosses. In Italy in the 1970s, for example, the three great national unions overcame political differences and formed a general alliance, which extracted many benefits from the weak central government. Wages were still indexed in Italy in 1983.

By contrast, Australia, loyally attached to the British system of craft unions, often offered a bewildering array of small, competing groups, which reacted to problems bureaucratically and insisted on costly strikes over petty demarcation disputes. The complex and competing union system in turn made it difficult for many unions to desire or afford an interest in migrant cultures or traditions. At least according to one migrant account, Australian union officials believed that there were only two languages in the world – English and 'New Australian'.[42]

It is thus easy to find bleak pessimism from some migrants about the Australian union system. As one Italian complained in 1970: 'At the union meeting I said very little because they would not have listened to what I had to say. For them I was a second-class citizen. At first, they would not let me speak. Then they would not listen when I spoke: "Shut up, bloody dago!" they would say.'[43] A number of Greeks working together on the factory floor expressed similar views: 'The union makes you a member only so that they can take your money off you, they don't give you any protection at all.'[44]

Other migrants had directly political reasons for opposing or rejecting the union system. East European or Asian refugees have sometimes feared that unionism meant communism. The sentiments expressed in a 1980 issue of the Vietnamese language paper *Chuong Saigon* are typical: 'We have seen how communist agents infiltrated the trade union movement in the former regime in South Vietnam. We see now in Australia some trade unions using industrial action for political purposes.'[45]

For some migrants, criticism of the union structure was extended into a deepening awareness of Australia's relative economic failure since the 1950s. Figures in 1982 showed that Australia, rated by gross national product, had fallen from fifth to eleventh place in the world, and OECD figures on health, education, and pension expenditure placed Australia even lower. Migrants from Germany and Holland have to bear the unpleasant knowledge that real wages have risen far more rapidly in their countries of origin than in Australia. Materially, it seems, their choice in the 1950s may have been a mistake. Moreover, while Australia has languished under unimaginative conservative governments, the welfare systems of many European states have been extended and refined. For Scandinavians, Dutch, Germans, but also for Italians and, if they are honest, for many eastern Europeans, social services in their country of origin are now far better than in Australia. Their homeland may well have been more a land of opportunity than Australia has proven to be.

Such information has only reached Australia fitfully. It is rarely emphasised in the generally conservative ethnic press and may often, in any case, be news that a migrant does not want to hear. In the 1970s, however, there were some signs of a new sense of combativeness among migrant workers. Among Italians, the Italian Federation of Emigrant Workers and their Families (FILEF), with its close ties to the PCI became influential, especially in Melbourne. Its weekly, *Nuovo Paese*, took to republishing pages from *L'Unità*, the PCI's national daily.

In 1973, stimulated by the general hope and excitement of the Whitlam years, the bitter Ford Broadmeadows strike broke out. During this strike, migrant workers were prominent in rallying the rank and file to the radical cause against the wishes of some Anglo-Australian trade union officials.

In the aftermath of the strike, the Whitlam government, along with the ACTU, sponsored a series of conferences on the migrant worker. The first of these was held in Melbourne from 5 to 7 October 1973. Two hundred delegates attended, and, as a symbol of multiculturalism, discussions proceeded in English, Italian, Greek, Serbo-Croatian, and Spanish. Ignazio Salemi, an official of the PCI, who was later discouraged by the Fraser government from remaining in Australia, was one of the spokesmen for FILEF. Niall Brennan opened the conference in his capacity as executive secretary of the Good Neighbour Council. His words reflected the new questioning of the assumption that all had really been well with the immigration programme:

I have spoken to too many migrants who believe they were lured out here, with specious promises, a life of surf beaches and luxury, when all they got when they arrived was the western suburbs ... We didn't even tell them what the award rates were, their very lack of the English language was a factor which made exploitation easier. And when there was the slightest sign of profits falling off, they were the first to be laid off: to spend Christmas on a surf beach with empty pockets because there was nowhere else to go.

Other speakers drew attention to more specific examples of errors and limitations in the trade union approach to immigrants and to the general disadvantages confronting the workforce. A Spanish-born woman delegate complained of the backwardness of Australia on questions of maternity leave, crèche or kindergarten facilities and on the simple issue of a greater recognition of the dignity of women. An Italian migrant, employed by BHP at Port Kembla, observed that 'I am witnessing migrant exploitation daily'. An Australian-born delegate remarked on the baffling problem of migrant diversity: 'One union official told me recently he went to the trouble of distributing a leaflet to his members in Italian and Greek, only to discover that his migrant members were mostly Yugoslav.' John Halfpenny made some enlighted proposals for reform, including separate migrant committees on the Amalgamated Metal Workers and Shipwrights Union (AMWSU), an exchange of language skills, and the establishment of a special advisory centre for migrants. The historian and social scientist M. P. Tsounis was quoted to emphasise that there was a long way to go – in 1971 there were only twenty Greek-speaking officials in all Australian trade unions. The tone thus varied from a pessimism about the past to an optimism towards the future. In that future, Niall Brennan proclaimed, the Australian working class would recognise that the migrant worker 'is no longer a threat, he is an asset. Now, for the first time [in Australia] the international solidarity of labour has a chance to be seen.'[46]

Such sentiment mostly remained however at the level of rhetoric. It is true that in 1975, the ACTU passed a resolution urging a major effort to improve communication with the non-English speaking membership. There was some discussion of more English classes and even of a greater attempt to preserve traditional cultures. But, in 1983, migrants continued to be badly under-represented in the union bureaucracy. Some progress has occurred but hardly at the rate predicted.

A study of union policies as much as those of employers advances, to some extent, the argument that migration acts as a useful tool for the manoeuvres of international capitalism. Yet, like most mono-causal explanations, this argument over-simplifies and is, in the final analysis, inadequate. 'Big business' in Australia as elsewhere is divided rather than united. Indeed, Australia's industrialisation has been so partial and so dependent on mining and agriculture (despite the growth of the 1950s and 1960s), that big business sometimes seems inappropriate in the Australian context. Moreover, Australian business interests have often been naive, insular, and ignorant – less the skilled manipulators of gigantic conspiracies and more the bipartisan carriers of ancient racial prejudices and ancient financial expectations that the Great Southland really ought to repay investment.

There are thus many areas of migration in Australia where a Marxist model built to cover the circumstances of western Europe does not fit.

Immigrants have not been imported as guest workers. Australians have expected that they would stay. Australian immigrants have not been discarded in the sense of being forcibly driven out of the country. Many migrants have abandoned Australia, but they have often done so after accumulating sufficient savings to be reasonably comfortable back home, and, by contrast, the poorest migrants by origin and the most vulnerable in Australia have tended not to leave.

Immigrants from non-English-speaking backgrounds often are located in a particularly disadvantaged segment of the workforce. But all sorts of myths and realities encourage migrants to be optimistic about the complex and terrible migrant experience and, therefore, to play up benefits accrued from coming to Australia. Centuries of peasant deprivation and exploitation make it hard for a migrant to accept that times have changed in a country of origin or that the changes are anything but cosmetic and short-lived. The grades of status and the sense of shame and honour in rural societies may also encourage reticence about admitting failure or alienation. Moreover in Australia since 1945, real wages may not have improved relatively as much as in some countries of origin, but they have increased greatly. A kind of prosperity is easy to see. A migrant has a house and a car and a washing machine, which neither he nor his wife had, nor could they imagine ever having, when they left their place of origin. Australia remains a country of vast open spaces and, although scarcely anyone visits them or lives there, the myth of Australia Unlimited survives. From Marrickville or Carlton, it is easier to believe than from Athens that, one day, there will be an escape from overcrowding and pollution.

Working hours may be long, labour may be harsh, the urban environment unpleasant, and the countryside an intermittent victim of fire, drought or flood, but the very nature of migration for many migrants makes any prosperity seem all their own work. As a couple from the Treviso who settled around Griffith declared:

We work hard, but we don't mind because we're working for ourselves. At harvest time we sometimes start at four in the morning and continue till all hours, but at other times if we feel like knocking off we can. In Italy we would have worked like slaves for a hard-boiled egg and a piece of *polenta;* here we set up our children and re-invest.[47]

Also relevant to migrant perceptions of their work in Australia is the question of the second generation. Gaps in Australian censuses have made this a difficult question for social scientists to probe with reference to post-war immigrants. Among earlier groups who have come to Australia, some social mobility does seem to have occurred. According to one analysis of the Chinese community in Sydney, those Chinese who were listed in the 1891 census came from poor, unskilled,

late 1950s: going to work in the fields in Sicily and, a few years later, at work in
the canefields in northern Queensland.

and illiterate peasant backgrounds; initially they had found work in cabinet-making, laundries, market gardens, and hawking. They had concentrated in the overcrowded and poor inner city area around Dixon Street. By the post-war period, those who were still alive had improved in status, with many entering restaurant, and fish and chip shop businesses. More significantly, however, their children and grandchildren were acquiring professional qualifications.[48] The squalor and heat of steaming laundries and exploited labour had, for the majority, become an element in their parents' pasts and their childhood memories.

Similarly, an analysis of the occupations of Greeks in Sydney revealed that 85.6 per cent of the first generation owned or worked in cafes, milk-bars, fish and chip shops, and similar small businesses. By 1956, just under 50 per cent of their offspring could be found in accountancy and commerce (13 per cent), skilled trades (27 per cent), and professions (6 per cent).[49]

The pattern remains the same for many other groups. Occupational and social mobility among first generation immigrants from non-English-speaking backgrounds generally occurs slowly. The pace, however, until the recent disastrous employment crisis, increased with the second generation whose members constituted one of the main lasting justifications for their parents' migration: 'We wanted a better future for our sons and daughters'. If educational attainment, occupational mobility, and material comfort are the yardsticks, then, for the majority of the first generation their hard struggles in an alien environment can seem justified. They may miss and eventually lose the social and cultural environment in which they grew up, but, for many, until recently it has been replaced by one of a material prosperity and security that they believed was unattainable or, at least as difficult to attain, in their regions of origin.

The fabric that makes up the story of migrant work is thus woven from many strands. There are differences between the work experiences of refugee and non-refugee migrants, of professionals and peasants, of one ethnic or regional or village group and another, of those who came in one year or in the next, of men and women, of first and second generation, of those who stay and those who go back to the country of origin. For many, work is harsh and has often involved active discrimination by bureaucrat, employer or union comrade in Australia as it would have done in the United States, Canada or South America. For many, too, while prosperity has increased, work has brought rewards, if not for the migrants themselves at least for their children, if not for their souls at least for their bodies. It is a myth that all migrants can be highly successful capitalists, though some are. It is a myth that Australia is a land of equal opportunity or that such opportunity has proved limitless. It is a myth that all migrants are exploited and in their work are no more than 'the wretched of the earth'. In any case, work, however essential, is only part of the migrant story; the part that pays for home, family, culture, or politics. And in each of these areas, too, the nature of migration promises an uneasy meeting between the knowledge of old worlds and the experience of the new.

Chapter SIX

Home, Health, and Happiness

Australia is the lucky country, or so Donald Horne deemed it in 1964. He intended to be ironic: our luck was already running out and it hid a multitude of problems. But the irony has often been missed and it is the self-congratulatory side of the term that has predominated. Certainly, for many of the migrants who left their old worlds for new Australia, if they understood anything about their destination, it was that Australia was a lucky country, fertile and prosperous, a land of opportunity where a person could make a fortune and discover happiness through the abundance of material comforts.

For those outside English-speaking networks, information about Australia was scanty. Rumour, stimulated by the occasional journalistic survey, did aver that Australia was rich and was still the working-man's paradise that had attracted so many British immigrants in the nineteenth century. Work in Australia could bring luxury and comfort unattainable in overpopulated, harsh, and competitive home countries. In 1903 an Italian writer had surmised:

To a country like Australia can and must be entrusted with a happy heart a section of our proletariat given the certainty that ... [in Australia workers] will soon turn themselves into rich landowners given the enormous quantity of fertile land ... available.[1]

The images persisted. All Australians, reported one Italian journalist in 1941, 'are well-off, so they hardly ever have children, they play sport and they drink a lot. Every worker owns a car, and, before the war, a worker every three years could afford to take off six months travelling around Europe.' The only real problem confronting an ordinary citizen was the difficulty of acquiring servants since the Aborigines had been massacred. In Australia 'upper class women shine shoes, cook, wash the dishes. It is even said that at official functions, the Premier makes his own daughters serve the guests.'[2]

In the post-1945 world from which new frontiers were rapidly disappearing, Australia improved its status as the new Eden. The United States no longer welcomed Europeans but Australia did, and its abundance of comforts supposedly provoked wonderment. The typical migrant was thought to be wide-eyed at the quantity of meat available. A refugee who had already settled in Australia extolled the virtues of Australian consumer society to compatriots still caught behind the barbed wire of displaced persons camps in Germany: 'Here you can buy everything on terms. For example, every seventh person owns a car. With a deposit of £300 in the bank you can start building your own home and pay it off for £12 p.w.'[3] Or, as *Good Neighbour* put it in a characteristic headline in 1953: 'From Kitchen hand to head chef. In 1947 – determination and hope. In 1953 – Happiness, a home, a car.'[4]

Government propaganda to the displaced persons camps or to migrant assembly centres placed particular emphasis on the Australian dream as made manifest in home ownership. Initial accommodation might be a little rigorous, but opportunity lay ahead. As a brochure explained: 'More than half the dwellings in Australia are occupied by owners or by persons buying them in instalments.' And it was ownership not just of small apartments, but of homes 'set in tree-lined streets' and of homes with 'front lawns or gardens, vegetable plots, fruit trees or sunyard at the rear.'[5]

For many migrants, the Australian way of being housed was unquestionably alluring. Central and eastern Europeans displaced by war may have felt a tug of nostalgia for their lost homes in the old world and for the maid who helped to polish the parquetry floors, clean the Persian carpets, and dust the piano, but even bourgeois migrants did not regret leaving behind some aspects of cramped living in a rented urban apartment. For less bourgeois migrants, the transfer to Australia has been seen as more obviously beneficial. One Maltese recalled that for him housing in Malta had been neither easy to find nor pleasant to live in. As a single man he had, at one stage, squatted in an allegedly haunted house. On another occasion, the dilapidated roof of the building where he rented a room collapsed. As a married man with a growing family, he had lived with his in-laws in their small village home. The prospect of acquiring land and owning a comfortable home in Malta (or Greece or Italy or the Lebanon) was an improbable, if not an impossible, dream. Australia made it seem possible. No wonder that migrants were impressed by the 'little books that showed how nice all the hostels were and all the beautiful houses – for someone arriving suitcase in hand'.[6]

Nor did arrival in Australia much shake these images. A Hungarian woman remembers her first glimpse of Perth, a city without tall buildings or rented apartments, where there were 'individual houses with gardens for each family'. Another migrant has treasured the experience of coming through Sydney Heads in 1951, and, then, from the main deck, using his binoculars to spy 'the little houses, the little suburban houses' scattered on the green of the foreshore in a way so different from Europe. However, neither romantic memoir, truth nor government propaganda has woven its spell evenly over all migrants. Some recall learning about a 'beautiful climate' and 'plenty of jobs', but 'nothing about land, housing, medical services [or] tax'. Others remember being misinformed: 'We thought Australia was all black and that you were given a block of land and had natives working for you.'

Nonetheless, the general impression remains that migrants have readily adopted the style of housing in the new world. Despite the usual ethnic and regional variations, statistics show that by 1970 more overseas-born owned their own houses than did Australian-born. In the 1980s, although the economy has deteriorated and home ownership is decreasing, migrant ownership rates remain high. Impressionist evidence is perhaps more telling. In 1978, a Yugoslav migrant identified himself thus: 'I am an Australian with an Australian wife and a fine brick house and some money in the bank.'[7] And many similar stories exist in which migrants proudly point to the rapidity with which they have been able to buy their own homes. A Latvian couple who arrived in 1949, moved into their own home two and a half years later; an Austrian couple arriving in 1956 managed to make their down payment on a home within eighteen months; and a 1970 immigrant from northern Greece asserted that his highest priority was 'to have a house, a nest'.[8] For Australian aesthetes this cosy nesting urge was rather disappointing. Robin Boyd had detected in 1960 that 'this transfusion [of migrants] was enormously beneficial to the patient [Australia] in many fields, such as coffee-making, ski-ing, and the stocking of delicatessen shops. But, contrary to some prophets, it did not assist in the broadening or sharpening of taste as manifest in the suburban street ... The desire to belong, it seems, overcame any inherent distaste for the scattered suburban mode of living.'[9]

High rates of home ownership hide the sacrifices frequently made to achieve that goal, just as they hide the often unpleasant initial living conditions, the diversity of immigrant life-styles and settlement patterns, and the possible disruption to individual, family, and community stability created by the tensions between old world and new Australian norms and values. Home and happiness may be the goal, but how easily or how well has it been achieved?

Immigrants rarely arrive with sufficient cash or confidence to set out at once to purchase a home. They need first to rest, become acclimatised, and find work; they need temporary accommodation. In post-war Australia a number of alternatives have been available: government-funded hostels; accommodation provided by employers; the houses of relatives and friends; or private boarding houses and rented flats. The choice, however, has not been a particularly free one. It has been largely influenced by the changes in Australian government policy and by the expansion and contraction of the building industry.

In the immediate post-war years there was a drastic housing shortage, and the plea to populate and develop was accompanied by a competing cry to house Australians. But it was also recognised that there were insufficient workers to construct the needed houses. Advocates of immigration offered a solution. In 1945, one ALP senator argued that it was not necessary to wait for accommodation to become available. After all, did Australia's pioneers wait for their houses to be built before they came to colonise the land? Immigrants could be temporarily placed in 'barracks'. Some years later, Liberal spokesman W. C. Wentworth, explained that in Queensland and Western Australia there were many under-developed areas that could be settled by immigrants living in 'temporary camps ... of log cabins with bark roofs'.[10]

What actually happened to the first post-war immigrants was not so far removed from these suggestions. In 1947 the decision to import displaced persons as workers under contract to the Australian government was accompanied by a promise to provide the new arrivals with accommodation. Until January 1952 and the establishment of Commonwealth Hostels Pty Ltd, it was the responsibility of the Department of Labour and National Service to find this housing and to cater for the initial needs of immigrants.

The quest was resolved with bureaucratic tidiness. Military camps with their wooden barracks and Nissen huts were converted to the purpose, as were old woolsheds; some new hostels were rapidly created from galvanised iron or sisalcraft. The civilian army of newcomers was received and processed through Bathurst or Bonegilla ex-military establishments. As the years passed, other camps – Williamstown, Endeavour, Fishermen's Bend, Westbridge, Wacol, Pennington, East Hills – would be used for the same purpose.

In the immediate post-war years, neither Australian authorities nor arriving migrants had to make much of a leap of the imagination in order to advocate or accept camp life. In Europe, refugees had been accommodated even in what had once been concentration camps as they waited for a new life and a new country. The Australian government had confined aliens and prisoners of war at Tatura, Hay, and Cowra during the Second World War. POW, alien, 'DP', 'reffo', migrant – for some bureaucrats, the labels changed, but the daily task, and many of the assumptions behind it, remained the same.

Government propaganda was soon employed to highlight the allure of the camps. An official pamphlet explained responsibly that 'new arrivals are not stranded on the wharf in Australia'. Instead, they could expect to be transported to a place such as Bathurst, 'a pleasant, inland town, where European newcomers are welcomed and accommodated at a special reception centre'. Here food was 'wonderful' with 'three big meals a day, and the canteen open for buying delicacies in between if you want them'. Moreover, 'here is sunshine and spaciousness, peace, and serenity'. As an accompaniment to the commentary, and useful for those whose English or German was shaky, there were photographs – a train chuffing to Bathurst; men and women eating white bread in the canteen; and smiling mother and daughter walking along the path set against a background of gum trees, open spaces, and solid-looking camp barracks.[11]

Some recollections of the camps justify this arcadian image. There are the stories, especially of the internment camps at Hay or Tatura, of attending a lecture series on Hegel or Freud, listening to records of Yehudi Menuhin playing Bach, enjoying golf and tennis, or even sipping black coffee at 1½d a cup at the 'Grand Cafe Tatura', which was managed by a former bar and restaurant owner from pre-1938 Vienna.[12]

With the more varied ethnic and class backgrounds and the more rapid turnover, camps like Bathurst were less like universities bizarrely functioning in the Australian bush (though an account does exist of a performance in 1950 of *Tosca* at the Bathurst camp).[13] Even among those not moved by Puccini, memories of the camps can be happy. One Polish refugee, whose health had been undermined by internment in Siberia, by the loss of family and friends, and by his political objections to communism, recalled his prolonged stay in Bathurst camp:

The fresh air, the fantastic food and hard physical work did me a lot of good. [When I arrived in Australia] ... I was so sore inside and outside. This war had ravished my body and soul. When I came to Australia, I was 54 kilos and after six months [at Bathurst] I weighed 86. I had breasts like a woman!

Another, who was a little perturbed to find that Australian 'brown bread' was not 'real', nonetheless has remembered the rapidity with which her fellow refugees were able to go shopping for motor-cycles, radiograms, chocolates, and dresses made out of 'genuine' not *ersatz* cloth.[14] Bathurst offered material paradise compared to the deprivations of war-torn Europe.

However, not all memories fit as tidily into the glowing picture that was being constructed in Canberra. Some new arrivals expecting heat were surprised by the cold of an Australian inland winter. They found 'unlined huts with stretchers', to which one had to wade with 'mud up to the knees', and which were marked by large gaps between wall and ceiling so that 'under six blankets we were still freezing'. The central heating which, for some, had made winter cosy in Vienna or Budapest seemed turned off forever.

Some new arrivals disliked the social dislocation that was part of camp life. Bonegilla was remembered as little more than 'two rows of beds, on each of which were a mattress, four blankets, sheets, a pillow and towels. On the ceiling near the light bulb sat two enormous moths, looking like a pair of small birds.' People who had clung together through the refugee experience were now separated: 'Married men were assigned one set of bungalows, the wives and children another, and the single adult members of families yet another.' Doubtless there was nothing deliberately oppressive in these arrangements and, in many camps and hostels, the Australian authorities were only trying to follow that variety of advice given in 1952 by Betty Archdale to the 3rd New South Wales Girl Guides Convention: 'The assimilation of new Australians would be helped if Australians made them feel: "one of the gang".'[15]

But, even among those who believed that they were doing new arrivals a 'good turn' by providing them immediately with government accommodation, incomprehension remained. Food often became the first symbol of the cheerlessness of the new home in Australia. In 1949, the newly established Estonian language newspaper *Meie Kodu* published an account of life at Bonegilla camp and noted that 'the most vivid memories were of kitchens smelling of mutton fat, and loudspeakers blaring all day amidst the bleak corrugated iron barracks ... [There was] a general mood of hardship and overcrowding felt at the time, but with a hint of optimism.'[16]

Some, too, resented the quasi-military administration of the camps, which were often markedly similar to the harsher side of internment camps during the Second World War.[17] One Polish-born staff member at the Scheyville hostel for women and children near Windsor has reported that most of the Australian-born members of the administration were ex-military men. She was not complimentary: 'I think they were people who couldn't fit into society after the war, and went into the department and couldn't cope well with the normal department work and were sent to the camps. Half of them were alcoholics ... [and] they were ignorant and poorly educated.'

The residents occasionally rebelled at being constantly queued for processing. Those from the refugee camps in Europe had had enough of being numbered, checked off lists, and endlessly organised. At Bonegilla, migrants were expected to assemble and join a daily ceremony of saluting the flag. W. D. Borrie argued that migrant children especially would benefit from such patriotic action. By honouring the flag, they would learn to forget their own backgrounds and yearn for integration into Australia.[18]

Over the years, as affluence spread, the camps turned into hostels, and initial government housing for immigrants improved, although it was not until 1970 that Philip Lynch could assert: 'About half of the unused [hostel] accommodation is being progressively demolished because of the substandard nature of the buildings'.[19] A visit to East Hills Hostel in Sydney in 1980 revealed belated but welcome improvements. Only a few Nissen huts remained and these were used primarily for communal and resettlement activities—religious services or the distribution of blankets and loans. Families now occupied small one or two room flats with their own bathroom. If bare brick walls, a vinyl covered divan, and linoleum tiles are still far from the full comforts of the bourgeois Australian dream, they are also a long way from dormitory accommodation in draughty wooden barracks.

Despite these changes, complaints and criticisms have continued. Not all hostels have been updated. In 1973 Geelong hostel still consisted of Nissen huts, 'albeit nicely painted ones',[20] and in the late 1970s Wacol in Brisbane reminded a visitor of the Bonegilla of earlier decades, thin huts set behind wire fencing facing a noisy road.

The quality and type of food has also remained not easily digested. In the 1940s and 1950s, European stomachs turned at the sight and smell of 'masses of lamb chops floating in mutton fat' or the unaccustomed prospect of 'mutton goulash'.[21] In the 1970s and 1980s the overabundance of mutton has been replaced by a more palatable menu, but it still provides a shock to taste buds and digestive systems used to different cuisines. As a Greek-born social worker noted: 'The food is not the kind of food Greek people are used to or even like.'[22] In 1979 a Vietnamese refugee admitted that, although he felt welcome and secure at Midway Hostel, he was happy to have the opportunity to move into accommodation with relatives, because 'we were not used to the food' in the hostel. At East Hills in 1980, the authorities offered Indochinese refugees over-boiled rice and curry-powdered chicken. It was not their traditional fare but, at least, it was better than the 'tea, jam and English cooking' that has so often confronted non-British arrivals. Ironically, two years earlier, British immigrants had complained that they were being pushed out of their hostels by Vietnamese who had successfully ensured that rice had prevailed over porridge.[23] Even a menu can become a battleground of national, regional or clan difference.

In any case, as an ALP Senator put it in 1967: 'It is clear that Commonwealth policy is not to make these hostels as comfortable as possible in case the migrants stay too long'.[24] Regulations had been quickly established setting down the length of time a new arrival could remain in the hostel. Nor was accommodation free. Even the first waves of occupants, the displaced persons brought out under a two year contract to work for the government, had to pay, and observers noted that the relatively high cost placed an unnecessary burden on new arrivals, especially on families.[25]

This situation has not changed much. Even in the 1970s, government-funded inquiries noted the particular difficulties for families who did not bring savings with them. While they remained in the hostels, they were unable to accumulate the deposit for a home or the capital needed to rent good private accommodation. Sometimes the migrants themselves have protested, but to little effect. In this sphere, the Australian government has remained loyal to its early pledge to migrants: Australia is a lucky country but 'you are expected to help yourselves'.

As assimilation changed into integration and multiculturalism, it was politic to dilute the practice of *laissez-faire* by offering an array of welfare information and assistance to hostel dwellers. But, even here, there are traces of the continuing belief that immigrants should do it on their own.

In the immediate post-war years and during the heyday of assimilationism, the greatest need perceived by the authorities was the provision of English language classes. Instruction was graded according to migrants' alleged ability to speak English, but it was a rough and ready method of differentiation and many of the teachers themselves were recent arrivals or were inexperienced in the art of teaching English as a second language. Lucija Berzins, who had been among the first wave to reach the Bathurst camp, captured this inexperience in her short story, 'The Berlitz Method'. In it, she described the antics of a young Australian-born, male teacher, as he demonstrated his approach to learning. He began by introducing his students to the nouns associated with clothes. 'Tie', 'coat', 'shoe', 'sock' were repeated, while he removed the item and then dangled it before uninterested eyes. The only spark of enthusiasm among the audience came when it seemed that he might remove his trousers. Otherwise, the ineffectiveness of the class was summed up by one participant who dispiritedly observed: 'I only remember one word "button" and what does it matter anyway. They want us to do the work, not talk about it.'[26]

Assisting new arrivals in the new land was, it seemed, not the only motive for teaching English. Even the *Good Neighbour* recorded with approval a comment in the Victorian RSL magazine *Mufti*: 'If it is rude to whisper in company, it is ruder still to pass remarks in a language that excludes from conversation most of one's hearers.' At least part of the political intention of language classes was to salve those Australian souls fearful of too many garish and polyphonic foreigners.

With the passing years, the crudeness and naivety of such assimilationism has faded. In the 1980s, English language classes are still given a high priority in the hostels, but the teachers are more adequately trained, and the courses are longer and more structured. Unfortunately, many immigrants have had to wait for some time before a place has become available. But for those with few linguistic skills, or whose mother tongue is far removed from the Roman alphabet and English grammar, twelve or even twenty-four weeks in a class with people of mixed ability is almost always inadequate. For others who move quickly into the workforce where they spend long hours labouring in alien and demanding environments, the English language courses are inaccessible. As a petition from one group of Vietnamese refugees at Wacol Hostel, Brisbane, argued: 'those of us who are working have no time to study the Australian language at the place of employment; those who are working have no time to pursue their studies at night because they are too tired'. But, they said, if we want employment here and if we are to succeed in having 'contact with Australians in all levels of society' then we 'must be able to speak Australian well' but how can we do this when all available time is devoted to work? They proposed that the English language courses should run for a year and that those who chose to attend the classes should not be required to go to work.[27] But, as the last Liberal minister for immigration, John Hodges, stated in early 1983, such a plea cannot be taken too seriously. Immigrants are still expected to learn and to learn quickly. If they want, they can get assistance to learn how to read bus destinations and safety rules, and how to ask for foodstuffs, but the acquisition of fluent English remains their responsibility.[28]

The creation of resettlement offices, government employment bureaux, social worker networks, and voluntary charitable organisations as part of the infrastructure of the hostels also reflects the recognition that immigrants need some assistance in adjusting to their new environment. But assumptions behind the processing and assistance have often been queried.

In the mid 1970s a group of community workers in the main Melbourne hostels criticised the inadequacy of the interpreting and information services. Only one Spanish interpreter was available for the 600 or so recently arrived Latin American immigrants. Communication about available services was thus a problem. The social workers also criticised the allegedly supercilious attitudes of the management towards the newcomers. It was said that the administration preached that 'migrants were lucky to be there at all and hence they had no rights and shouldn't complain'.[29] One ethnic affairs worker, who himself had been processed through the hostel system in the mid 1970s, summed up these complaints. He pointed to three areas of discomfort: the food; the attitude of the managerial staff, which was cool and uncommitted; and the cumbersome structure of the hostels. Responsibility was divided; the manager was in charge of catering and the day-to-day running of the hostel; English teachers looked after the English classes but were responsible to the Department of Education; social workers looked after the physical and psychological transition of migrants from hostels to the society outside, but they served the Department of

Immigration and Ethnic Affairs. Progress and humanity shattered against the barricades built by demarcation disputes, bureaucratic buck-passing or procrastination.

Not all tensions and complaints have emanated from the inadequacies, innocence or prejudice of Australian bureaucrats. Frequently, one group of residents has protested about another as national passions and politics have found expression within the hostels. In his observations of life at the newly constructed Villawood hostel in 1949–50, an Australian-born administrator quickly noticed the conflicts between various groups. A fight between Czechs and Poles had resulted from both claiming the border town of Těšín as part of their respective countries, and complaints about radio noise or other disturbances stemmed, he thought, as much from national animosities as from genuine irritation. He noted that 'where a Hungarian lodges a complaint it is generally a Yugoslav who is the offender. If it be a Czekoslovakian [sic] who is objecting, nine cases out of ten the radio involved is the property of a Pole ... they object to each other as a race'.[30] Looking back, a Polish-born man who had attended the English language classes at Bathurst camp allowed his national prejudices to show when he declared that the lowest groups were made up of 'Slavonic peoples who were illiterate or the Hungarians'.

Animosity and prejudice certainly were not the preserve of European migrants. In 1952 when British immigrants downed cutlery and refused to pay an increase in the tariff for hostel accommodation, their spokesmen cited two reasons. First, they claimed that the increase was unreasonable and had not been approved by the prices commissioner. Second, the protest was against 'Commonwealth Hostels Limited placing foreign migrants, particularly single men, in the same hostel as British migrants'. The British should be treated differently. They had been promised separate accommodation. Questioned before a special commission established to investigate the affair, the British representatives noted that the 'morals' of their children might have been affected by living too close to single foreigners.[31]

In the late 1970s, similar complaints could be heard from Europeans who objected to having to live, eat, and attend language classes with Indochinese refugees. In 1978 a two day riot in the Pennington Hostel in Adelaide was attributed by the manager to faction fights between the Chinese and Vietnamese. 'Maybe it's political', he observed.[32]

Despite such incidents and despite all other limitations, the hostels have at least provided new arrivals in Australia with a place to rest a little before embarking on a new life in an alien country. But only assisted immigrants and refugees are assured of accommodation in a government hostel on arrival in Australia, and the in-built biases in Australia's various immigration schemes have been consistently reflected in the national make-up of those who have occupied the hostels. In March 1967, for example, there were 18 746 people in hostels. Of these, 86.3 per cent were British,[33] at a time when British-born immigrants made up under 50 per cent of the total intake. The actual percentages have changed from year to year but, with the exception of refugee years when the hostels have filled with displaced persons of various nationalities, the pattern remained the same until the cessation of assisted passage schemes. By contrast, the majority of non-refugee migrants from non-English-speaking backgrounds have arrived without government assistance and, consequently, have had to find their own initial accommodation or to depend on sponsors to supply it.

Some immigrants have come with accommodation assured by their prospective employer. Included in these ranks are the business executives and the professionals selected for their expertise who, though technically migrants, avoid most of the perils and penalties of the migrant experience because they are wealthy servants of a multi-national and technocratic world.

Quite a different tale can be told when the migrant has been contracted for his labour, not for his expertise. Then, for some, the story reveals degradation more familiar in the story of slaves or indentured labour than that of free migration. One Italian left his village in the late 1940s impressed by the account of a fellow countryman who had set up business in Australia and who had then revisited Italy in order to enlist workers for his firm. This *padrone* had offered to pay fares and supply accommodation in exchange for two years labour. The work proved to be harsh and poorly paid, and the living conditions were deplorable. Those who signed the contract were accommodated 'in tin barracks ... in a field of mud'. At night, the men could be seen 'crying with frustration and disappointment and loneliness'.[34]

These stories are familiar to the history of migration anywhere, and in Australia they can be extended to include refugees who were placed in government employment with accommodation guaranteed. In retrospect, men who were sent to work for the New South Wales Railways and to live in the Chullora camp can recall the almost total lack of facilities they endured. They lived in tents surrounded by long grass and they occasionally sighted snakes slithering towards their unprotected sleeping quarters; beds were made of straw; rain seeped in through the canvas; and furniture had to be made from 'the bottom of a drum'. At Regents Park, the Water Board had made available a camp with 'concrete barracks, half barrel-shaped and concrete inside, and water running along the walls'.

Contract work, whether for government or private enterprises, involved other deprivations. Migrants bewailed the fact that they had become 'bachelors of misery'. A Slovenian-born man subtitled his account of life on the Snowy Mountains Scheme, that grand venture

Accommodation provided by a private company for their refugee workers during the housing shortage of the 1950s.

which imported so many male workers, 'Men without women.' It was a rugged outdoors life in poor accommodation and savage weather. Mateship had its limits: 'In these circumstances it was no wonder that Sergeant Carpenter had to shoot it out one day in the main street of Cooma with a man who had shot a woman in the leg and was holding her hostage.'[35] Nice Aussie girls stayed away, although prostitutes could sometimes be welcoming because at least migrants were quick. Married men arranged fleeting intercourse with their wives in dingy hotel rooms on the day off. Children spent months without seeing their fathers and grew to distrust or dislike them. Meanwhile Australian newspapers pontificated about the inevitability or extent of the vice that came with migrant settlement.

Sometimes chains of relatives and friends preserved other patterns common to the migrant story. There are accounts of wives or sweethearts left behind until the man returned or, more frequently given Australia's wealth and distance, until the woman was sent for. Even after the postman at last brought a ticket, the new country did not always offer a warm hearth and good cheer. One woman from Kastellorizo, who, in the early 1950s, joined her new husband in Australia, found 'the house she came half-way round the world to occupy was a small, four-roomed terrace with a ten-foot frontage in Woolloomooloo'. Undeterred, she sponsored five other siblings. As each arrived they moved for some time into these cramped living quarters. From there, they all worked at two jobs and they eventually moved out to find better housing and to begin a course of upward social mobility.[36]

Not all newcomers could claim sanctuary in such supportive structures or, indeed, in any structures at all. Some remember, rather, the high level of rents. Their independent Australian story began in the local camping grounds or in one-roomed flats (often let by fellow migrants), which were shared with wife, children, and cockroaches. For such accommodation, a Polish ex-serviceman recalls that, in the early 1950s, he paid three guineas out of his total weekly income of £5.17.6.

The housing and renting situation eased as the 1950s progressed into the prosperity of the 1960s. Yet it has remained hard to find adequate rented accommodation unless the person seeking a lease comes from a middle class background, can boast sound employment and income, and does not have too many children. Even in the 1970s and 1980s, there are repeated stories about parents who, when admitting to having four or six children, are immediately told that there is nothing available. Lies and subterfuge then, for some, become the only means of acquiring a lease. A Lebanese man gained his flat by saying that he only had two children. When the agent paid his weekly visit, the extra four children were explained away as the children of a visiting relative or the neighbours' offspring.[37]

Renting is also awkward when language and cultural barriers intrude. A lack of English-language skills can make still more opaque the legal clauses of a lease. Many migrants come from backgrounds where verbal agreements, a client's appropriate gesture to a patron, or the simple passing of money or goods were all that was necessary. In some European societies where renting is the norm and house ownership the exception, post-war left-wing local governments have blocked rents and thus made a major contribution to the social wage. In Australia, the concept of a formal contract has seemed to promise only the further expense of litigation on top of the already oppressive rent.

In these circumstances, predictable patterns of migrant settlement and services appear. In areas inhabited by particular national groups, estate agents soon employ people who speak the relevant language or dialects. Yet ethnic solidarity is as tenuous in the real estate world as it is in many other spheres. Dealing with a fellow national may provoke a sense of ease, but sometimes it has proved to be unfounded ease. A Dutch woman who arrived with her family just after the war was housed initially in Wallgrove Hostel. They found it expensive and unpleasant and so looked for private accommodation. This was offered by a Dutchman who visited the hostel: 'If you want a home or a garage or something to live in you give me £6 and I'll get you something.' The 'something' turned out to be an iron shed about ten feet square with 'hundreds of rats under the floor'.

Statistics bolster such impressions. Overcrowding and poor quality accommodation are disproportionately the lot of those who either have been in the country a short time or have come from regions low on Australia's current hierarchy of acceptability. Deprivation has also occurred in times of housing shortage or general economic crisis. It is equally plain that, sooner or later, most immigrants have sought the security of house and land ownership.

Sometimes the path to the fulfilment of this dream has been full of pot-holes. Some migrants believe that Australian banks and finance institutions have been more reluctant to lend money to migrants than to other clients. One Maltese has recalled in the 1950s always being told: 'Sorry, mate, can't give you credit or terms'. As he explained further: 'That's the day when they used to call us "wogs" and everybody looked at you and spat at you.' It is fair to add, however, that Australian xenophobia has been prompted by just the opposite belief, that refugees and migrants, because they stick together, acquire their homes unnaturally fast and may recourse to illicit financial deals in order to get them. Anti-Semitic remarks are well known in this regard. But the RSL was heard protesting about special loan privileges allegedly granted to Italians in inter-war Queensland.[38]

For some migrants, the battle for a family home has led only to despair. In 1981, the *Sun-Herald* reported the tale of the Kraljevic family. Since arriving in Australia in 1972, both husband and wife had worked frantically. Within ten months they had saved the $6,000 deposit required to get a loan for a unit. Their first child was born and, after a short period, Mrs Kraljevic returned to work as a machinist. Without a car, it meant leaving at 5 am each morning. After eighteen months the unit was paid off and the couple began saving for a house and garden. In 1978 Mrs Kraljevic opted for an abortion to terminate a pregnancy, but when six months later, she was again pregnant, she decided to have the child. There were arguments about money; Mrs Kraljevic became depressed after the birth of her daughter, Vesna; the couple rented out their unit and moved into a new home for which they paid $47,000 in cash. All this within six to eight years of arriving in Australia. Mrs Kraljevic's depression became worse; she was admitted to a psychiatric unit; on her release she killed her baby daughter and then tried to kill herself.[39]

The gods of surburbia seldom are so drastic in their demand for blood sacrifice. Yet the desire to prove that emigration has been worthwhile remains paramount. It becomes important to insist that the new home was better than what might have been in the place of origin. S. L. Thompson, in her study of emigrants who returned to Italy, has reckoned that only 6.8 per cent believed that their final accommodation in Australia was 'unsatisfactory'.[40] For those who stay in Australia, the family home, the new car, and the other material goods become what is scrupulously photographed and lovingly described or embellished in letters to those who have stayed in the place of origin. In the 1950s a Dutch woman, proud of her newly acquired radio but concerned about the bareness of her otherwise unfurnished room, spread a cotton bedcover on the floor. In the photograph, it looked like an intricately patterned carpet. Relatives commented on the grandness of it, all acquired so soon after arrival! At about the same time, a young Polish Jew carefully photographed his new car on a long stretch of country road outside Bathurst. As he explained:

I made this photo and sent it to my father with pages of explanation about distances in this country. I had to explain to him why I indulged, and why I did a thing [like] this. My father employed thirty five people in one shift in our factory, and he never had a car. Now his son, after two years working as a storeman in Australia, buys himself a car.

Two decades later material wealth, with its implied health and happiness, could be exhibited in more than cautiously written letters and painstakingly constructed photographs. Australian Valiants and Holdens can be sighted in small Greek villages or on dusty Italian roads; new houses built by the Australians' money dot the countryside; and relatives visiting from down under are obliged to distribute gifts among all those who had remained behind. Australia, like the United

A home, a car and happiness. This particular family had over-achieved the Australian dream: "We came from Holland, never having had a car, never having thought about it. At one time in Australia we had five cars . . ."

States before it and western Europe in the 1960s, demanded that its immigrants display their wealth and justify their emigration.

The Valiant, the Holden, the red brick house set in its yard, with the gaunt telegraph poles at the front, the fridge, freezer, washing-machine, colour television – these are the outward and visible signs of the migrant faith, the sacraments of the new world. But when ceremony is pushed aside, old habits die hard. As so often in the migrant experience, the new world has to co-exist with old worlds, preserved and re-invented within the walls of the hard-won family home:

> *For nineteen years*
> *We departed*
> *Each morning, shut the house*
> *Like a well-oiled lock,*
> *Hid the key*
> *Under a rusty bucket:*
> *To school and work –*
> ...
> *Back at 5 p.m.*
> *From the polite hum-drum*
> *Of washing clothes*
> *And laying sewerage pipes,*
> *My parents watered*
> *Plants – grew potatoes*
> *And rows of sweet corn*
> ...
> *For nineteen years*
> *We lived together –*
> *Kept pre-war Europe alive*
> *With photographs and letters,*
> *Heated discussions*
> *And embracing gestures:*
>
> *Vistors that ate*
> Kielbasa, *salt herrings*
> *And rye bread, drank*
> *Raw vodka or cherry brandy*
> *And smoked like*
> *A dozen Puffing Billies*[41]

The Old World can exist in material form; or it can exist in the things of the spirit, both grand and humble:

> *Fish and chips and Chiko rolls*
> *she cooks and wraps without a break*
> *while papa watches Soccer goals*

> *and mama makes more beef rissoles,*
> *prepares and stores tomorrow's steak,*
> *and fish and chips and Chiko rolls.*
>
> *Her schoolwork, books, she pigeonholes*
> *to help the shop, for mama's sake*
> *while papa watches Soccer goals*
> *...*
>
> *Back home were promenades, or strolls;*
> *long evening walks beside the lake,*
> *now papa watches Soccer goals,*
>
> *and school and dreams are rigmaroles*
> *of all the wealth we have to make*
> *of fish and chips and Chiko rolls,*
> *and papa watching Soccer goals.* [42]

Food, family gatherings, conversations, and even furnishings proclaim links to a non-Australian past. Backyards also sprout evidence of old environments re-invented in Australia. The members of a small Sicilian community who live close to each other in an inner-western suburb of Sydney are proud of their vegetable gardens. They grow fennel, artichokes, lettuces, lemon trees, fig trees (one *paesano* grew his fig trees from a cutting he took while on a visit to his home village) and essential herbs. It is almost a disgrace not to have vegetables growing in the backyard. [43]

For many immigrants, home and garden have become more than the realisation of the Australian dream: to retreat home to the past was, and is, also to find sanctuary from an alien Australian society. Europeans recall the Australia of the 1950s as a contradictory place: 'where you buy plants and flowers in the hardware store; cigarettes from the barber; glassware, watches and ice creams from the newsagent; and at the furniture shop they sell costume jewellery, toys and lots of other things.' [44] Olive oil was a medicine purchased at the chemist for an outrageous sum and in such small quantities that one bottle was insufficient to fry a small slice of meat. Shrugging dispirited shoulders, immediate post-war arrivals lamented the lack of coffee bars, the primness or the boredom of Sundays, and the unavailability of anything but lamb, white bread and cheddar cheese.

Pino Bosi, a successful journalist from Istria, has recorded his rejection of Australian emptiness in a book entitled *Farewell Australia*, which purported to be written by a departing migrant, though Bosi has stayed and (materially) prospered. In his first letter home, he remembered:

I wrote that walking down the dimly lit Australian streets was like walking in a cemetery at night. Even without ghosts, the small houses and cottages resembled mortuary chapels more than human habitations.

Australians didn't laugh, didn't weep, didn't sing, didn't swear against 'God'. [Australia was no more than] ... a country on the fringe of the world where one can so easily sit it out and watch the world go by.

Bosi's narrator seemed to find his only relief in sex, since in such matters, at least according to him, Australian girls were vulnerable to a little Mediterranean finesse. They could expect none from the Australian male who 'used to be like a wombat which eats, roots and leaves'.[45]

Even in sexual matters, some migrants have found a tension between old worlds and new Australia. Josef Vondra, in his novel, *Paul Zwilling*, revels, somewhat clinically, in the strains of different sexual mores. His Austrian protagonist is, at first, married to an Australian girl. The marriage fails; she drank tea and disliked him drinking wine: 'When they lay back in bed, waiting for the first impulse that would start their copulation, he would be conscious of the acrid, curled taste in her mouth from the cup of tea she had had minutes before. She was always drinking tea, strong stuff, milk, just a drop to make it mucky brown, no sugar!' By contrast, Zwilling's affair with an Australian girl who had been to Europe is happier, at least in bed. The girl knew 'German bed language' and thus could help to overcome Paul's frustrations: 'He was partial to love-language in bed. A word at the right moment would shoot that extra pleasurable wad of blood through his phallus.'[46]

Happiness has been more difficult for migrant women to find. So often in the minority and so often married or about to be married on arrival, they are denied the freedom and opportunities claimed by some of their male peers in this new and alien world. As in so many spheres, their lot can be particularly difficult. Many suffer from an attack on their own identity in the vague but powerful world of unspoken assumptions. Media images emphasise that tall and blonde is beautiful and desirable. Even a Greek language textbook, used widely in Australia, still depicts two characters, 'Maria' who is short, fat, dark and stupid and 'Aphrodite' who is tall, willowy, blonde and gets her man.[47] Husbands are no better. In one of her bitter stories about life in Australia, Vasso Kalamaras has depicted the plight of a down-at-heel schoolteacher who gives up her meagre existence in Athens in order to marry a Greek-Australian. Her new husband proves to be a brute who had wanted a worker for his fruit shop and a 'real woman' with 'breasts like mountains' for his bed. The woman has no family and no friends to whom she can turn. She is driven insane.[48]

Migrant men may muse about their sexual prowess and the different customs practised in their new environment; migrant women, instead, may lament a cruel world in which sex and marriage can help to isolate them. Australian bureaucrats and social scientists have rarely pondered such matters. But they have watched over marriage patterns as an indicator of the success, or not, of assimilation. Even in the 1970s, social scientists were still tidily constructing boxes to show who was marrying whom. Charles Price was a little perturbed that first generation southern Europeans still married 'out' less frequently than other immigrants, but he added that 'the tendency ... has weakened recently'. Balancing this inbreeding among southern Europeans, it was noted, were increasing numbers of English, German and Dutch immigrants, both male and female, who 'are now marrying heavily into the Australian born population'. Jews and eastern European refugees were also intermarrying more frequently, although they preferred other immigrants to the Australian-born. Predictably, in the second generation, the rate of 'out-marriage' zoomed ahead, with only a few exceptions. Price and his colleagues concluded that ethnic communities were breaking down as sons and daughters sought partners from the new world. But such analysts were also careful to hedge their bets. They bowed to the new respectability of pluralism and concluded:

At this rate Australia will be less a multi-cultural society – that is, a society containing many different cultures brought in from different parts of the world – than a mixed cultural society – that is, a society whose people inherit in themselves many different cultures and in themselves mix the cultural elements as seems good to them.[49]

Homogeneity remains the ideal. Yet, the blending has often created problems for those involved, whether they are the partners in mixed marriages or the Australian-born children of people from old worlds.

Looking at his own community in Melbourne, a Jewish social worker isolated the most common areas of conflict between children and their overseas-born parents. He pointed to the values of the *shtetl* which, for so many central and eastern European Jews, had somehow been passed down over the generations, and to the impact of the harrowing experiences of parents who had survived Nazi concentration camps. These two factors, he argued, helped to form the parental values, which were often at variance with the hopes and aims of children brought up in Australia. In particular, the honour and respect traditionally accorded to the learned in the community, reinforced the common migrant view that education is an important means to social status and material well-being. The case cited was of a single parent who sought assistance from Jewish Welfare to pay for his son's second attempt at matriculation. Why should the boy try again? 'Look at me, I lost my family in concentration camp, I survived myself, my business went broke, I am a sick man – what is there to live for now except to see my Chaim at university?'

Status and survival were also isolated as the main motives behind the strong desire that Jew should marry Jewess. How else can the group retain its identity? The potential conflict and disturbance were captured in the lament of a daughter who sought counselling: 'You should hear what Mum and Dad say about Tom – they're crazy – what they want for me is a nice Jewish boy, you know, one that stays up every night studying and wears short hair – just because he isn't Jewish, they think he's a criminal or something.'[50]

The Jewish community is certainly not alone. Culture conflict, the dilemma of balancing safely on the thin line between the old world and the new, is an integral part of the migration story everywhere. Some immigrants cope, some do not. There is the story of a young Greek girl in Melbourne who counted the blocks, houses, and then the fence palings between home and school. She marked the middle paling and on the way to school, as she passed it, said to herself 'Now I'm Australian' and, on the way home, 'Now I'm Greek'.[51] A young Indian girl expressed the same confusion when she wrote: 'Sometimes I feel that I split into two parts – the Indian and the Australian, having difficulty in compromising. Not only I have conflicts within myself, I very often have arguments in the family.'[52]

The influence of Australian life-styles, particularly the licence seen to be given to children and women, is often blamed as the cause of many conflicts. A Lebanese father did not want his daughter to wear slacks or any Australian fashions: 'Why should she exhibit her charms if she does not mean to sell or give them away?'[53] Similarly, a Greek woman reflected on the tension building up in her home. After a hard day's work in the factory, she came home to find her husband demanding immediate attention: 'before I put my bag down and catch my breath he asks me to make him coffee ... I get very angry with him and tell him to make one himself ... I know I am becoming a bad wife. But things are different in Australia.' Her husband had agreed but could not change his ways: 'I don't know any more who is the boss in this house. How can I call myself a man!'[54]

Nor does flight from Australia necessarily resolve such conflicts. Indeed, social change may have occurred more rapidly and more bewilderingly in the country of origin than in Australia. Catholic Italy now offers divorce and abortion. And in socialist Greece, there are the first feeble flutterings of an attempt to lift the yoke of the Orthodox Church from social and moral concerns.

Some commentators have claimed that the trauma of the migrant experience is further demonstrated by the number who seek psychiatric care. Since the 1950s, various studies have reiterated that migrants and refugees, particularly the displaced persons, have provided a much higher percentage of admissions to psychiatric institutions than have the Australian-born. These figures have given rise to sweeping generalisations about the nature of the migrant experience and its role in causing mental illness. In 1974, for example,

Alan Richardson endorsed an earlier claim that 'certain personality traits which belong in the constitutional background of mental disease predispose [individuals] to overseas migration'.[55] The real meaning of these figures can be, and has been, contested. Hospital admission rates are an inadequate measure in themselves. Some migrants may avoid such institutions through a lack of knowledge or for fear of the stigma attached. Other groups, particularly those without any community or family support systems, may over-depend on the succour offered by men and women in white. Closer analyses of the figures have also revealed that it is not the fact of migration *per se* that propels migrants to psychiatric care. Socio-economic factors, isolation from family and neighbourhood networks, the inability to obtain satisfactory employment or to acquire the material comforts so readily flaunted as the fruits of labour in Australia, all these push and pull the migrant man, woman or child between the closed doors of old worlds left behind and of a new world waiting to be discovered. And not all groups are affected equally. Refugees, the aged, women isolated in the suburbs and without English, and adolescents growing up in two worlds are more at risk and are more heavily represented among those in psychiatric institutions. Similarly, analysis by ethnic group has revealed the shallowness of lumping all migrants together. Polish refugees and Yugoslav migrants may have a higher representation than the Australian-born among psychotics in institutions but other groups, including Italians, have a much lower representation.[56] Yet again in the complex migrant world, generalisations hide more than they reveal.

A more notorious characteristic associated with migration is the migrant's role in the world of crime. In this regard, migrants have sometimes been seen to be importing into Australia, or wherever they land, sinister habits from their old lives. Prejudice has easily surfaced. Criminals are different; migrants are different. The conclusion to these twin observations has not been difficult to guess. 'Swarthy', 'dark', 'poor', 'feckless', 'undisciplined' – these are the adjectives associated with many criminal classes and with many migrants from south of the Alps.

Traditionally, Italians and particularly southern Italians have been categorised as 'prone to use the knife'. As Nino Culotta so smugly observed: 'They [southern Italians] are small dark people with black hair and what we considered bad habits.'[57] The stereotype has been readily picked up by Australian officialdom. In 1961 B. A. Santamaria expressed concern about the danger of keeping the Italian 'separated from his own women and with little prospect of marriage' because, without family life, he 'may become a prey to organised crime'[58] (though, in reality, in southern Italy, family life may well have been the first basis of organised crime).

The familiar and changing hierarchy of race appears even in comment on crime. In 1981, a district judge associated such habits no longer with the by now more respectable Italians but with the newly arriving Lebanese: 'it has been said the carrying of knives is a cultural matter in the Lebanese community. All I can say to them is: It is a cultural habit that should be discarded now.'[59]

In contrast, old Australians are presumed to be dutifully law-abiding – or at least more clever in their escapades. In 1981, Marrickville witnessed a dramatic increase in the rate of shoplifting. Shop-owners and police were in little doubt about the identity of the criminals. A manager of one department store said: 'We have a mixed league of nations in Marrickville but it's very rarely that an Australian offender is caught.'[60]

When prejudice is tested against serious research, very little evidence has appeared to indicate that crime is unusually high among immigrants or that the Mafia or any other overtly criminal organisations have been transported to Australia. That protection rackets, covert insurance and mutual aid groups, sometimes with illegal ambitions, have existed is undeniable and is plainly a natural part of the migrant experience. But investigations have always shown that organised crime has been a part of the Australian experience since well before the arrival of suspect Europeans and that, contrary to legend, most migrant groups are less likely to participate in crime than are old Australians.

In response to press and popular rumours about migrant criminality, in the early 1950s the Commonwealth government established an advisory council 'to investigate the conduct of migrants'. The chairman was a judge, W. R. Dovey, and the council had representatives from the Australian Workers' Union, the RSL and the National Council of Women. Successive reports in 1952, 1955, and 1957 concluded that 'the relatively low incidence of serious crime generally amongst migrants and the high standard of their behaviour in all aspects of their daily life reflects considerable credit upon those who have aided their assimilation and upon the migrants themselves.' The migrant crime rate was 'less than one-quarter' that of the Australian-born. Indeed, the 1957 report noted optimistically that migrants should be known in the press for their hard work and honesty, and not for alleged crime.

In the years which followed, the statistics have recurred. In 1981 Ronald Francis published *Migrant Crime in Australia* . Its tables showed that the crime levels of most migrant groups fell well below those of the Australian-born. Nor did hierarchies of race hold up very well, since the current criminal summit is held by New Zealanders, while Italians occupy almost the lowest level of all. Francis's research had evident inadequacies. He made no reference to class, except to note primly, and in characteristic prose, that, 'nativity groups are not homogeneous'.[61]

If crime and law have occasionally provoked discussion of the role of migrants in Australian society and the extent to which non-Australian backgrounds may adversely affect behaviour, the more consistent concern has always been over where migrants live. Commentators have sometimes expressed a distrust of migrants at play and have recounted the willingness of police to restrain parties in parks where the newcomers sing, strum instruments or sit on the grass. But the greater fear is that migrants cluster too close in their settlement patterns, preserving old worlds not just within doors but outside as well.

The interest in where migrants settle, and the anxiety that they might not disperse, has been at least partly motivated by Australia's traditional uneasiness before outsiders, and by the nightmare that a land so partially won might as easily be lost. Linked to such usually unspoken apprehension has been overt moralising. It was bad for the migrants to cling together. If they did, they would be relegated to the ghetto. As one commentator warned in an early *Good Neighbour*, 'If it happened in America it can well happen here unless we guard against it ... Without assimilation, a migrant scheme can be a tragedy of race riots, fostered enmity and malicious whispers – the ingredients of national dissension, turmoil and bloodshed.'[62] These fears had already surfaced from the very beginning of the increase in non-British immigration. Back in 1939, a Kings Cross real estate agent had bewailed the fact that Jews were treating his suburb as if they were 'at home'. 'One family visits the other, there is talking, singing, and merrymaking, and in the end we are inundated with shoals of complaints from other tenants ... The trouble is that many of them have very few inhibitions. They are not reserved like people of British stock.'[63]

Nor was suspicion directed only against Jews. A branch of the ALP at Port Kembla objected in 1948 to the establishment of a hostel for '400 Balts' in the area. 'We consider that these people should be absorbed into the community gradually and in a dispersed manner so that they may learn through necessity and contact with Australian people our way of life instead of becoming a foreign colony in our midst.'[64] In the House of Representatives, one politician warned against 'herding' immigrants together. Any concentration would only prompt expressions of 'discontent' and slacken the rate of assimilation.[65]

Such ideas have not vanished. Indeed, journalists writing of the 'coming crisis' of 'Vietnamatta' said much the same thing. An editorial in the *Sydney Morning Herald* remarked: 'With the continuing influx of Indo-Chinese refugees and their concentration in one area of Sydney it was inevitable that, sooner or later, racial and social tensions would arise'. Or, as a Yugoslav migrant, now community services planner for Fairfield, put it, 'The Indo-Chinese are much more "visible" than any of the other migrant groups because of their Asian features. When you see half a dozen Asians in the street you notice them straightaway. That's why people think they are taking over the place.'[66]

Social scientists too have gathered plenty of evidence about the clustering of migrants in particular suburbs at particular times. In Melbourne of the mid 1960s, Greeks and Italians occupied many houses in the inner industrial, and Maltese in the outer industrial suburbs. British and German migrants, on the other hand, were inclined to distribute themselves according to the Australian pattern.[67]

The Marxists are plainly right in arguing that it is naive to plot ethnic residential patterns with no reference to wealth or class, particularly when, on arrival and for some time after, the majority of immigrants live in low cost, working class areas. But it is also true that class or regional traditions and loyalties from the place of origin often influence settlement patterns. In Leichhardt, the first 'Italians' were Lipari Islanders; later they were joined by chain migrants from the towns of Spadafora and Comiso in Sicily, who could there experience or create some mutual identity as Sicilians or *paesani*. In the Renmark Irrigation Area of South Australia, peasant migrants from the Peloponnisos villages of Lakonia, Messinia, and Zakinthos have united with new settlers from the Aegean islands to create a Greek presence in their area.[68] Jews from different nationalities and class backgrounds congregated first in Kings Cross and the eastern suburbs of Sydney to provide an ethos that still exists. Other ex-Habsburgs have also tried to stick together. On a visit in 1968, comic writer George Mikes lost his sense of humour when confronted by Sydney's Hungarians:

Their society is the upper bourgeosie of Budapest of the thirties ... which is [now] as extinct as the dodo on the banks of the Danube, but preserved in methylated spirits near Sydney Harbour. Their bridge parties, their whole form of life, their feuds, their love-affairs, their badinage, even their turn of phrase, all belong to a bygone, almost historic era.[69]

Plainly, too, clustering has weakened over time. Indeed, what is most curious about the housing of non-British migrants in Australia is that the fears about ghettoes have proved largely groundless. The 1966 census figures revealed that even in the areas of highest concentration, the mixed immigrant component of the population did not represent more than 40 per cent of the residents. Later censuses have similarly shown that while some ethnic groups tend to cluster together for longer than others, no distinct ghettoes where a migrant population dominates the area have developed.

Why have migrant ghettoes not been created in Australia? Perhaps government policy, pushed by the ill-ease of public opinion, successfully discouraged them. The more likely answer is a less planned one. Until recently, the Australian economy has offered some upward social mobility and a much more powerful and all-embracing myth of it. In the land of opportunity why stay where you are? Migrants came here seeking a better life and, just as the Australian-born change their place of residence, so do migrants. Australia has often not offered much mobility in a real sense, or not as compared to what was happening in the place of origin. Yet, reality is often less influential than myth. The Australia that seems so empty, so lacking in traditions or history, and so unencumbered by a rigid class system has not posed a theoretical restraint on movement. In Sydney, Greeks expanded cautiously from Redfern to Stanmore to Marrickville and then to Kingsford and Earlwood; Italians from Leichhardt to Haberfield and Five Dock. In Melbourne, Italians moved from Carlton and Fitzroy to Brunswick. By the 1970s, in many Australian cities, the newcomers of the 1950s sold out their inner-city dwellings to incoming 'trendies' and left for a house and garden on the outskirts.

Much of migrant life in Australia has revolved around the problem of bricks and mortar, of acquiring a home and living in it, of collecting material comforts as evidence of the benefits of emigration. The conditions may at first have been and may continue to be nothing like the rosy picture of tree-lined streets and red-brick villas. To survive and achieve the Australian dream of home ownership may have meant disillusion for some, privation for others. But, migrants have conformed; they have even excelled and beaten the Australian-born at their own game. Now they can boast of their homes, cars and possessions. This is what new Australia has allowed them to acquire. In their turn, and despite the efforts of Australian assimilationism, migrants have also preserved parts of their own worlds. Kept alive, at first behind front doors, much of these old worlds has now spilled into the streets. There are foodstores, restaurants, doctors, real estate vendors, and all the other agents offering particular national or regional brands of goods and services in particular national or regional languages; ethnic groups picnic together, talk 'foreign' in the streets, and demand specialised health services. But this pluralism has not been achieved without great cost to many. The strains of living in two worlds and the prejudices of those worlds have caused many to falter. The fruits of emigration and labour have not always been home, health, and happiness. But, for those who have survived, they have given lie to the great Australian dream of homogeneity. It simply has not been achieved and perhaps one day, neither bureaucrats nor social scientists will seek it. Migration has not meant merely a life devoted to work and a home which becomes ever more Australianised. Instead, the flux of migration, its realities and its myths have driven the so-called Australian way of life to shift and vary. And this new heterogeneity has extended beyond house and family to leisure and culture, to politics and ideology.

Chapter SEVEN
Culture High and Low

Remember that Australia is a young country. It has not had time to develop a cultural life ... to the extent that the older countries of Europe have done. But it is a free country and you will be free here. You will be among friends.

Australia ... is a young country, which in many ways has been isolated from the main current of world thought, but there have always been standard-bearers in the arts and sciences.[1]

So the Department of Immigration began to explain to new immigrants after the war what sort of a cultural milieu they could expect in Australia.

When the migrants reached Australia, they were often unimpressed. A study published in the early 1970s of Polish, German, and British migrants in Perth found that only 4 per cent believed local culture to be better than it was in the country of origin.[2] A little before, a Ukrainian migrant knew his mind well enough. Australia, he said, was 'culturally ... the most backward country in the world'.[3]

The confrontation of one culture with another is always difficult. Metaphors become easily mixed, as one Polish migrant's comment indicates: 'I could not penetrate the Australian intellectual ebony towers'.[4] Incomprehension is common. Indeed, given that 'culture' is perceived and defined differently by different people, often according to their class, regional, or national background, the incomprehension is not surprising. What may be valued in Vienna could be scorned in Sydney; what may shape cultural identity in a village on the Canton delta could be non-existent or at least alien in the new world; what may be applauded as a cultural achievement in Adelaide or Melbourne could pass unnoticed in Rome, Prague or Peking. The story of migration to any land will often tell of a clinging to the old culture and of a nostalgic and stubborn assertion that the old ways were best. In that assimilationist Australia in which a migrant was often informed: 'People who come to this country should stop speaking their own yabba yabba. It's offensive',[5] many a migrant mind kept scrupulously protected a knowledge that these Australians were the barbarians who would never comprehend Vienna, Kiev, Athens, or even a village like Partinico.

This potential conflict was complicated by the many strains of Australia's own cultural values. These have often combined a cultural cringe – a belief that London, or perhaps New York or even Europe spawned culture – and new nationalism – an increasingly strident assertion that a koala-emblazoned tea-mug or a crocheted Harbour Bridge was the aesthetic equal of a Picasso painting or a Mozart opera.

In these circumstances, commentators have disagreed when they have tried to measure the extent to which immigration has affected Australia. Geoffrey Serle, in his standard history of Australian culture, was not sanguine about cultural exchange: 'The many continental European migrants, who mostly arrived after the 1939–45 war, have had relatively little impact on creative culture except in painting.'[6] On the other hand, Donald Horne declared that, but for immigration, contemporary Australia would reflect no more than the 'old dreariness'. With extraordinary statistical precision, he claimed that 'thirty seven per cent of people engaged in musical composition, literature, painting, sculpture and the theatre in Australia are immigrants, [as are] almost forty per cent of university staff.'[7] Al Grassby has even detected that migration has carried Australia to the edge of a 'cultural revolution'.[8] For Grassby, multicultural Australia will be able to stand on its own feet, and the Australian intellectual will no longer have to consider Henry Lawson's message:

My advice to any young Australian writer whose talents have been recognised would be to go steerage, stow away, swim and seek London, Yankieland or Timbuctoo – rather than stay in Australia till his genius turned to gall or beer. Or, failing this, ... to study elementary anatomy ... and then shoot himself carefully.[9]

Yet, for good or evil, Grassby's utopia has not arrived. Three or four generations after Lawson, any Australian still finds it difficult to steer successfully between the great cringe and the (new) nationalism. But, in appraising the character and impact of the complex of migrant cultures in Australia, another course can be charted. Migration, at least potentially, provides a chance to reject all nationalisms and to make Australia a place in which heterodoxy can outscore orthodoxy, in which each person can have his or her own culture.

But certain questions need to be asked about migration and culture. How and to what extent have migrant cultures been preserved (or re-invented)? What have they done to Australia? What has Australia done to them? When an official committee asserts that Australia 'will inevitably be influenced and infiltrated by the cultural traditions of incoming ethnic groups',[10] is it merely expending rhetoric or has Australia been culturally enriched by non-British immigrants? 'Culture' in this context becomes an open-ended category in which the 'high culture' of fine arts, music and literature jostles uncomfortably alongside the 'popular culture', expressed through folk traditions, sport and television; in which the 'national' culture promoted through Australian educational and religious institutions competes with the 'national' cultures preserved or re-invented in ethnic schools or through sectarian squabbles; in which the participants or creators of 'culture' play as important a role as the spectators. In all areas there is some evidence of the survival of old worlds, and of an uneasy meeting between these old worlds and new Australia.

One of the more noticeable fields of migrant penetration of Australian culture has been in the world of music. Werner Baer, 'Fred Blanks', Henry Krips, Rudolf Pekarek, Larry Sitsky, Felix Werder, Musica Viva – the names of performers, composers, critics and organisations at once record the impact that central European migrants in particular have had.

Before 1945, the Australian musical world had one manifest characteristic – a staunch cultural cringe, a provincially timid mimicking of what was done in London. Music in Australia moved to a tempo set in the metropolis of the British Empire, in much the same way that music did in Glasgow or Leicester or Leeds. An Australian Orpheus escaped automatically to London. *En route,* when passing through Europe, he sought out the British consul for introductions at Naples, was relieved to locate an English-speaker at Milan, caught a cold in Venice, and, at Bayreuth, organised eggs and bacon for breakfast: 'just the meal we wanted, and without any frills and fal-lahs'.[11]

Australian taste was narrow and provincial; knowledge of great performances was slight; the local repertoire was limited. Although Australia had been listed on the international music circuit for almost a century, the regular whistle stop tours by the 'world's best' bore some resemblance to similar off-season tours by great football teams. In exhibition matches or concerts, the faces were there, but the spirit or commitment was lacking. Music, too, was a victim of the time warp that accompanied the tyranny of distance. Thus *Tristan* was not performed till 1912, nor *Tosca* till 1911. *Fidelio* was still a novelty in 1930. (Similarly, staging Pirandello was *avant garde* in the 1930s, reading Croce in the 1940s, and in 1939, Modigliani prints were banned by the ineffable Australian censors who then still deemed Balzac unfit for Australian minds.)[12]

Entering this parochial world Europeans, nurtured in the traditions of the Habsburg empire, may well have gradually comprehended that 'many things which were quite contrary to our customs in Europe were quite natural in Australia',[13] but they also inevitably challenged and complicated some of the provincial simplicity. A well-known purveyor of Viennese taste has been Musica Viva, which has often seemed as though it were an organisation run by refugee migrants for refugee migrants. As one visiting German musician happily noted:

I wish to mention that which moved us most deeply of all, even more deeply than the experience of successful performances ... I cannot find words to say how happy my friends and I felt at meeting so many of our former fellow-countrymen as well as former Austrians, Poles, Hungarians, and Czechs.[14]

Musica Viva's founder, Richard Goldner, was a Romanian-born Jew who grew up and played music in Vienna, with experience in local chamber and radio philharmonic orchestras. The *Anschluss* cut short his Viennese career and, a year later, he arrived in Australia. He was unable to gain work in his vocation because the Australian Musicians Union black-banned all non-naturalised residents. Goldner fell back on other abilities. With his brother, he designed and manufactured brooches.

When war broke out, the Goldners' business was classified a luxury concern but it was saved as Richard Goldner put it, by *bonne chance*. An RAAF officer was doing his rounds of inventive manufacturers (Goldner had perfected a process for making his synthetic brooches look like wood), in order to find an efficient zip fastener. Goldner offered a suitable blueprint and his factory changed its name to Triflex. During the war the Goldners produced zippers for both the RAAF and the American forces, an achievement mentioned in the official history of Australia during the Second World War.[15] At the end of the war the patent was sold to a South African firm. It was with money gained through this business venture that Goldner financed the first Musica Viva concert.

The performance was held on 8 December 1945. On that evening the Sydney Conservatorium was plunged into darkness by an electricity strike. European nerve-ends jangled. Goldner has recalled that Charles Moses, head of the ABC, came to the rescue and provided an army generator. Then the concert went on, with the Conservatorium entrance lit by car headlights and the interior by small lamps and candles. On stage there were seventeen musicians who had been rehearsing for three months. They were an unusual group, not a chamber orchestra but four string quartets and a pianist, and there was no conductor. Goldner had resurrected a style of performance he had learned in 1930s Vienna. And 1930s Austria and Germany were also present in the audience. Participants recollect that there was a large contingent of central Europeans there, Jews and others, who had escaped from Hitler's Europe.

Walter Dullo had sent out many of the invitations. He had been born in Königsberg, and in 1933 he had just begun his compulsory three

years practice in the law courts. He joined the increasing stream of
professional Jews seeking to leave Germany and in 1937 obtained a
permit to come to Australia. Here, for him, the practice of law was out
of the question, and so he turned to the manufacture of a continental,
aristocratic delicacy – specially packed, rich chocolates. At first, his
market was restricted since he had not established a sales network.
Then war broke out and, like many of those fortunate enough to gain
sanctuary in Australia and who desired to assist in the war effort, he
found himself drafted into the alien construction corps, roadbuilding
at Alice Springs and Tennant Creek. The world of specialised
chocolates melted away before the heat, sweat, and flies of the
Australian interior. But at the end of the war, Dullo went back to
chocolate production, and to the task of finding those who desired a
taste of central Europe.

His first customers were Europeans and Goldner was among them.
In Dullo's own words 'we became friends by our common interest in
music'.[16] Dullo was a self-educated musicologist, who gradually built
up an enormous record and music book library, so large that he had to
construct a second home to house it. Until his death in 1978, Dullo's
expertise in music was reflected in Musica Viva's programme notes.
His commercial flair he had used earlier when invitations to the first
concert went out to those already buying his chocolates.

The list of central European names grew as Musica Viva grew. Five
out of the seven who attended the first executive meeting of Musica
Viva were Europeans. Early activists in Melbourne and Adelaide were
also central Europeans. Over the years the proportion of central
Europeans on the executive has lessened, but it has remained high.
The central European dominance in Musica Viva's administration
reflected, however, more than an importation of a Habsburg ethos. It
also marked the inaccessibility of established Australian music networks to non-Anglophiles. It was not until the 1960s and 1970s that
European credentials gained ready recognition and acceptance in the
higher echelons of Australia's dominant purveyor of classical music,
the ABC.

Musica Viva is not without its critics. To some, it is Musica Mortua.
The organisation has, however, attached Australia more firmly to
some international networks that lead beyond London to central
Europe and elsewhere. But it has also gradually become part of the
respectable Australian cultural world. For migrants, both original
refugees and those from the second generation, Musica Viva plays an
ambivalent refrain. The sweetness of romantic melodies comforts and
reinforces the nostalgia for a Europe left behind, and also for the
Europe that was and is not. For some, a Musica Viva concert can blot
out the harsh sounds of history, the hidden echoes of Auschwitz, of
Fascism or of the Red Army, and the real challenges of the present.

Musica Viva is only one instance of the migrant influence that has deeply, if ambiguously, affected Australian music. In opera, orchestral concerts, and even in some areas of popular music, similar tones can be sounded. Multicultural Australia has become a place to be toured by Italian pop, Chilean protest, or Greek folk singers. Local individuals or groups can also make a career on the ethnic club circuit. Non-British migrants have imported many of their musical traditions to Australia and have helped to condition Australia's previous insularity. But whether such traditions are now more alive than dead, and how likely it is that a country of Australia's size, wealth, and geographical position will for long lose its provincialism remain uncertainties.

The ceremonies of multicultural Australia often also celebrate literary endeavour. Angelo Loukakis wins prizes for his short stories; Antigone Kefala receives critical praise for her poems; and next to the stalls offering food or wine you can purchase the latest writings of Dmytro Chub, András Dezsery, Josef Vondra, or Pino Bosi. In Victoria, David Martin's *The Young Wife* has been included on the syllabus for Higher School Certificate English, and Judah Waten continues to be regarded as a major bard of the migrant tale.

Yet a paean of triumph cannot adequately explain the non-British contribution to Australian literature. Migrant literature can be separated into a number of types. There is writing in the language of the country of origin. The Estonian community, for example, is reputed to write much about itself in Estonian. Sometimes such refugee communities act as vendors for a literature that is linked to an international refugee circuit. The Ukrainian community offers for sale works translated into English and published in Canada. Typical is N. Prychodko's *Good-bye Siberia,* a propaganda piece about the evils of Russia and communism, and the supreme virtue of Ukrainian nationalism.[17]

Other first generation writers have also attempted to present their works in English. Some, like Vasso Kalamaras or Dmitris Tsaloumas have sought translators and have presented bilingual texts; others like Andras Deszery have less successfully done their own translations; and others such as Cecile Kunrathy and Josef Vondra have ventured to express themselves directly in English and have produced not so much literature as excellent source material for social history.[18]

David Martin and Judah Waten are writers who are normally assumed better to represent multicultural Australia, but they are not without ambiguity as authors who depict migrant life. Martin arrived here as an adult after an odyssey which began in Hungary and had then passed through Germany, Holland, Palestine, the Spanish Civil War, Britain, Hungary again, and India. A journalist, Martin's especial claim to fame at that time was probably his translation into English of the lyrics of 'Lili Marlene', most popular of all Second World War songs. His writings in Australia, which have included poetry, novels, and children's stories, have attracted critical acclaim. Reviewers have marvelled at his topicality and at his 'supra-nationalism', his ability to portray sympathetically the dilemmas of Somali blacks living in the Cardiff dockside regions, of Indians in post-Gandhi India, and of Greeks or Jews in Australia. Perhaps reflecting his journalistic training, Martin has certainly been adept at constructing plots from the headlines of the moment. His most well-known novel, *The Young Wife* (1962), is an exploration of problems of assimilation in the Greek community in Melbourne. Two decades later, his interests have kept up with the times and his 1981 publication, *Foreigners,* is a collection of short stories depicting the variety of backgrounds and problems that contribute to the migrant experience in Australia.[19]

A much more direct and well-known depictor of a migrant's lot is Judah Waten who, like John O'Grady, defines his writing as having a realistic intent. He has noted that his novel *Alien Son* (1952) was 'one of the first pieces about foreign migrants, written from inside a foreign community', to appear in Australia. Although set in the post-First World War period, it confronted, he said, the major issues of the post-Second World War migration, that is, 'loneliness, homesickness, language and cultural barriers, misunderstandings between the newcomers and the locals, divided families, or the sharp conflicts between parents and children brought up in Australia.'[20] Some of Waten's writing is mildly critical of Australia's unpreparedness for non-Anglo-Saxon migrants. Even his Australian Jewish characters are sometimes suspicious of new arrivals: one old citizen, for example, comments sagely on the persecuted Jews of post-1933 Germany: '[They] are a pretty arrogant lot ... They brought a lot of it on themselves.'[21] But Waten is also a comfortable writer. Despite his proclaimed allegiance to the left and his occasional dabbling with proletarian neo-realism, Waten is a serene revolutionary who is not sad that this is such a 'tranquil country' and who continues to portray a basically assimilationist Australia.

In a sense Waten exhibits from an earlier generation parallels to what seems to be true about some of the next generation of 'ethnic' writers. Antigone Kefala, Peter Skrzynecki and Angelo Loukakis arrived in their new worlds as children or adolescents and have passed through an Anglo-Saxon education system (Kefala at the Victoria University of Wellington, New Zealand, and Skrzynecki and Loukakis at the University of Sydney). As literary figures they really belong to a second generation, which, as is already known from America, explores and re-invents the experience of its parents, but is assisted in its 'success' both by its own assimilation and by the current trendiness of ethnicity. Their literature displays an aesthetic quality but, once again, and often unfairly, it is their status as migrants who have made it in the literary world and not their achievements as writers of literature that tends to win critical acclaim.

In the visual arts, the migrant presence can similarly be seen, as names like Judy Cassab, Maximilian Feuerring, Michael Kmit, Louis Kahan, Stanislaus Rapotec, Henry Salkauskas, and Andor Meszaros testify. For some, recognition has come in spite of the obstacles set by Anglo-Australia. For many, success has occurred after an induction into the networks of the established Australian art world. Judy Cassab is typical. Her journey to two Archibald Prizes began in Budapest and Vienna. Recommendations from there opened doors in London, which in turn opened doors in Australia. Her first portrait in Australia was of the wife of Charles Lloyd Jones. After this, further stints in London led to an exhibition there in 1959 and a commission to paint a portrait of Princess Alexandra (to hang in the ward-room of the P & O liner *Oriana*). Cassab may have kept her central European wires open but, in Australia, her fame had been bolstered from abroad through the usual patronage systems of Anglo-Australia.

If individuals through their work have played a role in the transmission of old worlds to new Australia, sometimes the importing has been done directly, often even bypassing the immigrants themselves. Foreign governments, for example, have tried to push their culture and language through institutions that they financed in Australia as elsewhere. The Goethe Institut, the Alliance Française and the Dante Alighieri Society still have branches in many Australian cities and teach the language of the country of origin, while also screening recent films and making some effort to publicise recent literary and artistic achievement and endeavouring to preach the nationalism of the country of origin. Such cultural bodies usually remain cosy associations where romantic and safe images of Italy and Italians (or Germany and Germans or Japan and Japanese) are imbibed:

I had no sympathy for Italians, until a friend of mine took me one evening to a function of the Dante Society devoted to Italian music. I was so thrilled that I decided immediately to become a member. I now realize that this is also the music of Melbourne's Italian migrants, towards whom my whole attitude has changed.[22]

As far as Italian high culture is concerned, a new initiative has recently been taken with the creation of the Frederick May Foundation for Italian Studies at the University of Sydney. With generous financial assistance from the Italian government, the Foundation has been able to bring to Australia historians as eminent as Giuliano Procacci, Renzo De Felice, and Franco Venturi; literary critics of the quality of Alberto Asor Rosa and Umberto Eco; avant-garde theatre groups; contemporary art exhibitions and more.

In many ways, the Foundation's achievement is also superficial. The

Italian government is perhaps not well informed about the value attached to high culture in Australia. A report in *Corriere della Sera,* averring that a May Foundation conference was 'the most important cultural event of the winter season',[23] had it been circulated widely, would surely have astonished or irritated many. Moreover, most ordinary migrants remain far from impressed by great cultural events. Semioticians, concrete poets and academic historians have little natural contact with ordinary Italo-Australians who, however far from the grandeur or glory of Michelangelo and Dante, are even further from the avant-garde of contemporary Italy.

In a more niggardly fashion, the Australian government (often through the Australia Council) does occasionally finance cultural exchange with migrant countries. Australian poets are sent to tour Italy; the Sydney String Quartet plays Bach to audiences in Salzburg and Singapore; German glass glitters on display in the Sydney Opera House; and a Zagreb theatre group confuses and amuses Australian audiences with its performance in Serbo-Croatian of 'The Liberation of Skopje'. The usefulness of such exchange, except for the individuals concerned, may be questioned, though perhaps a few pathways unknown to pre-1945 Australia have been opened.

But the most exemplary story of government and ethnic culture is that of television channel O/28. Inaugurated in October 1980 by the Fraser government, the channel screens ethnic films in the original languages and transmits many complex images of ethnic societies. It has done remarkably well on a purely intellectual level, perhaps because channel 2 goes on cringing so dispiritedly to mother England, but its ratings remain poor and its transmission limited. For the first two years it was available only to select areas of Sydney and Melbourne and the announcement of extensions to the service in July 1982 tellingly stated that the public service redoubt of Canberra would receive the channel before the migrant centres of Wollongong and Newcastle.[24]

A 1982 survey confirmed that of the 'ethnic viewing audience', only 15 per cent directed their attention to channel O/28 compared with 22, 27 and 32 per cent for the commercial stations; the ABC attracted a mere 4 per cent.[25] The fare simply is not appetising. Perhaps, as one explanation has it, the preponderance of films for language groups which only make up a small percentage of the migrant population drives away ethnic viewers. Not many Greek speakers automatically switch on to a Truffaut film with English subtitles. Nor are 'ethnics' necessarily delighted to see the latest art films from their country of origin. Back home, intellectuals probably demand to be and are treated very seriously, and their creations are approved and admired (though it was always alleged that the most popular programme on state-run Italian television was the ten minute slab of advertisements that came after the news and before the political debates). In any case, migrants may have left before being integrated into their own national culture, and their Australia scarcely stimulates much interest in or need for high art films. At most, many migrants may turn to channel O/28 for a glimpse of the home country behind subtitles and the involved dialogue, or for that overseas sport and news neglected by the rest of Australian television.

In the various areas of high culture, the list of non-Anglo-Saxon names and of non-Anglo-Saxon achievement is generally impressive. Yet to interpret such achievement is difficult. There is the problem of 'the industry of ethnicity', which forges into being migrant writers or migrant artists because bureaucracies or politicians want them to exist. There is the problem that much migrant success seems only to occur after an adaptation to basic Australian cultural structures and values. There is the problem that changes in communication have produced a smaller world now than existed in 1945 and that these changes would inevitably have reduced Australian provincialism with or without immigration. The achievement may be ambiguous, superficial, idiosyncratic, and limited, but it is there. The greater problem is what does all this high culture mean to a country of Australia's intellectual values? Is not Australia a place where it is rather popular culture that matters? And have not most migrants themselves been people who imbibed more deeply the popular culture of their village than the high culture of their nation?

The 'popular culture' of pre-literate peoples at once conjures up that world of costume, dance, and festival, the depiction of which has rocketed *Annales* historians like Emmanuel Le Roy Ladurie to historiographical stardom. The local equivalent of the peasants of Montaillou still await their historians, but they will have rich material on which to work. During the 1940s and 1950s, the press and government publications abounded with photographs of adults and young children in their national costumes. Calwell, Holt and other ministers for immigration were photographed kissing young girls who were adorned in the aprons, garlands and gaily patterned clothes of their country of origin. At the third citizenship convention, in 1952, proceedings began with a patriotic display. The hall was decked with 'a twin row of alternating Australian flags and Union Jacks'; drums rolled and the curtains opened to reveal 'a tableau symbolising migration and its part in the development of Australia'. The tableau included a mother with two children, flanked by representatives of the Australian armed forces, a farmer 'with a sheaf of wheat' and 'a mechanic in overalls'. Representing 'the migration flow' was 'a Scot in busby and full Highland regalia; [and] ... a new Australian from Europe in the national costume and head-dress of her land.'[26] There was no need to distinguish which land the new Australian came from. After all, what

difference did it make since in Australia it was Australia that
mattered?

Occasionally some European gagged at the squishy diet of such
occasions. One actually complained that these ceremonies hindered
the construction of a genuine relationship between old worlds and new
Australia. He observed:

Australians probably get the impression that European migrants are quaint and
charming people wearing funny costumes, singing exotic songs and performing
their national dances; the migrants, on the other hand, get the false impression that
Australians are childish people who are 'intrigued' by their old-fashioned
costumes, songs and dances – long forgotten in their own countries in Europe.[27]

By now such shining innocence has dimmed. But the ceremonies go
on. An Oktoberfest at Fairfield Oval in Sydney, the blessing of the fleet
at Ulladulla, the annual Holland Festival in South Australia and the
Italian Arts Festival in Melbourne all bear witness to the continuing
popularity of representing ethnicity by folk-costumes, folk-arts and
folk-music. The Moomba festival or the 'Carnivale' [sic] in New South
Wales are also stuffed with folkloric moments. Nor has naivety completely disappeared. In 1977, the *Sydney Morning Herald* reported on
the organisation of that year's festival: 'Mr Jose Perez, who migrated
from Spain, was appointed ethnic group coordinator, so that when
participants ring Carnivale's headquarters, the phone is answered with
an accent.'[28]

Australia is not unique as a venue for folkloric nostalgia. In the
Americas, similar ceremonies are frequently held as, indeed, they often
are in countries of origin. Moreover, non-English, British migrants
have long engaged in similar activities, as any who have watched the
bekilted Scottish-Australians tossing cabers in the heat of a Sydney
new year's day will know.

For some ethnic groups, folklore is a genuine matter, at the heart of
their self-definition. The small Liminotto community in Sydney
provides an example. Memories of life back in their Sicilian home
village abound in images of the *festa*, the annual holiday dedicated
theoretically to the village saint but really to a celebration of humanity.
Stories are told and re-told about the procession that carried the saint
from one end of the village to the other. A particular sparkle comes into
the eyes of older members of the community when they recall the *lotta*,
which had been a traditional part of the procession until it was stopped
by the local priest as being too vulgar.

We used to have a *lotta* [a struggle or tug-of-war] to pull the saint from one side
to the other. All the shepherds would be on one side and all the tradesmen on the
other. It was a struggle of strength. It could be dangerous. They would pull the
saint about, throw him on the ground . . .

San Fulippu would always fall down. I remember him falling down with his feet sticking up in the air ... Another time ... he got stuck in the mulberry tree because of the *lotta* and nobody could get him out...

It was such a *lotta*. People would come from all around to see it. They had to watch it from their balconies because it was dangerous.

The *lotta* and the *festa* symbolise for Liminotti now living in Sydney their sense of community. It is their common birthplace, their *paese*, Limina and its myths, which bind them together and, to ensure that this bond remains, the Liminotti have recreated their version of the *festa*. There is no village saint and no procession. Instead, they book a reception hall as if for a wedding and there everyone gathers to eat and dance, to 'keep in contact with one another' and to remember 'the customs that were used in Limina'. The folk tradition, altered in an Australian environment, remains central.[29]

But folklore can readily shade into a purposeless nostalgia, a one day of the year on which to remember so that the rest may be forgotten or overlooked more easily. Folklore is pretty; folklore is safe; folklore is non-political; folklore looks good on television; folklore can touch the heart; folklore can anaesthetise the brain.

Often folklore is linked to religion and goes public in the various ethnic religious festivals. Again the cameras whir as migrants carry imported replicas of their saints in processions through the streets and schoolyards of Australia's cities. Religion, folklore and ethnic colour become comfortable bedfellows in multicultural Australia.

In Australia, religion has, in a sense, always been an ethnic matter. The ruling élite was English and Anglican and looked to London or Canterbury; the working class was Irish and Catholic and looked to Rome via Dublin. In between, Scots, Welsh, and northern English dissented and kept themselves apart from both traditions. These divisions have been weakening with the general growth of secularisation. They have also been overlaid by a further complexity with the arrival of migrants from so many different backgrounds and with so many different churches and religious practices. Initially, ancient feuds sometimes surfaced as Catholic spokesmen endorsed the usefulness, particularly the numerical usefulness, of Catholic Italian, Maltese, Croatian, or Polish migrant stock, while Masons and Protestants were fearful that Australian virtue might be sullied by too close a relationship with the Catholic Whore of Babylon.

But this dispute rapidly lost its relevance. Instead Roman Catholic migrants soon demonstrated that, contrary to Nino Culotta's view and to the hopes of many from within the Catholic hierarchy, mass is not 'the same all over the world'.[30] The church universal has, instead, many varying national and regional characteristics. In the United States, Italian migrants long ago had already established an enviable reputation for a loyalty to the religion or popular culture of their *paese*, for a reluctance to hand over money to priests or bishops, and for their profound distrust of national or transnational religious institutions.[31]

Similar attitudes and behaviour patterns can readily be discerned in Australia. As one Italian priest tried to explain: 'Australian Catholics ... knew more doctrine and they thought much more, but religion in Italy was innate, was felt in the heart, was very simple.'[32] He should, perhaps, have added that the rituals and the needs were just different. In her study of Italians in Griffith, Rina Huber touched on this matter when she noted that neither the Calabresi nor the Trevigiani showed much interest in the established Irish Roman Catholic church in the region. It was not until each group built its own regional church and, in the case of the Calabresi, had imported a plaster cast of their saint, that interest and attendance increased. Similarly, in Melbourne, the Capuchin Fathers' shrine of San Antonio has provided a haven for a number of village saints unrecognised by the local Australian parishes in which their migrant followers live.[33]

Other regional, linguistic or village groups have been equally anxious not to join Irish-Australian Catholicism. The small Ukrainian Catholic community has clung firmly to its own identity and, in 1958, managed to have its own bishop appointed. The use of the Ukrainian language, an emphasis on anti-communism, and dreams of a free Ukraine remain central tenets of this particular version of Catholicism.[34] Similarly, Polish, Croation, and Maltese Catholics in Australia are catered for in their own languages and with the national trappings of their version of Catholicism.

Yet, despite the importation and re-creation of varieties of Roman Catholicism, the equivocation noted elsewhere about the real impact of this pluralism has remained. The top of the Australian Catholic hierarchy remains in Irish hands. Intellectually, too, Irish Catholicism transmuted to Australia is that expressed by figures such as Patrick O'Farrell, John Molony, John or Des O'Grady, and Thomas Keneally. But the foot-soldiers of Australian Catholicism are no longer as homogeneous as they were in 1945.

Catholicism is only one of the religions changed by the migrant influx. The numbers of the various Orthodox churches, of Muslims or of Buddhists have multiplied since the Second World War. Sometimes, the development of such religions has not always been devoid of conflict and schism. The Greek Orthodox Church's politics are particularly closely linked to those of Greece itself, and the Church has acted as a conservative moat for the Greek state against besieging communists, socialists or democrats. Such conflicts have been transported to Australia. In particular, the appointment of a new head of the Greek Orthodox Church in 1959 was accompanied by a restructuring of church organisation. It was an attempt to break the tradition that had developed in the early days of Greek settlement in Australia,

Leichhardt, Sydney, 1981: celebrating the *festa* of San Giuseppe, patron saint of the Sicilian town of Spadafora.

whereby the lay Greek communities had an equal, if not controlling, say in the management of church affairs. With approval from the Greek government, the newly established Greek Orthodox Archdiocese of Australia set about establishing its suzerainty. In its view, there were now too many Greeks in Australia to leave their management to local forces whose politics were suspect. The result was a split between the Archdiocese and those lay communities whose members held on to their practice of appointing their own priests and having an effective say in the running of church life. For some, this meant tragedy or, at least, humiliation. Church and state lived in close ménage in Greece; now in Australia, the Archdiocesal authorities proclaimed that marriages solemnised in the breakaway Greek community churches would not be recognised under Greek law. Any couples who were married in the schismatic churches in Australia but who had retained their Greek passports could find, on return to Greece, that their children were labelled as bastards.

Saints, schisms, and solidarity bind migrants into groups whose loyalties invariably extend beyond Australia. Religion shades into folk tradition and nationalism, and the hierarchies of the different religions now represented in Australia strive to keep their flocks within national or regional or factional folds. Some succeed; others do not. But, certainly, for many migrants, religion and the various religious institutions and conflicts remain pivotal in defining their identity.

If religion is thought to be central to many migrant and peasant lives, sport is conventionally thought to define much that is Australian. In the 1950s, assimilationist Australia was anxious to introduce its new settlers to this crucial aspect of the Australian way of life. Nino Culotta got it straight: 'Soccer ... is a lousy game. Only dills play soccer ... Italians are dills ... They play soccer.'[35] *Good Neighbour* was more reticent: 'It is most unlikely that New Australians will ever figure prominently in cricket, rugby or national code football [Australian Rules]. These games are largely unknown in Europe and good players are not made overnight.' If prospects were dim in these areas, they were less so in others. 'There are Olympic hopes among New Australians', one article noted joyously. And especially in 'association football' or soccer ('wog-ball' as it was soon termed in high schools), migrants could improve Australia's pitiful record. 'Migrants lift our soccer standards' proclaimed another *Good Neighbour* headline.[36]

Undoubtedly, soccer has expanded in Australia since 1945. Its authorities are probably justified in their claim that recently it has attracted an increased participation among Australian boys. Australia (with a Yugoslav coach) qualified for the finals of the 1974 World Cup and was not disgraced, though the World Cup campaigns of 1978 (with an English coach) and 1982 (with a German one) failed dismally. By 1984, in both Sydney and Adelaide, as well as in smaller centres such as Wollongong and Newcastle, soccer offers a very serious challenge to rugby league or Australian Rules.

Yet the growth has not been unified, nor has it been achieved easily. Ethnic tensions have been frequently displayed on the football field and on the terraces when Greek played Italian, Croat played Serb, or English played Argentinian. The sporting press, an Anglo-Saxon fortress, has lovingly exaggerated such conflicts and has been very ready to moralise about the flabbiness or over-exuberant temperaments of the proponents of 'wog-ball'.

Off the field, the conflicts have continued in management, in selection, and even in the naming of teams. In the 1980s the National Soccer League has tried to put its terminological house in order in a way that would satisfy the most tidy and prudent assimilationist. It has become illegal to call a team JUST; 'Footscray' was thought to be less divisive. Sydney Olympic or Brisbane Lions or even Newcastle K-B United were okay; but the names Hakoah or Hellas or Azzurri could only be whispered abroad. This process is all rather reminiscent of what has occasionally happened in Europe and of what regularly happens in South America, when the street known as St Mary's Street suddenly has its name changed to honour the latest dictator of the latest glorious, if ephemeral, revolution. The signs then say 'the Street of 35th October', but the populace talks about 'St Mary's Street' all the same. So, in Australia today, the press talks about Leichhardt, but the crowd remembers it as APIA and knows that it is an Italian club.

If 'wog-ball' can promote passion and debate, other less popular sports have a more tranquil history. Take the sport of *arijaso,* rock-lifting. In Trebonne, a tiny town in north Queensland, there is a small Basque community. From the old world of their mountains, they have brought their annual festival in which rock-lifting is the great activity. Rocks have been carried to Queensland from the Pyrenees and Basque-Australians, perhaps with a can of Fourex beside them, strain to see how often they can heave a specially imported piece of their native-land from ground to shoulder.[37]

Somewhere in between, lies the sport of *bocce* or *boule.* In Europe, *bocce* is traditionally associated with drinking and the best fraternal aspects of village life. In Fascist Italy, the middle-class authorities in a bout of puritanism tried to ban it but ended up having to accept what they deemed to be a 'genuinely popular sport'.[38] Now the sport is quietly spreading among Italian, German, Yugoslav, and Spanish migrants, and Australia competes with modest achievement and with an Italo-Australian team in international tournaments. But in Queensland in 1981, the state federation had an Irish-born president who liked to claim that Sir Francis Drake was playing *bocce* and not bowls as the Armada sailed up the Channel, and in New South Wales Benson and Hedges acted as a benevolent sponsor of yet another healthy sport. Perhaps there is hope as well that one day certain RSL bowling clubs will dig up their grass, replace it with sand and offer glasses of red wine instead of schooners of beer (though feminists might not find much to admire in *bocce*).

The nature of migrant participation in sport becomes more shadowy when it involves more traditional Australian activities. The careers of Barassi or Jesaulenko, Peponis or Raudonikis, indicate that barriers are not rigid. But they do exist. In cricket, traditionally a sport of middle-class values and, to many migrants, a sport epitomising English phlegm and stupidity, players of European background have been rare and have not been much welcomed by Anglo-Australians. Perhaps the story of Lennie Pascoe is emblematic: 'My father came here at an early age. We've eaten steak and chips as long as I can remember.' Asked why then he had become 'Pascoe' instead of Durtanović (a name change which coincided with his first selection in the New South Wales state squad), he said that he had dropped Durtanović simply because Pascoe was easier to pronounce.[39] But, it seems, when 'sledging' was being used against Pascoe, Ian Chappell at least knew that Pascoe was a Croat.

Foreign names, imported sports, quaint folk traditions and religious practices are now all accepted and praised by multicultural Australia. An even more remarkable change has come over language policy. In the days of assimilationism, the chief aim of government often seemed the extirpation of migrant languages. Public opinion was alarmed by this most audible sign that aliens had entered Australia. The Department of Immigration was soon carefully explaining that all newcomers 'are told that they should speak English at all times to help them become absorbed into the community more quickly, and most of them follow the advice to the letter.'[40]

Throughout the 1950s, the Australian authorities continued to attempt to assimilate migrants through the compulsory use of English. In 1952, the federal executive of the ALP characteristically passed a motion that 'all publications that contain any extracts in foreign languages should have the English version printed in full.'[41] In 1960, a poll conducted in Perth indicated that 70 per cent of Western Australians still believed that migrants should not use their languages publicly.[42] Even when it was gradually and reluctantly admitted that adult migrants might preserve their old languages, governments and experts laid great stress on making sure that migrant children spoke English and only English. In 1951, a headmaster of a primary school in a migrant holding centre put it this way: 'the child must learn to think in English from the start ... It is the avenue to mutual understanding. It is the key to the success of the whole immigration project ... English must be spoken to the pupils and by them, all day and every day, in every activity, in school and out of it.'[43] In 1963, H. S. Wyndham, the New South Wales director of education, bluntly stated: 'We deliberately refrain from collecting any statistics in regard to school pupils from overseas ... Once they are enrolled in school they are, from our point of view, Australian children.'[44]

As the years passed, the sterility and insularity of this behaviour became more evident. So did its failure and simple irrelevance. By the late 1960s some Australians were becoming troubled both by the parochiality of previous policies and by the increasing evidence that many migrant children were being unfairly penalised by the existing education system. In this regard, important work was done by Eva Isaacs on the Greek community. Isaacs had migrated to Australia with her Polish Jewish parents in 1930. In the preface to her *Greek Children in Sydney* (1976), she recalled her own experience with the inter-war education system:

Within six months of arrival, as a candidate at the Matriculation Examination, I had to answer questions on five different subjects in a language I had scarcely begun to understand. The method I used was to translate the questions into Polish, the answers into German or French and submit these together with an appropriate diagram to clarify points I was unable to transmit linguistically.

A woman of formidable energy and stubbornness, and of unusual honesty, Isaacs triumphed over such ordeals and in 1963 became a district counsellor for the New South Wales Education Department. She began to specialise in the social problems of the inner city and taught herself Greek so that she could better comprehend one ethnic group. When her research was finalised, it drastically contradicted much of the cosy optimism of earlier work. 'In the primary school,' she reported, Greek children's 'meeting with Australians generally begins and ends in the classroom.' Indeed, she added 'to most of the parents I was the first non-Greek to enter the house'.

Isaacs also noted that many Greek children endured a double education system. They went to Australian schools but they were also expected to attend Greek school, in the afternoon or on Saturday mornings. There, they learned the Greek language or, rather, the purist (and politically conservative) version, καθαρευουσα. They also learned Greek history and Greek culture often with a strong nationalist bias.

I am proud of being Greek because of things my father does and because of our family. We buy houses whereas Australians buy cars, drink and gamble. I really like being Greek, they were the first people to give the world medicine and literature. It is a privilege to be Greek, to be connected with their contributions and their history.[45]

COLOURFUL FINALE TO MUSICAL FESTIVAL

This was the gay scene that ended the musical festival in the Albert Hall during the Citizenship Convention last month. After the last item the artists gathered on the stage and were thanked by Mr. Holt (at the microphone on right). Artists from all over Australia performed at the festival. Fifteen nationalities were represented and the items included singing, dancing and music. Many of the artists performed in their national costumes. The performers included about 100 children who came from the Cowra Holding Centre and presented many of their national dances. Performances on both nights had capacity houses.

Finale to the 1950 Australian Citizenship Convention. *The New Australian* (Department of Immigration Journal), 14 February 1950.

Australians have traditionally reacted to these ethnic schools with considerable suspicion. As late as 1974, a report to the director of primary education in Victoria observed: 'The present after hours ethnic school system only encourages a deep sense of independence by migrants, drawing them further away from any form of integration with the rest of the community.'[46] Less commented on was the more serious problem that many of these schools were dominated by the political right and were endeavouring to impose what a nineteenth century Italian bishop, G. B. Scalabrini, termed *religione e patria*. Thus Greek schools were likely to offer a distorted version of Greek history as approved by the Orthodox hierarchy or by the colonels. Armenian Saturday schools openly declared their purpose was to foster Armenian nationalism. Poles, the various Baltic peoples, and, in a more complex way, Jews, kept to the same purpose.[47]

Multiculturalism has thus curiously reversed some of the assumptions of assimilationism. Australia now seems to accept community languages – they can be studied for the Higher School Certificate (although not necessarily without some penalty as was indicated by the 1982 debacle in New South Wales when community language candidates had their marks scaled down); every Australian city is full of signs saying *agenzia di viaggio* (travel agency) or ὀδοντογιατρός (dentist). Al Grassby has even campaigned for a future in which each Australian can speak at least two languages fluently.[48] Meanwhile social scientists probe the educational achievement of the various migrant groups and have characteristically invented a new term, the 'eth-class', to explain why, in a formal exam structure, a bourgeois from Latvia 'out-performs' a peasant from the Lebanon.

Much of the achievement is also brittle. Sometimes it seems that a sort of concordat of nationalisms (itself a concept as bizarre as the Fascist International) has been reached. Migrants can receive some instruction in their own nationalism as long as all is finally dedicated to an integration into Australian nationalism.[49]

Government subsidies for this school or that, for a dancing troupe here, a religious festival there, an extensive ethnic media, university conferences on one ethnic culture or another – Australia in the 1980s provides a much more cosmopolitan image than it did in 1945. It is easy to be cynical about the reality behind this image – urbane foreign diplomats stimulating society ladies with invocations of Renaissance art at Alliance Française or the Dante; bourgeois Jews trying to blot out the cacophany of the present at Musica Viva; writers hoping that ethnicity will be enough to capture some government money; priests and businessmen keeping their clientele safe through saints, sport, and fireworks; patronising Anglo-Australians dabbling in something beyond the parish pump; self-interested politicians who believe or declare that politics can be kept out of the intellectual and spiritual worlds. All these naive and unattractive elements can still be detected in any history of migrant culture. Sometimes it seems that, for the majority of Australians, our vastly diverse migrant intake has only had one cultural influence, and that a very partial one, on habits of cuisine. Deep springs have been tapped only for the odd bottle of mineral water. And even in regard to cuisine, that most obvious and remarkable aspect of the new Australia, a recent commentary has been inclined to doubt the crucial impact of immigration. These days we eat falafel and curry, and drink retsina or chianti because we are richer, because the Americans did so before us, and because many have visited or long to visit Delphi, Florence or Paris.[50]

Few Australians and few of the leaders of migrant communities have had much interest in a genuinely critical analysis of the diverse cultures now represented in this country. It may be true, as one migrant has inelegantly stated, that from a world of 'races, beer, pies, and gambling [and] outspokenness' has been created a new society changed 'cultural-wise, food-wise, even clothes-wise'. It may even be true that the change has sprung from 'the influence of the uneducated as much as the educated European – after all we now have salami as well as Musica Viva'. What is less clear is the extent to which migrant cultures can remain in contact with the growing and developing cultures of their countries or places of origin. Migration since 1945 has enhanced Australia's opportunity culturally to escape the tyranny of distance and to favour a new cosmopolitanism, a celebration of the diversity of mankind. It is not yet clear whether Australians will have the energy and humility to allow this continent to be the place in which a genuine synthesis can occur of the cultures, not just national but regional and local, of old and new worlds, and in which such an array of cultures can at the same time survive in genuine antithesis.

Chapter EIGHT

Immigrants and Old World Politics

In 1950, many Australians were unsure if their culture was really up to the standard of that of many immigrants. Few Australians had any doubts that their political system was immeasurably superior to that of the old world. For immigrants, politics should be left at home. The last thing Australia wanted to import were those class and ideological feuds that had so often torn apart the old world.

Nor has this particular viewpoint much changed over time. In the aftermath of the Hungarian uprising of 1956, the Roman Catholic bishops of Australia commended the cultural benefits that sprang from Australia's acceptance of migrants from diverse backgrounds but trusted 'that the infusion of older cultures ... will not bring with it a transplanting in our soil of old national feuds and enmities'.[1] In 1963 A. R. Downer, who was near the end of his term as minister for immigration, responded to ALP accusations that extremist Croatian activists were at work in Australia and declared that no one wanted this country 'to be made a springboard for future European battles'. He also asserted that there was no reason for extremism because Australia offered immigrants 'a new life – a life that we hope will be in many respects better, and not just a continuation of the old life, the old prejudices, and the old hatreds, which we hope they will leave behind in the Old World'.[2] Even in 1978, the Fairfax press still enunciated the common preference that foreign quarrels not find expression here, lest Australia become 'a training ground or arsenal for every dissident faction overseas'.[3] Many commentators have been especially anxious to quarantine Australia against what they depict as the foreign virus of political terrorism. For them, what is most genuinely lucky about Australia's history is the peaceable nature of its political traditions.

Nor have migrants themselves disagreed with this opinion. In his 1978 Meredith Memorial lecture, Jerzy Zubrzycki affirmed that

Multi-culturalism ... does not stand for ethnic separatism and by the same token it does not mean the existence of ethnically based political groups with

151

activities aimed at the country of origin which might be incompatible with the foreign policies and interests espoused by any democratically elected government of Australia.[4]

To a conference at the ANU in December 1981, Senator Misha Lajovic echoed these sentiments and asserted that migrants only wanted to be left alone. It was useless for eager political scientists to approach them with their questionnaires. Migrants would only lie anyway. They had come to Australia and preferred it because it was a place of peace and quiet where they could enrich themselves. The refrain has been repeated many times throughout the decades since 1945. 'What I like most about Australia is that there are no politics here', remarked one Greek technician in the 1960s.[5] 'Australians just treat every –ism as if it were warm beer', complained a disgruntled journalist.[6]

There has been, therefore, a widespread public acceptance that Australians old and new could be kept safe from the savageries that had so often broken through the genteel façade of the old worlds. British two-party parliamentarism, British law, the British monarchy, British trade unionism—these were the systems that all Australians must honour. Australian politics, by nature, were not vulnerable to the snares of 'extremes of right or of left'. In Australia, men could rely 'on the peaceful growth of opinion to bring about changes in the society and in the way in which our nation is governed'.[7] In Australia, there was neither corruption nor violence. Politicians were well-meaning; police were honest; judges were fair. *Good Neighbour* set the tone, which, in this case, has never varied:

Australian elections are quiet affairs. An election is another name for a riot in some parts of the world I have visited. But in Australia there are no bands playing, no street fights, no disturbances. Election day is just like an ordinary business day. I suppose it is the Australian temperament and the fact that they already have a great deal more than most people in other parts of the world.

In Australia a policeman is a friend who will help you when you need help. He is there to protect you and your family against anyone who might try to do you harm. The policeman will not worry you if you are doing no harm. He will not interfere with your work, your play or worship.[8]

Immigrants, at least as far as politics were concerned, must be truncated beings; they must be born anew in Australia or alter their politics and adapt them to the Australian way of decision making and power broking. Whatever tolerance and pluralism might be possible in relation to art or sport, assimilation was the only method that could be applied to immigrant politics. Anyone who disagreed should either keep silent or be deported.

Most social scientists long endorsed this view. Even more than loss of language or intermarriage, rate of participation in Australian politics became the most severe standard against which the success of immigration policy could be determined. Where exceptions have occurred, there has been some puzzlement. A study published by Paul Wilson in 1973 began by regretting that 'little of substance' had appeared on 'immigrant political behaviour'. But his own comparative study of the activities of certain British and Italian migrants in Brisbane came to the conclusion that Italians were 'almost totally absent' from local politics. The reason, he suggested, was that Italian political culture discouraged political participation—an explanation that may have had some merit in 1910 or 1939, but which seemed bizarre when applied to the Italy of the 1970s. Untroubled by such thoughts, Wilson declared, in now familiar phrases, that the Italians of Brisbane 'only wanted to be left alone, to make money and to attend to their family affairs'.[9]

Such certitudes have begun to waver. James Jupp, so often the pioneer of the more profound and wide-ranging ideas about migrant communities, had already noted back in the 1960s that immigrants 'bring the beginnings of a political culture with them'. He had even argued that migrant politics did exist and were not necessarily all bad. 'Like all emigrant movements, Australian ethnic parties are inbred, factional and unrealistic. They may waste talent. But they do no real harm to the society which houses them.'[10] When Jupp penned these words, few paid much attention. It has only been in recent years that some social scientists have begun to probe more deeply into migrant political behaviour. One reason for this development has undoubtedly been self-interest. Migrants, as Wilson had noted in 1973, might turn out to be a 'potentially powerful political group'.[11] It was as well for political leaders and commentators to know how migrants voted in Australia, and even why they voted the way they did. This last issue has stimulated the thought that maybe the explanation lay not always and not completely in Australia, but rather in the country of origin. It might be that the partisanship of immigrants' parents in their former countries could influence the later party identification of their children in Australia.[12]

June Hearn has added the suggestion that a person who emigrates as an adult could have been influenced by childhood experiences and forces. She cites the case of one Greek migrant. At the age of seven, he watched while soldiers 'dragged a political prisoner through the streets then shot him and left the body to the dogs'.[13] Hearn does not reveal the date of the incident, or the political colouring of the soldiers. But she does make the obvious point that such an experience was memorable and that the memory had not been erased by the later peaceful and materially successful years in Australia.

Her one example can be extended to many of Australia's immigrants since the Second World War. They have brought past political ideas and loyalties with them. What is the nature of these ideas? How much are they denied or destroyed in Australia? How much are they retained or re-invented and for what reasons? What variations are there between the different migrant communities? And how have migrant ideas about politics affected multicultural Australia? These questions are much easier to ask than to answer. But perhaps the problem is not merely created by deficiencies in research or by the fearful or self-interested reticence of refugees and migrants. Often in Australia, politicians, the press, and the populace have not merely argued that Anglo-Australian parliamentarism is good and that foreign systems are bad, they have also sought means to expel or repress those who practised or preached ideas which seemed outside the Australian way of life.

Thus, in 1947, when there was a predictable and justifiable reluctance to offer sanctuary to any Nazis, Calwell declared that no 'person who fought against us during the war' would be allowed entry to Australia.[14] Three months earlier, the creaky machinery of the dictation test had been hauled out and applied to a German immigrant named Lerch, who had falsified his documents in order to hide his Nazi past. He failed a test in Romanian and was deported.[15] Others were not caught out, and some commentators began sighting swastikas attached to every refugee. Les Haylen, a senior Labor spokesman on immigration matters, asserted in 1950 that at least 10 per cent of the IRO immigrants 'are, or have been, Nazis'; the communist *Tribune* reported that 'Balts' were wearing Nazi uniforms to work at the Woomera rocket range; the RSL, in unaccustomed comradeship with *Tribune,* launched a hue and cry about immigrants who allegedly stepped off boats wearing old uniforms of the *Wehrmacht;* and the Jewish press claimed that there was 'anti-Semitic bullying of the worst kind' carried on by 'ex-Nazis from Hungary' in one of the displaced persons camps.[16]

On the conservative side, a distaste for Nazism was soon forgotten in the face of Cold War imperatives of making the world safe for capitalism. As one Liberal Member of the House of Representatives, William Lawrence, observed in 1950, displaced persons must be 'decent people' since they were, by definition, 'sincerely opposed to communism'.[17] Politics could reinforce old preferences about migrants. Thus, following the riots of Italians at Bonegilla in 1952, Henry Gullett argued: 'I say that Italians are unsatisfactory as immigrants. Let us not bring any more of them to our country. If those who are here are trouble-makers, let us send them back.'[18]

Even in the 1970s, many Australians feared that migrants could be the tools of an extreme right or an extreme left unfamiliar in Australia. At that time of crisis in late 1975, the halls of Australia's federal Parliament resounded while government and opposition bandied words about which refugees were the most politically detestable and disruptive. Michael MacKellar, then Liberal spokesman on immigration and soon to become minister, accused the government of discarding that ample, humanitarian mantle under which refugees had always gained entry into Australia and replacing it with narrow, political concerns. Specific criticism was directed against the government's treatment of a small group of ex-Vietnamese army officers who had been required to sign a declaration that they would not become involved in any political activity in Australia. Former Liberal leader Billy Snedden maintained that this was a denial of civil rights; it was forcing immigrants into the role of second-class citizens; and it was exposing the government's bias. After all, he queried, would the government take this action against Chileans or Greeks or against the Italian left-wing organisation, FILEF, which 'is supported by the Communist Party in subverting our democracy'?

But Labor could play tit for tat in any game about the purity of democratic principles. In the continuing debate, Bert James, Labor member for Hunter, found that history was on his side, even if he had problems with dates and geography. Pointing an accusing finger at the opposition, he singled out the refugees 'from Hungary following the uprising in that country in 1958' [*sic*]. Among them, 'for every decent citizen ... we got 2 or 3 scum, professional criminals who came ... because they knew their chance of survival in Hungary under communist law was nil'. Many 'so-called freedom fighters' were also accepted. All they 'had to say was "I hate communism" and that was nearly a passport to come to Australia'. Finally, he queried, what about those 'fascist-minded people', the 'Croats from the Greek region' [*sic*], were they not the refugees who have 'caused great turbulence and trouble in Australia'?[19]

The manifestation of such error or prejudice has sometimes had a more practical side. The most logical area in which most migrants would express their political beliefs was their own language press. But, for a long time and within the limits of their ignorance, the Australian authorities remained suspicious of the politics possibly concealed in local non-English newspapers.

An ethnic press has had a long history in Australia, dating back to a German language paper published in Adelaide in 1848. Such papers often had a definite political colour. In the interwar period, for example, anti-fascist communists, socialists, or anarchists tried on a number of occasions to rally Italian migrants to their cause through newspapers and news-sheets, while the German language *Die Brücke* proclaimed the virtues of Hitler's Germany. During the Second World War the threat of internment discouraged most alien editors but, with peace restored, no sooner did the displaced persons reach their holding centres than they began publishing their own bulletins. From Bathurst camp, for example, came the roneoed *Der Neu Siedler* with its advice about the Australian political system. Once out of the camps, the IRO refugees swiftly produced their own weeklies and monthlies. Greek migrants, too, at once demanded their own papers. For them, the *Hellenic Herald,* which had continued publishing since 1926, was soon challenged by post-war competitors. Notably in 1957, the Greek left began to publish *Neos Kosmos* in Melbourne. By the 1960s, eight rival Greek–Australian papers circulated in Victoria.[20]

For a considerable time, non-English papers were produced under major disadvantages. They had to have official approval and be registered, and at least 25 per cent of each issue had to be in English. There was a traditional concern that foreign languages could veil evil sentiments, and Australian authorities demanded that the editors of such papers should pledge that 'nothing be published which was likely to foment disaffection or sedition, or to cause a breach of the peace, was offensive or objectionable, or was in conflict with the Government's policy of assimilation of new settlers'.

As the years passed, such governmental severity was relaxed. In 1958 a report by a Commonwealth Immigration Advisory Council committee asserted that the papers were helping migrants assimilate: 'They provide a valuable safety-valve for migrants for letting off their grievances ... They commented favourably on such things as citizenship conventions and the Queen Mother's visit, and various aspects of Australian life'.[21] But the liberalisation in Australian attitudes percolated only slowly into migrants' consciousness. Most of the papers remained reluctant to express too many or too firm opinions about Australian politics. In December 1960–January 1961, Evasio Costanzo, the Piedmontese editor of one of the main Italian papers, *La Fiamma,* had to explain away his journal's fervent support for the Italian tennis team's challenge to the Australian holders of the Davis Cup. During the next December his paper abstained from any editorial comment before Menzies's narrow federal electoral victory.[22]

A dislike of too ardent a display of political loyalties in migrant newspapers remained the commonplace in Australia. Evidence of this can be found in the chief analysis made of the migrant press by M. Gilson and J. Zubrzycki, *The Foreign-Language Press in Australia 1848–1964,* published in the mid 1960s. Although the book collects much useful information, it also carries a plain, if unstated, political message: politics are much more tolerable on the right than on the left. It is noted that Baltic migrants 'as people no longer under communist political restriction', were often encouraged by their newspapers to use their new freedom to act 'as genuine spokesmen for their countries'. *Il Globo,* a far right-wing Italian paper inclined to support the neo-fascist MSI, is also praised, while leftist papers such as *Neos Kosmos* or *Il*

Nuovo Risveglio are condemned. The book concludes confidently, however, that such radical leftist papers are unlikely to last since they cannot attract advertising revenue: 'The chauvinistic press receives little support from the rank and file of European settlers in Australia once the major political causes and movements which justified the continued existence of these papers disappear or lose their urgency.'

From these comments, it might be pondered whether, by the end of the 1960s, the real problem about migrant newspapers in the Australia so dominated politically by the Liberal-Country Party was becoming not so much how to keep politics out of them, but how to keep those politics conservative. As Gilson and Zubrzycki remarked, the foreign-language press is 'a powerful instrument of social control in an immigrant community'.[23]

It was not only Australians who had these thoughts, but also the leadership of some of the migrant communities. The history of *La Fiamma* serves as an example. Established in 1947 by Catholic sources in Sydney, and blessed by Archbishop Gilroy, the paper took up a markedly conservative stance. Costanzo, who became editor in 1951, published Santamaria and displayed some sympathies for the Democratic Labor Party (DLP). On Italian politics, the paper's guarded opinions were also conservative. Revanchist about foreign affairs (especially on the Trieste question), the paper bitterly criticised the 'Opening to the Left' policies advocated by the Christian Democratic leaders Amintore Fanfani and Aldo Moro after 1959.

But, as times changed in Italy and Australia, so too did the opinions of Costanzo. In 1972, he was only another of those attracted by the charismatic qualities of Gough Whitlam and by the ALP's newly enlightened solicitude for migrants. Costanzo, who, in 1975 had been bought out by financial interests with contacts to the conservative side of Italian politics, has retained a political interest by helping to organise the *Amici del Partito Laborista* ('Friends of the Labor Party').

Although Costanzo had moved definitively to the Labor camp, *La Fiamma* was less partisan. In 1979, the paper changed hands again. The new owners were the Valmorbida family, who also controlled *Il Globo,* the ostensible major competitor to *La Fiamma.* In 1983, anyone who read a number of *La Fiamma* would find detailed accounts of the latest football results, pictures of pop stars and starlets, a horoscope section, tales of murders and kidnappings from villages in the South of Italy, and scanty accounts of Australian and Italian political life. There are no editorials.

As the *La Fiamma* story implies, migrant politics are certainly not merely a tale of old ideas soon forgotten or abandoned on a welcoming Australian shore. The interests of capital and of labour and a continuing attachment to the politics of the country of origin are readily discernible, as is a desire to be commercially successful and not to antagonise what are believed to be Australian and, often, readers' susceptibilities.

What else can be said about the politics migrants bring with them to Australia? First, and most plainly, there is the kaleidoscopic complexity of the migrants themselves. For migrant politics, simple national or political labels do not work. Take, for example, the Hungarians. Hungary lies behind the Iron Curtain, and commentators on Hungarian behaviour often assume that it will reflect a generic anti-communism. Some Hungarians, certainly, have been zealots of such causes. Cecile Kunrathy, the Hungarian-born novelist-memoirist, has noted that even ex-members of the wildly fascist Arrow Cross (it had advocated something called 'Hungarism') had managed to slip into Australia as IRO refugees. In her novel *Impudent Foreigner*, she recounts the reception in a displaced persons camp of news about politics:

'I've heard of this international organisation', said one of them. 'Its called I.R.O. ... Anybody can emigrate if he is healthy, able to work and has no police record.'

'And the Arrow Cross people? What about those? Will they get a chance to emigrate, too?' somebody cut in excitedly.

'The leading figures have been executed at home by now. The others? They don't stir up much dust, theirs was mostly empty talk; but they had better not mention anything about having been in the Arrow Cross Party when it comes to being registered.'[24]

In the 1930s, while Hungary was administered by the reactionary regime of Admiral Horthy and threatened by the proto-fascist activities of Gyula Gömbös and the Szeged movement, Hungarians who fled could be liberals or socialists or, most often, Jews who read correctly the messages of enveloping anti-Semitism. One was Emery Barcs, who subsequently became foreign editor of the Sydney *Daily Telegraph*. By his own account, Barcs fled Hungarian anti-Semitism and took refuge in Fascist Italy, where he obtained a doctorate from Rome university. Only when anti-Semitism spread to Italy did he move on to Australia, where he was interned during the Second World War. After his release, Barcs helped set up the Association of Refugees, a body that had its political bona fides guaranteed by Roden Cutler as 'Assistant Deputy Director of the Security Service'.[25]

Publicly at least, successive 'vintages' of Hungarians have diluted their ideology into a general nationalism, whereby all Hungarian–Australians are urged to pull together in the cause of a Greater Hungary. An extraordinary and lavish display of such opinions was given by the Hungarian Council of New South Wales in June 1980, when a ceremony was held at the Seymour Centre of the University of

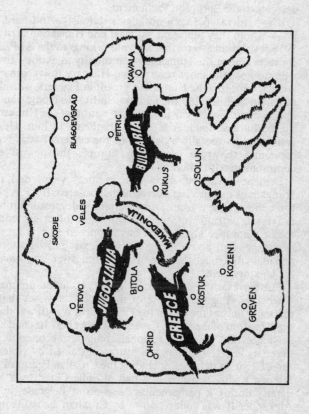

An illustration from *The terror in Aegean Macedonia under Greek occupation*, n.d. (1980?), produced by the Macedonian Cultural and Educational Society for Australia, one of many organisations in Australia concerned to promote political causes of the home country.

Sydney. Its purpose was to mourn the sixtieth anniversary of the Treaty of Trianon, by which modern Hungary was re-established at the end of the First World War but forced to acquiesce in a major loss of territory to Romania, Yugoslavia, and Czechoslovakia. These old wounds were opened anew in Australia. The audience was regaled with an 'historical re-creation' paralleling 'Trianon Hungary' with an imaginary Australia which, through involvement by no fault of its own in a British imperial war, had thereafter been deprived of its coastal strip and left to console itself with the Simpson Desert, Alice Springs and the odd dingo. But the most breathless moment of the evening occurred when a message of sympathy and support for all at hand was read out. It had been penned by Otto von Hapsburg, the historian-heir to the twin-crowns of Austria–Hungary, who is now also a Bavarian delegate to the European Parliament.

It is hard to take such nostalgics seriously. And hard, indeed, to know whom they represent. At least one Hungarian arrival from the 1956 revolution asserts that his vote belongs to the ALP, and that his contacts among the Hungarian community in Sydney are with those who do not talk about resurrecting Hungary to its former grandeur. Associations like the Hungarian Freedom Fighters, with their aim 'to maintain and develop the national spirit, the Hungarian heritage ... and to maintain the existence of the nation of the Hungarians within the traditional boundaries',[26] are anathema to him. He is also un-convinced by too glib a defence of the current Kádár regime as the economic showcase of eastern Europe, the newest example of communism with a human face.

Evidence available about the political views and practices of Hungarians in Australia thus remains scattered. But it is plain that the three most evident factors are a certain widespread, but by no means universal, patriotism, a certain nostalgia (often accompanied by a major ignorance about what has happened in Hungary since their departure), and, above all, a great complexity and variation in attitudes and ideas that make the general label 'Hungarian' anything but a useful explanatory term.

Further examples of complexity can be found among Australia's Yugoslavs. Yugoslavia, one of the successor states that came into existence only at the end of the First World War (it was then known as the Kingdom of the Serbs, Croats and Slovenes), has had an embattled existence. Its political, regional, religious, economic, and social diversity is extraordinary. Its history is stained by violence: in 1928 three Croatian deputies, including the Croatian Peasant Party Leader, Stjepan Radić, perished in a hail of bullets fired by a Montenegrin deputy during a parliamentary session at Belgrade; in 1934, King Alexander II was gunned down by Croatian assassins in Marseilles. During the Second World War, Yugoslavia's history became still more terrifying. Invaded and divided between Germany and Italy in April 1941, the demise of Yugoslavia gave further prominence to internal nationalisms. The Croats, Catholic and ex-Hapsburg enemies of their Orthodox and ex-Ottoman brothers, the Serbs, proclaimed the era of an independent Croatia. They chose as king an Italian princeling who took the title of King Tomislav II (a park in Sydney has been named after him), who prudently never visited the country. He has been aptly called 'the King who never was'.[27]

Real power in wartime Croatia was shared by the Axis forces and the Ustaša, a native fascist movement led by Ante Pavelić and among the most bloodthirsty of all the varieties of fascism. At least according to one Italian journalist, life with Pavelić had its drawbacks:

'The Croatian people', said Ante Pavelić, 'wish to be ruled with goodness and justice. And I am here to provide them'.

While he spoke, I gazed at a wicker basket on ... [his] desk. The lid was raised and the basket seemed to be filled with mussels, or shelled oysters – as they are occasionally displayed in the windows of Fortnum and Mason in Piccadilly in London. Casertano [an Italian diplomat] looked at me and winked, 'Would you like a nice oyster stew?'

'Are they Dalmation oysters?' I asked ... [Pavelić].

Ante Pavelić removed the lid from the basket and revealed the mussels, that slimy and jelly-like mass, and he said smiling, with that tired good-natured smile of his: 'It is a present from my loyal *ustashis*. Forty pounds of human eyes'.[28]

During the war, the Ustaša had other allies and rivals – Serb fascists, Bosnian Moslems, Macedonian freedom fighters, Albanian nationalists in the Kossovo. All contested one against the other, and, from time to time, were friends or enemies of the two major competing groups, the *četniks* who were Serb nationalists and monarchists, and the partisans who wanted to reunite Yugoslavia under communist rule. The memoirs of the Montenegrin communist Milovan Djilas provide one English-language account of the horror and unpredictability of these times.[29] On another level, so do the memories of an Australian woman, born in Belgrade and a teenager during the war years. At one stage during the war her family took refuge with some peasants in a village outside the capital. The village itself, she recalled, was full of Mihailović *četnik* supporters who were co-operating with the occupying forces: 'Their presence in the village was incredibly public. They just walked around and you could recognise them ... they wore beards and black clothes and they had black sheepskin caps with a skull and crossbones in front.' Across the river was the opposition. The woods were filled with partisan supporters and, regularly, the two groups would take pot shots at each other over the water. For a lively girl, she recalls, swimming was a little hazardous.

It should cause little surprise that a country that could harbour so many opposing loyalties and so many hatreds, could also produce politically active emigrants. Ustaša followers, along with a variety of anti-communist and royalist sympathisers, fled as the partisans marched to victory at the end of the war. Another wave of refugees joined the *émigrés* following the 1948 split between Tito and Stalin. As one Australian woman who came in this wave recalled, she felt uncomfortable and unsure about the future. She had been a committed member of the Youth Communist League and then, 'suddenly, overnight ... you're just supposed to change your mind ... we didn't know it was going to happen until it did and then the gradual disillusionment came in as ... a number of people we knew and whom we thought were quite reasonable and respectable communists got arrested and put into goal.' Only then did she accept her family's decision to emigrate. Refugees continued to trickle out of Yugoslavia and, with the 1960s relaxation of that country's emigration restrictions, they were joined by increasing numbers of Yugoslavs who left and sought a new life for more avowedly economic reasons.

These succeeding Yugoslav emigrant groups, with their diverse regional backgrounds, have pursued their political commitments in a variety of ways in Australia. The most notorious have been the activities of Croatians with apparent links to the surviving international Ustaša network – Pavelić had fled to Argentina at the end of the Second World War. In October 1963 the future deputy leader of the ALP, Jim Cairns, produced photographs and reports as evidence, not just of an Australian branch of the Ustaša (under the name of the Croatian Liberation Movement), but also of members of that organisation being involved in paramilitary training programmes. The twelve months following these allegations were punctuated by press reports, and by questions and debates in Parliament querying the nature, aims, and activities of the organisation. Its leader, Fabijan Lovoković, appeared on the ABC television programme 'Four Corners' declaring that he and his fellow supporters of Croatian separatism were in Australia to reorganise and to prepare for the overthrow of the communist and Serbian rule of Croatia. There was the occasional 'political' bombing; a 'Croatian embassy' was established in Canberra and then disbanded; in 1963, 1972 and 1981 some Croatian women revealed that their husbands had returned, armed, to Croatia; and *Spremnost,* the Croatian language newspaper, set few bounds to its Croatian patriotism.[30]

With the death of Tito in 1979, television news reports carried film of Croatian Clubs throughout Sydney celebrating the death of the 'tyrant' and drinking to a future independent Croatia. All this suggests that, back in 1964, Hubert Opperman may have been displaying ignorance and innocence when he admitted attending a Croatian gathering where the Ustaša flag fluttered. But, as he recalled, it was just a smoke-filled hall with people enjoying themselves 'drinking beer and eating pies and saveloys and all the strange foods that are eaten at such gatherings'. Anyway, he argued, 'if, over the noise of the band that was playing, anybody could have heard and understood any political talk, by people speaking in broken English in any case, his hearing would have been better than mine.'[31]

However, the public face of Croatians as extremists is a stereotype because, yet again, the factionalism and division make the Croatian community far more complex than is usually suggested. Many may still dream of a future, separate Croatia, but there are various views about the nature of this independent nation and how it can be established. There are the few extremist Ustaša supporters who see an armed battle between Croatians and their oppressors as the most effective means to a free Croatia; there are others, including many who came as displaced persons after the war, who see independence as possible only with assistance from the democratic west; and others who yearn for assistance from the Soviet Union. There are also a number who accept the existence of Yugoslavia but advocate a Yugoslavia freed from communist rule. Regional diversity can also affect political attitudes. Emigrants from Dalmatia cannot be relied on to share the history and prejudices of those from Zagreb. Croatians in Australia may be bound by their national ambitions, but they become unbound by the factors of class, ideology, region, and period of departure.

Among both Hungarians and Yugoslavs a nostalgic nationalism has been noted. Such patterns recur in the history of other refugee migrants. Clouded by sentiment, the political views expressed may be based on unrealistic and inaccurate assumptions. One Ukrainian poet has invoked her homeland with scant recognition of its sombre social and political history:

> *O my Ukraine, beloved land of mine,*
> *Bright homeland where I spent my childhood days!*
> *Carpathian heights where sky-blue spaces shine,*
> *How often in my dreams on you I gaze! ...*
> *Without your welcome, through the world I've gone,*
> *Wandering on in many a foreign part;*
> *But my Ukraine, my native land, lives on*
> *As an eternal treasure in my heart.*[32]

Similarly, an Estonian woman, when interviewed, stated wistfully that interwar Estonia was 'the most democratic country that ever was'. Its economy boomed, she said, and benevolent guidance was provided by Konstantin Päts, the father of his people. She did not add that the ethnic minorities of Estonia were then under-represented in the halls of power, and that Päts, repelling an attempted coup by the fascist

Association of Freedom Fighters, after March 1934 ruled by decree. Estonia had become a 'democracy' with a prorogued Parliament.

More recently, some Vietnamese refugees have repeated behaviour familiar to their eastern European counterparts. In 1978, Vo Dai Ton, the chairman of the Greater Overseas Alliance for the National Restoration of Vietnam, observed: 'We have not come here to enjoy the life but to continue the fighting'. Four years later, Vo Dai Ton's capture near the Vietnam–Laos border and his public refusal at a Hanoi press conference to betray any of his contacts, allegedly gave renewed impetus to the anti-communist movement among Vietnamese refugees in Australia. Through an international network, financial support began to flow from Australia to resistance movements within Vietnam. One spokesman emphasised that the money was for goods not guns and that the goods could provide moral uplift. 'A refugee told me', he said, 'that the spirits of the resistance fighters get new life when they see a can of Coca-Cola or a packet of Dunhill.'[33]

As the years pass, hopes for the 'liberation' of Vietnam may fade, just as the hopes for the return to a free Hungary or a free Czechoslovakia have faded. Action may be postponed and replaced by romantic dreams about how sweet life was before the revolution.

Perhaps the images are too smug. The leaders of such refugee groups do create and maintain contacts with fellow political sympathisers who have emigrated to other countries. The historian of Melbourne's Polish community has recounted the fluctuating story of Poland-in-Australia. In May 1949, the Polish Association of Melbourne had already been established, and it developed and retained its links with Polish nationalist groups in London, who were themselves the heirs of the wartime conservative government-in-exile. The Polish Association is said to have many claims to achievement: it has run the Polonia soccer club; purchased a Polish ('Kosciuszko') House; organised an annual Festival of Youth, Beauty and Strength at Werribee; fostered the use of Polish (the Victorian government submitted to pressure that it be acknowledged a high school examination language in 1973); and co-ordinated scouting and girl guide movements (which are also affiliated with London). The Association owns a campsite on the outskirts of Melbourne near Healesville. It has been planted with beech and poplar to invoke the scents and images of the Polish countryside. The Polish Association is strong, too, in rhetoric about the Rousseauian beauties of the constitution of 1791, and about the traditional heroism of Polish soldiers who, it claims, were in 1939, as always, 'fighting against tyranny and [for] the freedom of all men and nations'. Unattractive aspects of Polish history are rather less remarked. A revised constitution in 1966 declared the Association to be 'non-political', but barred from membership any communists or communist sympathisers. Similarly, the Association is no friend of the Jews: 'Why should Polish Jews join our organisations when they've got everything they want among themselves, only a hundred times better?'[34] In December 1981–January 1982, groups such as the Polish Association loudly proclaimed their sympathy for Solidarity supporters suffering beneath the communist and military heel of General Jaruselski. If Polish events produce a major emigration to Australia, or even if General Jaruselski achieves his ambitions to be a Polish de Gaulle, a sort of born-again Pilsudski, it may be doubted whether the local Polish community will go on displaying such unity for long. Already, on the eve of the military clamp-down, a leading member of Sydney's Polish community argued that it would be better for Solidarity supporters to stay in Poland. They were needed there to carry on the good fight.

If Melbourne's nationalist Poles look to London for sympathy and legitimacy, the more common centre of anti-communist refugee politics is North America. A familiar example is the Captive Nations Council, which has branches in various Australian cities. They are linked to an international organisation, the Assembly of Captive European Nations (ACEN), which, in the atmosphere of the Cold War, was established in New York in 1954 to represent those nations formerly independent but now under the suzerainty of the Soviet Union. The avowed aim was, and is, to work toward the restoration of self-government for these countries, preferably through the military 'rolling back' of communism. Denounced by the Soviet authorities as an organisation controlled by fascist *émigrés*, the Assembly and its affiliates throughout the world never tire of presenting their case to governments and the public, and of pressuring for official recognition of their aims. A permanent ACEN Australian delegation was established in 1959 and, within a year, sponsored a Freedom Photographic Exhibition imported from the United States. The Australian delegation and the bodies associated with the Captive Nations cause have been active ever since in promoting Captive Nations Week, in protesting against visits by Soviet artists and officials, and even in political campaigns.

The most notorious example of direct political involvement occurred after the Whitlam government's *de jure* recognition in August 1974 of the USSR's *de facto* ownership of the Baltic states. However justified in terms of Australian national interest, Whitlam's decision blighted the carefully nurtured hopes of many Baltic refugees. In 1939, they had dreamed of a British 'white ship' that would save them from a choice between Germany and the USSR. After the war, they had made their way to Australia, but many had gone on telling themselves that one day, Uncle Sam would launch another white ship to carry them home.

In defence of these unrealistic or perilous hopes, their leadership, encouraged by the Captive Nations Council and by similar groups outside Australia, cried betrayal. Release of the news of Australia's change in policy was ascribed to Reuters of Moscow, and a local Baltic sculptor produced a bust of Whitlam disfigured by an exaggeratedly large nose. In these circumstances, many Labor politicians began to back down. In South Australia, the usually progressive Don Dunstan assured Baltic leaders that he personally objected to Whitlam's policy, and that he had conveyed these objections to Canberra. In return, the Baltic spokesmen promised that they would underline to their followers the differences between the ALP in Adelaide and in Canberra. As Dunstan reports in his memoirs: 'At the [next] state election a former Baltic Minister of Justice toured the state saying to Baltic migrants: "It's all right – you can safely vote for Dunstan".' But, he adds, they certainly were not willing to say the same about Whitlam's ALP.[35] After Labour was defeated in 1975, the Fraser government reversed Whitlam's decision.

The percentage of refugees actively expressing commitment to some brand of old world politics is uncertain. Few are willing to admit to more than inchoate feelings of attachment to the country of origin, and most shy away from overt declarations of loyalty to political movements whose _raison d'être_ appears to have little relation to Australia or Australian politics and may well have even less connection to real politics in the country of origin.[36]

What of those immigrants who were not refugees? Do their political inclinations and activities reveal a similar complexity? It is commonly assumed that much of what is true for refugees is false for 'economic' migrants. For some commentators, 'dispirited peasants' are simply 'too backward' to have any politics anyway.[37]

In these circumstances, it is frequently stated that 'northern Europeans' have assimilated or integrated most easily into the Australian way of life. One student of the Dutch presence in Australia has hypothesised that the rapid absorption of most Dutch into the Australian system is because the Dutch are 'naturally internationalists' and possess 'a collective open-mindedness'.[38] This may be one reason, but other factors do exist: the relatively slight linguistic problems which have confronted Dutch immigrants; the relative graciousness with which Australians have welcomed the Dutch; and, perhaps most significantly, the relatively high return rate of the Dutch.

Nor have the German migrants who have come here since the Second World War been particularly visible politically, although occasionally, signs do exist of the development of a German-Australian literature which hints at times not forgotten. The most bizarre example is a novel published under the pseudonym of 'Hans Richard' and entitled _Mary my Hun: a Novel with a Purpose_ (1976). The book is hardly a novel, but rather records a farrago of tired ideas from the interwar world. Australians, Richard's protagonist complains, lack the most important thing of all, loyalty to one's country: 'They are nothing but a stinking bunch of lost humanity ready to sell their bloody selves for a few dollars.' He goes on to suggest that Australian babies would be better fed on hand-collected garden snails than on pre-packaged baby food, that fascism is a word used too loosely, that 'a small group of scientific academics must be trusted to govern the world' and that the Jews are taking over in the Real Estate Institute, the big retail shops, and the Australian Medical Association. Journalism offers still greater problems: 'Today no one in Australia ... has any chance to be someone in ... T.V., unless he or she is first of all a Jew.'[39] Hans Richard published his book at his own expense in Campsie and hopefully represents no one but himself.

More interesting is Josef Vondra's novel, *Paul Zwilling*. Vondra, who has gone on to a career in ethnicity and journalism, depicts the ideas and experiences of an Austrian migrant trying to come to grips with his identity in his new country. The protagonist displays an Austrian patriotism and integralism that would not have seemed out of place in the conservative Austria of the 1930s. As a schoolboy in Australia, forced to chant 'I love God and my country ... he always whispered: "My country is Austria, I am Austrian born, I will always be loyal to Austria".'[40]

These are mere impressions hinting at a survival in Australia of the values of pre-1945 Germanic Europe. More needs to be known about such cultural values, and more also about the economic bonds which have linked Australia to nostalgics in West Germany. For the Federal German Republic, the 1960s seem to have been a crucial moment for the legitimation of democratic ideals. It would be interesting to know how delayed was this changeover in 'society and democracy' among the various segments of Australia's German community.

Economic links to the place of origin remain almost as obscure (and perhaps even more important) for the Maltese, Italian, and Greek communities, but among these 'dispirited peasants', politics is alive and well.

The Maltese story is one of division. Australia's Maltese are numerous and are relatively concentrated. Almost half of them live in Victoria, with the majority in Melbourne itself. There they have pursued the parochial politics of 'saints and fireworks', much loved in anthropological accounts of Malta.[41] Maltese from Egypt separate themselves from islanders (and owe allegiance to an organisation based in London). Maltese from the second island of Gozo proudly assert their independence from emigrants who have come from the main island. These divisions are carried into the formation of clubs and the sponsorship of newspapers. Levantine Maltese, it is reported, delight in discomforting their islander brothers by switching into Italian, French, or Arabic on meeting.

Influential too, are the drastic changes that Maltese politics have experienced since the Second World War. In 1968, the previous conservative and Catholic government was replaced by the socialist and nationalist Don Mintoff regime, which has since pursued an adventurous and idiosyncratic course, including flirtations with Colonel Gheddafi. At the time of political changeover, Australia's high commissioner on Malta was Hubert Opperman. He took up the post after Holt dropped him from the ministry.

In Malta, by his own account, Opperman encouraged Australo-Maltese relations. Opperman, who has declared his dislike of extremists ('I had always without reservation voted anti-Labor as I considered Labor a radical Socialist organisation'), was a partisan of the Borg Olivier regime and was appalled by the triumph of Mintoff. He made his views apparent, particularly disapproving of the Australo-Maltese businessman whom Mintoff chose to be his new delegate in Australia. Opperman was soon recalled.[42]

Future historians may well find it interesting to pursue the economic hints that accompany this story. The only available analysis of the Maltese community in Australia admits class and social divisions as well as regional ones. Yet, it is also evident that these divisions are in turn conditioned by surviving political contacts and probably by very significant commercial ties between the rival Maltese communities in Australia and Malta itself.

The politics of the Italian community in Australia are also characterised by regionalism. But regional diversity explains only part of the story. Through the efforts of the Triestine migrant Gianfranco Cresciani, a great deal is known about the politics of Italians in interwar Australia. Australia had the dubious honour of having welcomed Franco Battistessa, a Fascist squadrist who established the first *fascio* in Bombay. Reformist socialists, communists, and anarchists also nurtured Australian organisations. These, in turn, were linked to party or general anti-Fascist structures in Paris or in other places where Mussolini's downfall was plotted. One Italo-Australian from North Queensland even joined the International Brigades in Spain and came back to recount his experiences to his colleagues on the canefields. The Roman Catholic Church, too, kept a weather eye on politics, ready to step into the breach lest the *connubio* with Fascism ended in divorce and conservative forces needed to create a new ménage.

The interregnum that followed the first collapse of Fascism in 1943 proved to be just such a moment. In a fascinating microcosm, which displays again the truth of A. J. P. Taylor's maxim that 'the Cold War was a ... capitalist invention from start to finish', power over the Italian community was contested by left and right. Schiassi, Alcorso and others, through an organisation called *Italia Libera,* tried to transmit to Australia the social radicalism of the Italian resistance. They were outmanoeuvered, however, by the right, whose forces were marshalled by a businessman, Gualtiero Vaccari, and a priest, Ugo Modotti. Cresciani has revealed that both Vaccari and Modotti had been severely compromised with Fascism in the 1930s. But, now with the blessing of Archbishop Mannix, a prelate who in September 1943 still regarded Mussolini as one of 'the big men of the century', and of Arthur Calwell, Vaccari and Modotti were able to deflect the radical ambitions of *Italia Libera*.[43]

Less detail is available about the practice of Italian politics in Australia since the establishment of the Italian Republic. Although the multi-party structure of that state sometimes makes it seem especially impenetrable to Australian eyes, it is known that the various Italian parties do have organisational links with Australia. The most open is that of the Italian Communist Party with FILEF, the Melbourne-based Italian Federation of Emigrant Workers and their Families. A number of Christian Democrat ministers and under-secretaries have visited Australia and the Social Democratic President, Giuseppe Saragat, came here in 1967. Forces on the Italian right, allied to the neo-Fascist MSI, also have networks in Australia, as they do in South Africa, Argentina, the United States, and other countries not inhospitable to the far right. It was at least rumoured that Prince Junio Valerio Borghese, a Fascist relic of the Salò Republic, found sanctuary for a time in Australia after his coup attempt with the Forest Guards in 1970. Some sections of the Italian business community appear to endorse such activities and stimulate it with funds and other assistance.

Nonetheless, it is probably generally true that for most Italo-Australians such political activism is exotic indeed, and far from the life they hope will bring material success, the chance to 'set up our children and re-invest',[44] and even eventually to return to their *paese*. Politics, for them, still means local social action, within the family and among fellow *paesani*. In the Fascist period, some Italian diplomatic officials tried to encourage a greater national spirit among Italians in Australia. Such attempts were only partially successful and were not prosecuted with much zeal by diplomats rarely anxious to mix too closely with people they regarded as 'the great unwashed'. Since 1945, diplomatic attitudes have altered only a little and slowly, but, by 1983 there was a developing sense that the Italian Republic, which has itself changed greatly since 1946, is more interested in its migrants in Australia.

It is a commonplace that Greeks have played their politics harder in Australia, and that they are better organised and more united than are the Italians. From 1453 to the 1820s, the Greeks had no state of their own, but, within the Ottoman Empire, some of them became familiar with wandering, with sea-faring, and with commercial activities, bearing some similarities to the role assumed elsewhere by Jews, Armenians or Chinese. The Ottoman Empire's recognition of the special character of the Greek *millet* reinforced a sense of religious and national identity. Although there were regional variations, it was natural for the Greeks in Australia before 1945 to possess their own religious, political, charitable, and patriotic structures.

Probably more influential, however, were more contemporary political factors. Greeks arrived in Australia after 1950 in the wake of a particularly vicious civil war won by the right only through Anglo-American intervention. The war, as historian Michael Tsounis has noted, 'forced people to declare their political ideologies'.[45] More significantly, it meant that the Greeks, unlike the Italians, contained a radical segment anxious to rally support in Australia against the various conservative regimes that misgoverned Greece until 1981. In return, the Greek right could not rest easy in the knowledge that apathy, or keeping sport on the front pages of the newspapers, would serve its cause as well as any other, more active, approach.

Australians should be neither surprised nor dismayed to find that post-1945 migrants have brought most varieties of their own politics to our shores. After all, Australia's largest non-English migrant group, the Irish, have long fought out their politics in Australia. Since the Second World War, in the far more complicated world of so many migrant groups, much about these politics has been kept hidden because of inherited fearfulness or through Australian ignorance, scorn and active suppression. Much *émigré* politics is wildly unrealistic, a doomed attempt to kindle the ashes of a dead past that bears even less relation to the present politics of the country of origin than it does to structures of power in Australia. Often, too, except in times of political crisis at home (especially crises which encourage further emigration), developed ideologies fade into a generic and sentimental nationalism. At the same time, it is obvious that all the old worlds are not dead. What is not yet clear is whether such old world politics have in turn been grafted into the Australian political system.

Chapter NINE

Immigrants and Australian Political Structures

There is evidence that migrants have preserved the politics of their country of origin and even occasionally re-invented them in Australia, but how have migrants penetrated Australia's political structures? Have migrants occupied an important place in the Australian political world, directly in Parliaments and councils, or indirectly in the federal and state bureaucracies? Do the different migrant groups form electoral blocs? Is Australia providing any parallels with the earlier experiences of the United States, where, for example in New York, successive waves of the Irish, Jews, Italians, Negroes or Puerto Ricans physically replaced each other in certain neighbourhoods and, as a result, took over the politics of those neighbourhoods? How have migrants affected Australia's Anglo-Saxon political structures and ideas?

From time to time, certain individuals have been put forward as the chief spokesmen of the migrant vote. B. A. Santamaria, whose parents had come originally from the Lipari islands, has both spoken out in the 'migrant interest' and used migration issues as evidence for his more general political concerns. In Australia, he argued in 1945, 'the crying need is for people', and he has preferred 'families with strong bonds and a strong Christian tradition'. Emigration, too, he stated, might be necessary as a safety-valve for the host societies and could, for example, help to forestall those who would permit the 'handing of Rome, the Holy City, over to the Communist agents of Stalin in the Italian Peninsular [sic].'[1]

Other figures including some immigrants themselves, wrote in the 1950s and 1960s as 'migrant spokesmen'.[2] But they were too exotic or too reticent to have much impact or following. Before the 1970s, the products of the new immigration programme were perhaps too inexperienced in the ways of Australian politics and too preoccupied with establishing themselves in a new land to produce effective representatives from their own ranks or to elicit more than superficial

171

support from Australian politicians. Equally, the rank and file was also generally quiescent. The major exception to this occurred in the Bonegilla incidents of July 1952 and July 1961. On the first occasion, Italians, who had been kept in the receiving camp near Albury during a particularly cold and wet winter for over two months without receiving employment, rioted. As a contemporary journalist explained: 'They have no money, they say – not even enough to buy soap, and yet they have families back in Italy to support.' The Australian government reacted with considerable alarm to the prospect of aliens revolting. Some armoured cars and troops were put on alert at the nearby Bandiana base. The *Sydney Morning Herald* used the occasion to preach against bad manners from those living 'at the taxpayers' expense'. 'The Italians at Bonegilla have behaved very badly. There can be no toleration or condonation of their threats of violent action to obtain redress of grievances. They must learn, if they are to become useful citizens, that such tactics have no place in Australian life.'[3]

In fact, the migrants seemed still to have perceived their politics as functioning in the context of their old world. When the Italian consul hastened north from Melbourne, he was stoned by the rioters. Traditional anti-clericalism could also emerge: 'We started to revolt. We burned two or three huts and set fire to the church, not because we didn't like the church, but because the Italian priest there used to say, "Have patience, God is on your side" and we were fed up with him.'[4]

In 1961, a similar winter of economic discontent precipitated another riot. The Sydney *Sun* told how 'one policeman was injured when screaming migrants turned over his car, punched him to the ground and kicked him'. The camp commandant, Colonel A. H. Guinn, was bruised and cut; he was persuaded that 'communist agitators' were to blame. For two nights, armed patrols guarded the camp, and the injured policeman, having shrugged off his dislocated shoulder, returned, saying ominously: 'They know I am out of hospital and that I know their faces, and they are keeping well out of sight.' The incident contained as much evidence of old politics as of new. The Italian vice consul turned up to mutter ineffectually to Australian audiences about the absence of communism among his own emigrants. Much of the conflict seems to have been between rival Italian, Yugoslav, and German groups, with special resentment being directed against the alleged preferential treatment being granted to northern Europeans in their employment applications.[5]

In both 1952 and 1961, there was some moralising about the inefficiency and inhumanity of drafting migrants into an economy in crisis. Each incident did lead to a short-term reduction of intake, although the economy soon recovered and immigration figures swiftly returned to their old levels. In 1961, the *Sydney Morning Herald* was reassured because, although the news of the riot had been published in

London, everyone there knew that no British migrants resided at Bonegilla and the incident, therefore, would have no effect on British emigration.[6]

At least according to an Italian migrant, there was one, more sinister effect of being a rioter in 1952: 'Later when I came to apply for citizenship I was refused, when I applied to visit Italy I couldn't go because I was refused a re-entry visa to Australia.' Perhaps such experience prompted many migrants to believe, as one Italian advised: 'An Italian proverb says, "When in Rome do as the Romans do". I wish to say to all Italians who have arrived or who are about to arrive in Australia, "When in Australia, do as the Australians do".'[7]

Such sentiments reflected the prevailing atmosphere in Australia where officialdom wanted immigrants to remain silent politically or, at most, to express themselves through established political structures. To this end, a series of organisations was sponsored, usually with the stated aim of smoothing an immigrant's path into the Australian way of life and thus educating him or her about Australian politics and attitudes. These organisations often were directed as much at all Australians as at the newcomers.

In the 1940s, the Australian authorities had anxiously fostered bodies which might lessen a xenophobic backlash from the national electorate.[8] Even while war continued, in 1943, the government had formally approved the foundation of the Association of Refugees under the direction of Max Joseph. Made up of a group of central European, and primarily Jewish, refugees this body was reported to have gained 1350 members in its first two weeks of existence. Its aims, initially, were to represent those refugees already here and to assist family and friends to come to Australia.

In 1945 the name was carefully changed to the more homely sounding Association of New Citizens and, from 1946 to 1954, a monthly newsletter, *The New Citizen,* appeared. It reflected the concerns of what remained the Jewish and central European refugee core of members. There were articles about events in Europe, particularly concerning the status and plight of Jews surviving there, about vestiges of anti-Semitism in Australia and elsewhere, and about taxation and other matters of practical interest to new citizens. There were also regular theatre and music reviews, and the leading article was often a reprint of a talk, broadcast or paper given by some prominent Australian on the nature of prejudice, the state of politics in Germany, or the unpleasantness of the White Australia Policy. The advertisements provided an ideal directory of the services available for Jews and central Europeans in Sydney at the time, and the letters to the editor reflected the current topics of debate. In 1950 there was heated criticism of the proposed migration agreement with Germany. As Julius Stone, professor of international law at the University of

Sydney, noted elsewhere, the government could not be sure who was an ex-Nazi and should remember that 'refuge ... is for the oppressed not the oppressor'.[9] There was also a tendency to discuss terminology. One correspondent disliked the title New Citizens because 'we preferred in fact to remain the old Association of Refugees ... always in a non-splendid, pseudo-ghettoish isolation, a small group consisting exclusively of central Europeans'.[10]

In fact, the narrowness of the social, religious, geographical, and class base of the Association ensured its demise. Although its secretary emphasised that it would receive any newcomers, he also regretted that many had refused to 'cut off their pasts', and cease 'to be Germans, Hungarians, ... or Czechoslovakians' and assimilate. Those who rejected the chance of becoming New Citizens lacked citizenship: 'To us Australia is the terminus of our earthly itinerary, to many of *them* it is just a station where to gather the strength to make them fit to return from where they came.' Other members stressed that newly arriving Italians or Greeks could apply to join, but the welcome was unenthusiastic: 'The main body of our members is still made up of those who were forced out of Europe by Hitler's persecution ... These people, of whom I am one, had little or no assistance, whereas the new influx of migrants are well catered for by the various Government agencies.'[11]

By the time of the collapse of the Association in 1954, the government was sponsoring more directly the wide-ranging organisation called the Good Neighbour Movement. This group had grown rapidly from small beginnings. Launched in 1949 under parliamentary auspices, the Good Neighbour Movement was given the task of promoting 'a good neighbourly spirit towards all migrants, so that they can become happy citizens of Australia'. The subsidy from the Department of Immigration began at $1,300 in 1949–50, and rose to $60,000 (1959–60), and $100,000 (1963–64). Most of the money was spent on publicity. In 1948, Calwell had set up a small news-sheet entitled *Tomorrow's Australians*. Soon after, its name was changed to *The New Australian*. In January 1954, this bulletin was merged with the more flourishing monthly *Good Neighbour,* which had been published since August 1950. The monthly had soon expressed that mixture of cloying friendliness, hortatory counsel, and determined assimilationism that became the hallmark of the whole movement. The first number of *Good Neighbour* set the tone by recounting the tale of a Spencer Street, Melbourne, ticket collector who had just decided to Teach Himself German and Italian, and by displaying a muted picture with caption: 'In New Guinea Migrant Doctors tend Fuzzy Wuzzies'. A migrant named Attila Bujdoso was interviewed about his new job in Sydney (he had left a wife and baby son at the Bathurst camp):

I started my work in the factory. Everyone was nice. My workmates were all sad that I had to leave ... [my family] so far away. They all promised to help. In a fortnight [I managed to rent] ... a little room; we're all together and I can see my wife and my little boy when I come home from work. I have to thank all my Australian friends who stood by me.[12]

A year later, *Good Neighbour* had further happy news to print: garlic was being grown near Mildura. It was explained carefully to those readers who kept doggedly to mint sauce with their Sunday lamb that 'Garlic is a bulb and one of the oldest plants known to man. It was used by the Romans and later became popular in Spain. New Australians have caused a sharp increase in the demand for garlic. One Melbourne emporium is selling it in pound lots over the counter'.[13]

The Good Neighbour Movement also set up a structure outside Canberra. Councils were established in each state and, in turn, organised sub-branches. By 1958, the secretary claimed that twenty-five separate branches and nineteen liaison groups were flourishing in New South Wales. She added that, in some country towns where numbers could not justify a full branch system, the Country Women's Association had rallied to the cause and its members were arranging the welcoming functions that were such a part of Good Neighbour activities.[14] As Mrs Z. Kaldy of Launceston was reported to have declared, Hungarian rhapsodies were all very well but what did you do after the ball was over? The answer was easy—go to an Australian home and have a nice cup of tea, since, in such genuine exchanges, 'we take away something of our host's personality and we leave behind us something of ourselves'.[15]

Not everyone was ecstatic at this solid world of tea, cakes and jam, and slices of delicious ham. As one migrant soon remarked, such naive do-gooding was 'frivolous, superficial and unrealistic'.[16] Perhaps it was worse than that. Good Neighbour activities in the 1950s oscillated uneasily between patronising pretty migrant girls doing pretty migrant dances and preaching hard-line assimilationism. As early as July 1954, Cairns had announced its very own Miss New Australia Quest and it was not long before each state branch of the Movement was running a contest aimed at unearthing a national Miss New Australia. In 1959, *Good Neighbour* was especially triumphant when a migrant (a blonde German) was named Queen of Melbourne's Moomba Festival. Photos of assimilated girls on page 3 of a newspaper might help to convert migrants to Australian ways or at least encourage them to forget their home-grown politics.

Sometimes the benevolent veneer of the Good Neighbour Movement wore a little thin. Not far beneath the surface was the constant message that British Australia was best. Between 1952 and 1954, the accession and coronation of Elizabeth II and the subsequent royal tour

brought tears of monarchist pride and joy to Good Neighbours. As one
poor migrant poet wrote in 1952:

> *God save our noble Queen*
> *With Royal Coron* [sic]
> *We are ready now – and have been*
> *To defend her Empire's Lion*

And on the occasion of the royal tour in 1954, *Good Neighbour* found
this message in a shop run by Germans:

We, the people of many lands who have lost there our family, our friends and
our freedom, greet our lovely Queen and her husband, the living symbols of
British liberty, humanity, and justice and we give thanks to God and the people
of Australia for having given us a new happy haven, a home, and a new heaven
of happiness.[17]

It was also predictable that the Good Neighbour Movement would
cheerfully act as paladin of the Bring out a Briton scheme in the late
1950s and that the much publicised one millionth post-war migrant,
kissed in a good neighbourly way by Harold Holt in 1955, should be
young, female, married and British.[18]

Gradually, some criticism began to be voiced about the Movement.
A Romanian remarked: 'Associations like the Good Neighbour
Council, supposedly there to help migrants, do their best to care for
British migrants and deal with other nationalities only as a sideline.'[19]
His comments were increasingly endorsed by other migrants. Even
when, finally in the 1960s, some non-British figures began to appear on
the executive of the various Good Neighbour Councils, most migrants
continued to find that its members ignored them.

An occasional effort had been made to establish select Nationality
Advisory Committees, which were meant to act as a channel between
the Good Neighbour executive and the various communities. But
passage was made arduous by the diversity of the alleged communities
and by surviving paternalism among the Good Neighbours. Characteristic were the discouraging comments in 1958 of J. T. Massey who,
from a past in the YMCA, had become Commonwealth Co-ordinator
of the Good Neighbour Movement. Massey stated defensively that the
temporary existence of any foreign clubs, press or churches could only
be justified while they did not 'discourage assimilation and cultivate
the preservation of foreign aspirations'. Any alternative would lead
migrant organisations to be deemed 'subversive and hated by
many'.[20]

As rhetoric switched from assimilationism to integrationism, the
Good Neighbour Movement continued its preaching of Australia
Unlimited. In 1963, its monthly noted that a Dutch-born Shepparton
family were 'most naturally Australian': the father was prominent in

Speak dinkum Australian

the tongue which says you put fat in the banjo!

AUSTRALIAN	ENGLISH	GERMAN	ITALIAN
Abo	aboriginal	eingeborener	aborigine
arvo	afternoon	nachmittag	pomeriggio
also-ran	person who is a failure	pechvogel	sfortunato
argue the toss	to dispute a decision	einen beschluss anfechten	contestare una decisione
art union	lottery with non-money prizes	lotterie ohne geldpreise	lotteria d'oggetti
Aussie	an Australian	ein Australier	un Australiano
Aussieland	Australia	Australien	Australia
Aussie Rules	Australian Rules football	Australische fussball regeln	Regole Australiane del giuoco del calcio
All Blacks	New Zealand Rugby Union footballers	fussball spie ler im Neu See-land Rugby Verein	calciatore della Rugby Unione Nuova Zelanda
Australiana	collection of Aust. historical or other records	sammlung hisorischer oder sonstiger Dokumente uber Australien	Collezione di documenti storici od altri Australiani
Apple Island	Tasmania	Tasmanien	Tasmania
back of beyond, back of Bourke, backblocks	the remote inland	das weite inland	interno lontano
bagswinger	bookmaker	buchmacher	allibratore
bail up	to rob	berauben	rubare
bald as a bandicoot	completely bald	vollkommen kahl	completamente calvo
ball of muscle	energetic, strong person	ein starker tatkraftiger mensch	una persona energica e forte
banjo	frying pan	bratpfanne	padella
Bananaland	Queensland	Queensland	Queensland
banker	river in flood	uberschwemmter fluss	Torrente in inundazione
barney	argument	argument (streit)	discussione
barrack	shout for or against a sport-ing side	parteinehmen fur oder gegen beim sport	essere parziale pro o contra di un incontro sportivo
bathers	swimming costume	schwimmanzug	costume da bagno
belly	person's stomach	ein bauchlein	stomaco
beer-up	get drunk	sich betrinken	ubricarsi
be your age!	don't be childish!	sei nicht kindisch!	non faccia il bambino
big smoke	a city	eine stadt	una citta
bilge artist	careless talker	ein schwatzer	chiacchierone
billabong	small lake or pond in river	kleiner see oder tiech in einem fluss	laghetto nel fiume
billy	tin can for boiling tea	blechener teekessel	brocca di latta per fare bollire il te
bit hot, a	unreasonable	unvernunftig	irragionevole (assurdo)

How to cope with Aussie slang, published in *Migrant Voice*, October 1960.
Migrant Voice was a short-lived magazine produced privately by Philip Luker
and had as its sub-title 'The National Magazine of Immigrant Australia'.

'six community organisations' and the mother was active on local church, Girl Guides, and mothers' clubs committees. In 1965, the Gertrude Kumm Citizenship Award went to an Italian couple 'representative of the many new citizens who make considerable sacrifices to help their children enter the professions'. Their three sons had graduated in engineering, medicine, and law.[21]

These were almost the last flourishes of the Movement. In 1968, the Department of Immigration withdrew its sudsidy of the monthly. Following the recommendations of the Galbally Report (1978), the Good Neighbour Movement was slowly dissolved amd its staff dispersed. The multicultural 1970s were demanding a new bureaucratic approach to immigration.

In its own fashion, the Department of Immigration had been active and generous in sponsoring an organisation which, by constantly reiterating the superiority of Australian ways, had aimed to detach migrants from their old cultures and thus, by implication, from their old politics. The bureaucrats had laboured hard and long for assimilationism. Australia's own politicians, by contrast, searched more intermittently for mechanisms to attract or to control the migrant vote.

By 1961, the party that was popularly supposed to be most open to migrant membership and sympathy was the DLP. Its Catholicism, its endorsement of the family, and its bitter, even hysterical, anti-communism were thought to bring together peasants from southern Italy and refugees from eastern Europe. Yet the DLP's public face seemed a long way from Catanzaro or Warsaw. Stalwart Irish Labor bosses such as Jack Kane, Frank McManus, and Vince Gair were not notable students of foreign customs and were among the bearers of Australia's isolationist traditions.

In 1958, the DLP did establish a New Australian Council in Victoria, but its historian has argued convincingly for its peripheral and eccentric nature. The DLP leadership regarded the Council as an outlandish body useful mainly because it could appeal to the 'quaintness of new Australians'. As one party faithful emphasised, 'there was nothing ulterior about it'.

Another recurring problem for the Council was the division between one migrant and another. A Czech-born member (who was prone to writing fifteen page reports to be presented at executive meetings) explained confusedly that a Latvian-born delegate could not be trusted:

I must understand that Latvians were like this; after three centuries to the German overlords, they had been servants, they bow and scrape. If he is boss, a Latvian, oh he is big and hard and powerful, orders and parades, but if they are below, it's yes sir, no sir and thank you sir ... the only good Latvians were those who had been educated in Russia [before the 1917 Revolution].

Faced with continual quarrelling of this kind, the DLP executive in 1967 made the best of a bad job and disbanded the New Australian Council. The party president took the occasion to observe that the migrants had not properly comprehended Australian procedures: 'Some got terribly excited, and waved their arms around, and got terribly emotional.' Thereafter, the DLP would await its coming doom without special provision for the migrant vote.[22]

The major parties have been still more careful about becoming too embroiled in a foreign world. In Victoria, the New Australian Liberal and Country Movement was established in 1952, but was dissolved only two years later, on the grounds that the existence of a special section of the party machine catering for migrants was divisive. Since 1954 the Liberals, and even more their Country Party allies, have made few attempts to attract migrants as distinct from other Australians. As the special bearers of the myths of Australia Unlimited, the lucky country, and of anti-communism, perhaps the conservative leadership has believed its virtue to be so evident that there was no need to translate it into foreign tongues.

Many Liberals probably had such opinions confirmed by the Lyenko Urbanchich case of the late 1970s. Urbanchich migrated to Australia from Yugoslavia soon after the Second World War. In a Cooma paper, he wrote that displaced persons were 'those who left their own countries because they preferred freedom or because they ran the risk of losing their lives if they did not agree with the Red bosses'. He was not yet reconciled to all aspects of the Australian way of life:

The migrants are here – homesick, always prepared to criticise puritanical and silent Sundays, exaggerated interest in horse racing, and mutton sausages. They are irritated by the many flies in summer, they laugh at Australian husbands who wash the dishes for their wives, they condemn women who smoke in the street and those who are too fond of drinking beer. They complain that Australians envy them if they save money to buy cars and houses. Australians do not invite them to their homes and do not like to listen to any language but English. General criticism – Australia and culture are our enemies.[23]

By the late 1970s, Urbanchich was again prominent. He had become a major force in the Ethnic Council established by the NSW Liberal Party. Early in 1978, Urbanchich was associated with forces of the extreme right (including some Europeans and a group of former officers from the South Vietnamese army) who were allegedly involved in a right-wing attempt to take over the Liberal Party. His real notoriety came, however, in August 1979 when rumours began to spread that he had been a leading anti-Semite and pro-Nazi in wartime Slovenia. Questions were asked in state and federal Parliaments; Urbanchich was suspended from the presidency of the Ethnic Council; and inquiries were instigated by the NSW Attorney-General, the NSW division of the Liberal Party, and by the Ethnic Council itself. Urbanchich narrowly avoided expulsion from the Party although the executive was sufficiently embarrassed to dissolve its Ethnic Council.[24]

If the Liberal Party has abstained from embracing its migrant electors too closely, the ALP began as a still more reluctant wooer of alien voters. Don Dunstan can remember in 1951 campaigning among the Italians of Norwood after his opponent had publicly stated 'these immigrants are no use to us – a few of them are tradesmen but most of them have no skills at all. And when they intermarry we'll have all the colours of the rainbow' and can also claim thereafter to have been one of the most tenacious and outspoken opponents of the White Australia Policy.[25]

Certainly, any formal move to organise ethnic voters faced a rocky road within the ALP. In Victoria the Party's various New Australian Councils were dissolved three times between 1954 and 1970. In any case they contributed very little to decision making and scarcely offered any entry to real power. When, in reaction to such exclusion, Giovanni Di Salvo sought endorsement for the federal seat of Batman in 1966, using the local Italo-Australian community as a power base, he was easily defeated at branch level. With suspicion and active discouragement augmented by knowledge from their place of origin that national politics for the poor only spelled trouble, it is not surprising that many migrants thought that Australian politics were not for them: 'I vote so as not to get into trouble but I don't care who gets in; all politicians are crooks, so I just put a cross on the piece of paper. My husband does that too.'[26]

Nonetheless, despite the many real and psychological obstacles, some migrants by the 1960s did begin to penetrate the national scene. The 1961 elections were a first step. In the lead-up to that election, the *Sydney Morning Herald*, at the time bitterly critical of the economic policies of the Menzies government, ran a series of articles about the electorate. It cited *La Fiamma* saying: 'The migrant will vote with a feeling of boredom and gratitude ... because they have employment and ... a full stomach. Don't ask them for anything else.' The *Herald* was a little perturbed by such cynicism, but its analyst, pointing out that only 287 600 of a possible 873 200 non-British post-war migrants had been naturalised and thus earned the vote, concluded: 'Migrants may swing a seat but not the elections.'[27] But it was these elections when Jim Killen saved the day for Menzies through those famous donkey communist preferences. A seat could decide an election; 287 600 voters could not be taken for granted.

Despite a deepening acknowledgement that the migrant vote could be politically significant, few migrants yet won places in the formal structure of Australian politics. An occasional councillor was elected –

for example, an Italo-Australian took a seat in the Griffith shire in 1962. By 1966, fifteen migrants had been elected to various local bodies in Victoria. In Western Australia, Hungarian-born Andrew Mensaros even won a state parliamentary seat in 1968, and went on to a ministerial career.

But for every such success, there were many more failures. In 1966, 30 per cent of the population of the inner Melbourne suburbs of Collingwood, Prahran, St Kilda, and Sunshine were from non-English-speaking backgrounds. Not one migrant sat on the councils in these areas. In most state assemblies and in federal Parliament, members who proclaimed their ethnicity did not emerge until well after Grassby's proclamation of a 'multicultural society for the future' in 1973. For example, Franca Arena (ALP) was elected to the New South Wales upper house in 1981; in Victoria, the lower house gained Theo Sidiropoulos (ALP) in 1978 and Giovanni Sgro (ALP) in 1979; and in Canberra, the Senate gained Misha Lajovic (Liberal) in 1975 and Nick Bolkus (ALP) in 1980, and the House of Representatives, Andrew Theophanous (ALP) in 1980. Nick Greiner, Hungarian-born, although married into the Anglo-Australian establishment, in 1983 became parliamentary leader of the New South Wales Liberal Party.

Even before these individuals surfaced, political scientists had kept a precise surveillance of voting patterns among migrants. Although their categorisations hid as much as they revealed, they could demonstrate that northern Europeans were as divided politically as ordinary Australians, that eastern Europeans were eternally repelling the Red menace by voting Liberal, and that southern Europeans had begun by voting Liberal–National Party. Recently, they have also shown that, as names like Sidiropoulos, Sgro or Theophanous suggest, southern Europeans have been switching in large numbers to the ALP. In Victoria, there have been recent instances of Greeks taking over particular branches and even conducting the business in their own language.[28]

Commentators have been less confident in explaining why this pattern is emerging. One possibility lies in the ALP's general abandonment of xenophobia with its surrender of the White Australia Policy in 1971. Another is the more broadly based humanitarianism that characterised much Labor theory in the 1970s. Probably still more significant in the ALP's increased attractiveness to southern European and other migrants has been the personality of Gough Whitlam. It was Whitlam who unleashed Grassby and who publicised the new legitimacy being granted to social heterogeneity in Australia – although he also tried to ride the dangerous tiger of new nationalism. More importantly perhaps, Whitlam looked like a politician from the old world. He was literate and urbane; he took trouble to pronounce foreign words and was rumoured to speak Greek and Italian passably. Certainly he was a Latinist. But

Whitlam's apparent intellectuality was, among many Australians, an electoral liability. But his stature – intellectual, moral, and physical – was admired by many immigrants and, at least in retrospect, seems to be encouraging the creation of a myth about the lost leader.

In practice, the Whitlam years may only have demonstrated the limitations of reformism in Australia. But, at least symbolically, his government did offer new sympathy towards migrants. In fact, much legislation had been drafted under John Gorton and William McMahon, but, under Whitlam and Grassby the tide became a flood. There were reforms in adult and child education programmes for migrants (1969, 1972, 1973); citizenship requirements were loosened in 1973; a government-financed interpreter service was begun; an anti-discrimination law was passed in 1975; and the Commission for Community Relations was established under Grassby in 1975. Meanwhile, committees of inquiry investigated poverty (1972–73), community relations (1973), the teaching of migrant languages (1974), and manufacturing industry (1974).

Nor were such bureaucratic labours curtailed by Malcolm Fraser after 1975. Legislation was passed to establish the migrant broadcasting and television service in 1977. New commissions pondered ideal policies on welfare and health (1976), and interpreters and translators (1976); in 1977, that perennial legal advocate of public migrant causes, Frank Galbally, headed a review of post-arrival programmes and services to migrants and proposed far-reaching reforms. Some of the Galbally recommendations were duly implemented and, in 1982, a review of the review was undertaken by the Australian Institute of Multicultural Affairs, one of the institutions created after the Galbally Report, and itself by 1983 a body under review.

To appraise all these reports and to implement all this legislation, multicultural Australia has seen the creation of a formidable new bureaucracy. Taking over where the Good Neighbour Movement left off, Ethnic Communities Councils were inaugurated in all states. Control of these councils was firmly in migrant hands. In 1975, Bill Jegorow, the aspirant chairman of the New South Wales Council, declared proudly that for 'the very first time in the history of N.S.W.... Australians of ethnic minority origin, born in Australia, born overseas and migrants [*sic*] have come together to speak for themselves rather than being spoken for, as in the past.' The organising committee, he announced, had 'representatives of almost all ethnic communities'.[29]

The age of fully fledged participatory democracy, however, had not yet arrived. The Councils were to be 'above politics' and, thus unencumbered, would be better able to act as a sort of transmission belt through which migrant wishes could pass to the Anglo-Saxon controlled and trained bureaucracy and power brokers. The leadership, however, has often been faction-ridden and decidedly political, at least with reference to the countries of origin. The search for one Australia has similarly not been abandoned.[30] In other words, although the Councils have been active in promoting reforms and although the membership has changed from the days of the Good Neighbour Movement, much of the ideology of that organisation lives on.

The Ethnic Communities Councils have also had their influence balanced by competing bureaucratic bodies. New South Wales (1979), South Australia (1980), and Victoria (1983) established Ethnic Affairs Commissions and other states can boast Ethnic Affairs Divisions, usually as part of their premiers' departments. All, to varying degrees, have been active and have done useful work in publicising the many areas in which Australians from non-English-speaking backgrounds suffer active discrimination. The New South Wales Commission, for example, was officially established after the publication of its initial report, *Participation* (1979), which detailed and illustrated the means whereby 'minority groups [could] achieve total participation in the Australian and New South Wales political and social systems.'[31] It was as much a blueprint for action as a documentation of the inaction of previous governments and bureaucracies.

While government departments slowly began to implement some of the new policies, migrant welfare organisations have also blossomed under the gentle zephyr of the 1970s. Co.As.It., Greek Welfare, the Indo-Chinese Refugee Association, and the plethora of charitable organisations effectively demanded that private enterprise also win a (subsidised) place in multicultural Australia.

Critics of such organisations do exist. It is difficult not to fear that such welfare organisations are more capricious or political in their definition of the deserving poor than government agencies would be. The very number of the groups involved hints at another obvious limitation. Personal, political, and ethnic rivalries cause such bodies to form, break up, and re-form, so that sometimes the real intention is far from the simple one of a rapid and equitable distribution of charity to those growing numbers of migrants who not only discover an Australia that is spiritually empty but also one that is materially barren.

Similarly such bodies merge uneasily into the numerous religious and social clubs that characterise any migrant society. In multicultural Australia, over 1000 such bodies can be enumerated, such as the Albanian Club, the Armenian Church Sevan Dance Organisation, the Nederlands Bridge Club, and the Cyprian Brotherhood Evagoras. The focus of such bodies can be cultural or religious or even military. But few offer charity without political strings attached and without some reference back to the nature, real or imagined, of old worlds.

In reaching this position, this story has turned a full circle. In a sense, the history narrated here has been a simple one. With respect to political participation as to many other matters, the aggressive insularity of the assimilationist Australia of the 1950s has given way to the more complex plurality of the multicultural 1980s. No longer are sponge cakes or lamb chops forced down the throats of bemused or costive newcomers by the ladies of the Good Neighbour Movement. Australia in 1983 had become sufficiently sophisticated to admit that the contrasting sounds of Lajovic or Theophanous, FILEF or the Captive Nations' Council, the Greek Orthodox Church or the Vietnam Veterans' Association are part of the voice of Australia.

Of course, not all are satisfied.

> *If I was the son of an Englishman,*
> *I'd really be an Aussie,*
> *I could be a High Court Judge,*
> *Or an actor on the telie,*
> *I could be a Union Boss,*
> *Or a co-star with Skippy,*
> *I could even be Prime Minister,*
> *Or comment on the footy,*
> *If I was the son of an Englishman,*
> *I'd really be an Aussie.*[32]

Yet even such expressions of discontent seem a world away from that time in which Arthur Calwell blithely assayed his 'choice specimens' or in which W. D. Borrie wondered whether 'white Australia' could cope with more Italians. In multicultural Australia, my brother Jack may turn out to be Greek or Vietnamese, Polish or Tongan, Chilean or Maltese, and may even be proud of it.

Chapter TEN

Many Little Australias

Since 1945, politically and culturally, socially and financially, Australia, through immigration and other events, has been connected to a wider world in a way that was not so before the Second World War. Australians preserve within these shores no longer just a 'fragment'[1] of the British Empire, but in addition, fragments of Greece or Italy, the Dodecanese or Sicily, Kastellorizo or Limina, and many more. It is the histories and experiences of these many little Australias that has been recounted here.

War, Lenin said, is the locomotive of history and certainly the Second World War propelled Australian immigration policy into an area previously disdained. The shibboleths of British Australia were infringed by politicians who had seen Japan come too close and who now demanded that Australia populate or perish. At the same time, post-war reconstruction stressed a growth in manufacturing industry which would help to convert Australia into the 'Great White Southland'. In the factories of GMH or on the construction sites of the Snowy Mountains Scheme, all hands, any hands, were needed. Almost without admitting it, politicians, bureaucrats and perhaps the population at large shifted the pendulum of racial acceptability to encompass migrants from Norway, the Baltic states, the Mediterranean, Asia Minor and eventually even Asia itself. However privily, the new immigration policy was revolutionising Australian society.

It has been a very odd revolution. Denied by its makers from old Australia, the revolution for a long time was not publicised by its participants, the newcomers. These immigrants from non-English-speaking backgrounds came to Australia having learned to be careful and to be silent. Inevitably, they carried with them parts of their old worlds as cultural and social, economic and political baggage.

The baggage was complex. For an emigrant, neither time nor place were matters to be taken for granted. The maps may say 'Australia' and the calendars '1984', but for many an inhabitant of this country at least part of his or her mind still resides in Vienna before 1938, Riga before 1941, Thessalonika before 1945 or Saigon before 1975.

But even here a commentator needs to be careful. In the 1980s, the nationalisation of the masses seems so complete as to be natural and permanent. Yet this nationalisation is a process that only began in 1789, and then varied immensely in its pace and nature across Europe and the rest of the world. After 1945, newcomers might be listed as 'Maltese' or 'Yugoslavs' or even as 'southern Europeans' when their real identity was framed by that traditional village and family which did not know the nation.

In this sense, some migrants brought to Australia structures of the world before 1789. But even as historians acknowledge this, they cannot rest secure. Nationalisation has advanced on all fronts. Sometimes the labelling by Australian authorities, sometimes the requirements of ethnic politicians, sometimes fashion aped from the United States have nationalised migrants into the culture and even the politics of their country of origin here in Australia.

Moreover, one group of migrants has diluted or helped to foment another. In the countries of origin, television and mass education have continued to strike at old localism in the interests of the homogeneous nation. Even peasant migrants who reach Australia in the 1980s are more likely to feel that they belong to their nation than their predecessors would have done a generation ago.

Until very recently, these structures of a history left behind or even of one comprehended in Australia were revealed or re-created only slowly and hesitantly. Migrants hesitated to flaunt their identity partly because Australians spurned their backgrounds, resented their willingness to work hard and save, frowned at their funny foreign voices, and were horrified by their alien politics. These newcomers were expected quickly and rapidly to assimilate into the Australian way of life, although no one was willing to define what this meant or to offer much assistance in achieving such a goal. Immigrants became numbers in the workforce, a percentage of home owners, people in pretty costumes, and, on occasions, the scapegoats for economic strife.

Then, after two decades of boosting the Australian population figures by importing non-British immigrants, it became apparent that these newcomers were not easily discarding old ways. They had kept alive many of their familiar customs – many still 'spoke foreign' at home, many were choosing to return to their countries of origin, some were even labouring to have their Australian-born children learn a non-English language, many had kept themselves apart socially from old Australians, and some were still practising outlandish forms of religion and were even building places of worship in which to do so. Prompted by critics on the left who, both in Australia and in the countries of origin, were inclined to see only the exploitative side of migration, Australians began to notice that immigrants had not always been comfortably absorbed into the workforce. Often indeed, on tables of employment or affluence or educational performance, they came second last ahead only of those oldest Australians, the Aborigines. Migrants became a problem.

And, by the end of the 1960s, problem-solvers could readily be found. The expansion of Australia's universities and the liberal messages of the Great Society which could be seen on television induced a growth in welfare policies and personnel. Rhetoric began to change from assimilationism to integrationism. Immigrants were no longer expected to adjust to living in Australia all on their own. They could obtain assistance from bureaucrats, social workers and even from fellow migrants, and, if they were lucky, some bits of their own cultural traditions might be recognised as part of the Australian way of life.

The industry of ethnicity began to grow and its growth coincided with changes in immigration policy. It was no longer fashionable or politically astute for Australia to sustain its White Australia Policy or, indeed, any obvious preference in its selection of potential new citizens. Equally, it became unfashionable to be seen to discriminate against Australians who could not claim an English-speaking background. Integrationism shaded into multiculturalism. Australians from immigrant backgrounds had the right to sustain old world cultural traditions if they so chose, the right to obtain equal access to social resources, and the right to be represented at all political levels. A new spirit would be kindled at last by the new immigration policy, and a new Australia which would discard all discrimination and which would welcome diversity as its catchcry would arise. A. J. Grassby would be at the forefront of those optimists who have seen not a hidden social revolution but a complete cultural one.

A more pessimistic interpretation is possible. In many ways, Australia remains an intensely parochial country anxious to fob off any suggestion that economic ties should be made with Asia or cultural ones with non-British Europe. Despite multiculturalism, Australians seem even more reluctant than in the past to learn any languages other than English. Australian culture and particularly Australian historians, foreswearing the cultural cringe, don with enthusiasm the newest nationalism. And our politicans seem to believe that they can preside over a winged-keel or Davis-Cup-led economic recovery. We Australians whom only a few years ago Manning Clark found 'comfortless on Bondi beach' can overcome all practical and spiritual troubles simply by clinging to the boxing kangaroo.

By this interpretation, the Australia of the 1980s which hopes to become the Great Southland but fears that it may not, is not so different from that of 1945. Then we humbly made obeisance to British ways, British blood and British institutions. Now, sometimes it seems, a British Australia has merely been replaced by an avowedly Australian Australia.

But does Australia really have to move from its accustomed cringing colonial deference only to a strident and homogenising nationalism? In many old societies since 1945 there have been some welcome signs that nationalism is weakening and that the age of the masses does not always have to imply a tragic destruction of individuality in the interests of the nation. It would be nice to contemplate a relatively rich and relatively safe Australia that was proud to state that our nation, so varied and complex, is little more than a mere geographical expression. In those circumstances, mass migration, despite its frequent sacrifice of the individual migrant, would prove the happiest event so far in our history. And historians, those natural manufacturers or forgers of the national myth, could reveal how happy is the fortune that has made the history of Australia a chapter in the history of migration and has mingled, and continues to mingle, so many old worlds into new Australia.

Notes

Oral history material

Unless footnoted, the oral history material used comes from two sources:
1. 'Refugees: intellectual origins and impact of European migration to Australia 1933–1956.' This was a research project carried out by the authors between 1978 and 1980. Subject to the interviewees' agreement, the tapes, transcripts and other material will be passed to the Mitchell Library, State Library of NSW. The research was funded by a University of Sydney Special Projects Research Grant.
2. The Oral Histories Project of the Ethnic Affairs Commission of NSW. This project has been in operation since 1981 and the material collected to date includes a series of oral history interviews conducted by Janis Wilton as consultant to the Project and a number of interviews conducted by members of various ethnic communities. As well, the Project has unearthed letters, diaries, photographs and other source material. Again, most of this material will be eventually deposited in the Mitchell Library.

The endnotes refer only to specific quotations and information cited in the text. For further references, a number of bibliographies on Australian immigration studies provide a useful starting point, for example:
CHOMI Das (A quarterly documentation and abstracts service on migration issues published by the Clearing House on Migration Issues, 133 Church St, Richmond, Vic. 3121.
C. A. Price et al. (eds), *Australian Immigration: A Bibliography and Digest*, Canberra, No. 1. 1966; No. 2, 1970; No. 3, 1975; No. 4, 1979; and No. 4 Supplement, 1981.

Chapter 1   The New Immigration Programme: attitudes and policy

1.   A. A. Calwell, *How many Australians tomorrow?*, Reed and Harris, Melbourne, 1945, p. 1.

2.   A. Grenfell Price, *Australia comes of age,* Georgian House, Melbourne, 1945, p. 97; C. E. W. Bean, *On the wool track,* Angus & Robertson, Sydney, 1945, p. 99.

3.   A. J. Grassby, 'Australian ethnic affairs policy for the 80's', *Journal of Intercultural Studies* 2, 1981, p. 55.

4.   C. M. H. Clark, *A History of Australia, Vol. V,* Melbourne University Press, Melbourne, 1981, p. 202.

5.   R. M. Crawford, *'A Bit of a Rebel': the life and work of George Arnold Wood,* Sydney University Press, Sydney, 1975, p. 310.

6.   B. Hornadge, *The Yellow Peril,* Review Publications, Dubbo, 1976, p. 104.

7.   N. O. P. Pyke, 'An outline history of Italian immigration into Australia', *Australian Quarterly* XX, 1948, p. 105.

8.   G. Blaikie, *Remember Smith's Weekly,* Rigby, Adelaide, 1966, p. 227.

9.   C. A. Price, *Southern Europeans in Australia,* Oxford University Press, Melbourne, 1963, p. 205.

10.   W. D. Borrie, *Italians and Germans in Australia,* Cheshire, Melbourne, 1954, p. 144.

11.   A. Fitzgerald, *The Italian Farming Soldiers,* Melbourne University Press, Melbourne, 1981, p. 33

12.   Australian Archives (Canberra), Dept. of the Interior, A433, item 39/2/909, Inspector R. S. Browne to the Director, CIB, 31 May 1939.

13.   H. Gullett, *Not as a duty only,* Melbourne University Press, Melbourne, 1976, p. 11.

14.   J. Lyng, *Non-Britishers in Australia,* Macmillan, Melbourne, 1927, pp. 5; 10–11; 22; 94; 107.

15.   Pyke, 'An outline history of Italian immigration', p. 103. Also his 'Some reflections of Italian immigration into Australia', *Australian Quarterly* XVIII, 1946, p. 40.

16.   M. A. Petrover, The attitude of the Sydney press to the immigration policy of the Labor Government in the years 1945 to 1947, BA Honours thesis, University of Sydney, 1974, p. 26; and P. Y. Medding, The Melbourne Jewish community since 1945, MA thesis, University of Melbourne, 1976, p. 11.

17.   NSW Parliament, *Debates,* 1948, 2nd series, no. 188, p. 221.

18.   R. M. Crawford, *Australia,* Hutchinson, London, 1952, p. 11.

19.   H. Gepp, *When Peace Comes,* Robertson and Mullens, Melbourne, 1943, p. 116.

20.   *Sydney Morning Herald,* 29 March 1939.

21.   Australia. Senate, *Debates,* 1945, no. 185, p. 6017.

22.   Calwell, *How many Australians tomorrow?,* p. 66; Australia, Senate, *Debates,* 1945, no. 185, p. 6294.

23. Australia. Senate, *Debates,* 1945, no. 185, p. 6019 cf., W. D. Borrie, *Immigration: Australia's Problems and Prospects,* Angus & Robertson, Sydney, 1949 for a discussion of the various projections of the time.

24. S. Kelen, *Heed McGlarity,* Mingay, Sydney, 1945, pp. 5; 26; 35; 111; 130.

25. J. Jupp, *Arrivals and Departures,* Cheshire-Lansdowne, Melbourne, 1966, p. 8.

26. For example, see chapters by J. Collins and M. De Lepervanche, in E. L. Wheelwright and K. Buckley (eds), *Essays in the Political Economy of Australian Capitalism,* ANZ Book Co., Sydney, 1975; and M. De Lepervanche, 'From race to ethnicity', *Australian and New Zealand Journal of Sociology* 16, 1980.

27. The main model used is S. Castle and G. Kosack, *Immigrants Workers and Class Structure in Western Europe,* Oxford University Press, London, 1973.

28. Borrie, *Immigration,* p. 11.

29. P. Weller and B. Lloyd (eds), *Federal Executive Minutes 1915-1955,* Melbourne University Press, Melbourne, 1978, p. 542.

30. C. Kiernan, *Calwell,* Nelson, Melbourne, 1978, p. 82; and Borrie, *Immigration,* p. 90.

31. *Sydney Morning Herald,* 30 January 1952.

32. NSW Parliament, *Debates,* 1948, 2nd series, no. 188, p. 221.

33. Viscount Dunrossil, 'The Powerful Magic of Australia', *Digest* (Report of the Twelfth Australian Citizenship Convention), Canberra, 1961, p. 6.

34. A. A. Calwell, *Be Just and Fear Not,* Rigby, Adelaide, 1978, p. 107.

35. K. T. Henderson, 'Migration: an Australian view', *Contemporary Review* CXXXV, April 1929, p. 496.

36. L. F. Crisp, *Ben Chifley,* Angus & Robertson, Sydney, 1961, p. 319.

37. Australia. House of Representatives, *Debates,* 1947, no. 195, p. 2948.

38. L. F. Fitzhardinge, 'Immigration policy – a survey', *Australian Quarterly* XXI, 1949, p. 11.

39. H. L. Harris, in W. D. Borrie et al. (eds), *A White Australia,* Australasian Publishing Co., Sydney, 1947, p. 137.

40. Australian Archives (Canberra), Dept. of the Interior, A434, item 46/3/10627, especially A. Barclay to Calwell, 26 October 1946.

41. *Age,* 24 July 1947.

42. Commonwealth Immigration Advisory Committee, *Report,* 27 February 1946, pp. 6–7; 11; 31.

43. Australia. House of Representatives, *Debates,* 1947, no. 190, p. 1015.

44. Calwell, *Be Just and Fear Not,* p. 103.

45. H. Strakosch, 'National and international significance of immigration', *Australian Quarterly* XIX, 1947, p. 52.

46. Z. Holt, *My Life with Harry,* The *Herald,* Melbourne, 1968, pp. 84–5.

47. *Sydney Morning Herald,* 27 July 1933; and Australian Archives (Canberra), Prime Minister's Dept., A461, item V 349/1/2, J. D. Connolly, London, to Senator McLachlan, 16 December 1937.

48. *Reveille,* May 1951; Jupp, *Arrivals and Departures,* p. 12.

49. Crawford, *Australia,* p. 11.

Chapter 2   From Assimilationism to Multiculturalism: immigration policy 1949–83

1.   *Digest* (Report of the Third Australian Citizenship Convention), Canberra, 1952, p. 10.

2.   *Australian,* 26 July 1969.

3.   L. F. Fitzhardinge, 'Immigration policy – a survey', *Australian Quarterly* XXI, 1949, p. 15.

4.   J. Jupp, *Arrivals and Departures,* Cheshire-Lansdowne, Melbourne, 1966, p. 117; Australia. House of Representatives, *Debates,* 1951, no. 215, p. 1694.

5.   On Heyes, see 'Niche in history for Immigration "Boss"', *Sydney Morning Herald,* 3 November 1961. cf., Heyes's own comment in *New Era* 32, February 1951, p. 22.

6.   N. W. Lamidey, Partial success. My years as a public servant, December 1970, pp. 40; 72; 75; 81.

7.   RSSAILA., Annual Report, 1950, p. 22; 1951, pp. 29–30.

8.   W. D. Borrie, *Immigration: Australia's Problems and Prospects,* Angus and Robertson, Sydney, 1949, p. 88.

9.   *Good Neighbour,* February 1958.

10.   W. D. Borrie in A. F. Madden and W. H. Morris-Jones (eds), *Australia and Britain: studies in a changing relationship,* Sydney University Press, Sydney, 1980, pp. 101–2.

11.   A. Grenfell Price, *Australia comes of age,* Georgian House, Melbourne, 1945, pp. 86–7; 136.

12.   C. A. Price, *German settlers in South Australia,* Melbourne University Press, Melbourne, 1945, pp. 3; 13–4; 81. Price did note that the First World War had put a severe strain on Germans in S.A. But, he said, 'like "Brer Rabbit" they "lay low" to see what happened' (p. 29).

13.   C. A. Price in *Anatomy of Australia: proceedings of H.R.H. The Duke of Edinburgh's Third Commonwealth Study Conference,* Sun Books, Melbourne, 1968, p. 111; J. Wilkes (ed.), *How many Australians?,* AIPS Summer School Papers, Sydney, 1971, p. 192.

14.   J. Zubrzycki, *Settlers of the Latrobe Valley,* ANU Press, Canberra, 1964, pp. 160; 183. J. Zubrzycki in M. Bowen (ed.), *Australia 2000: the ethnic impact,* University of New England, Armidale, 1977, pp. 130; 137. See also *Quadrant* VIII, 1969, pp. 61–6.

15.   R. Taft, 'Opinion convergence in the assimilation of immigrants', *Australian Journal of Psychology* 14, 1962, pp. 47–9.

16.   A. Richardson, *British immigrants and Australia: a psycho-social enquiry,* ANU Press, Canberra, 1974, pp. 24 fn. 1; 37.

17.   J. Yeomans, 'Nino Today', *Walkabout* 31, March 1965, p. 24.

18.   J. P. O'Grady, *They're a weird mob,* Ure Smith, Sydney, 1957, pp. 204–5.

19.   Borrie, *Italians and Germans in Australia,* Cheshire, Melbourne, 1954, p.xiv.

20. Quoted by J. I. Martin, *The Ethnic Dimension,* George Allen & Unwin, Sydney, 1981, p. 27.

21. See R. White, *Inventing Australia: images and identity 1688-1980,* George Allen & Unwin, Sydney, 1981; and 'A Backwater Awash: The Australian Experience of Americanisation', *Theory, Culture and Society* 3, 1983.

22. Wilkes (ed.), *How many Australians?,* p. 169.

23. R. G. Menzies, *Speech is of time,* Cassell, London, 1958, pp. 18-20.

24. Australia, House of Representatives, *Debates,* 1958, no. 18, p. 288.

25. See reports in *Good Neighbour,* March 1956, February, June, August, November 1958, April 1959.

26. ibid., February 1959.

27. H. I. London, *Non-white Immigration and the 'White Australia Policy',* Sydney University Press, Sydney, 1970, especially pp. 107-142; 173-7; R. N. Rosecrance in L. Hartz (ed.), *The founding of new societies,* Harcourt, Brace and World, New York, 1964, pp. 316-8.

28. C. Kiernan, *Calwell,* Nelson, Melbourne, 1978, p. 133.

29. P. Blazey, *Bolte: a political biography,* Jacaranda, Brisbane, 1972, p. 240.

30. Australia, House of Representatives, *Debates,* 1972, no. 80, p. 2051.

31. A. Richardson and R. Taft, 'Australian attitudes towards immigrants: a review of social survey findings', *International Migration Review* 2, 1968, p. 48 cf. London, *Non-white Immigration,* pp. 148-9.

32. Apart from London, for the White Australia Policy see A. C. Palfreeman, *The Administration of the White Australia Policy,* Melbourne University Press, Melbourne, 1967; A. T. Yarwood (ed.), *Attitudes to non-European immigration,* Cassell, Sydney, 1968.

33. London, *Non-white Immigration,* p. 38.

34. Grenfell Price, *Australia comes of age,* p. 44; Borrie, *Immigration: Australia's Problems and Prospects,* p. 76.

35. Australia, House of Representatives, *Debates,* 1973, no. 83, p. 1909.

36. Jupp, *Arrivals and Departures,* p. 15.

37. Australia, House of Representatives, *Debates,* 1967, no. 56, p. 947.

38. L. Oakes, *Whitlam P. M.,* Angus & Robertson, Sydney, 1973, p. 163.

39. Quoted in Bowen (ed.), *Australia 2000,* pp. 50-1.

40. A. J. Grassby, *The Morning After,* Judicator Publications, Canberra, 1979, pp. 9-10; 18, 24, 51.

41. F. Daly, *From Curtin to Kerr,* Sun Books, Melbourne, 1977, p. 250.

42. Australia, House of Representatives, *Debates,* 1973, no. 83, p. 1914.

43. *Sydney Morning Herald,* 7 July 1980.

44. *Australian,* 28 February 1978.

45. M. J. R. MacKellar, *The population challenge,* AGPS, Canberra, 1977, p. 13.

46. Review of Post-arrival Programs and Services for Migrants, *Migrant Services and Programs,* Report, AGPS, Canberra, 1978, p. 4; *Sydney Morning Herald,* 11 March 1983.

47. *Good Neighbour,* August 1950.

48. *Good Neighbour,* September 1959, January 1961, April 1963.
49. For example, see, A. L. Putniņš, *Latvians in Australia,* ANU Press, Canberra, 1981, p. 13; A. Giordano, *Marco Polo ... and after,* published by the author, Adelaide, 1974, pp. 9; 13; A. P. L. Stuer, *The French in Australia,* ANU Press, Canberra, 1982, p. 20.
50. B. H. Travers, Speech Day report to SCEGS, 1981, p. 18.

Chapter 3 'Reffos' Old and New

1. *People,* 15 March, 2 August, 13 September, 22 November 1950, 14 February 1951.
2. *Bulletin,* 9 July 1977.
3. *Daily Telegraph,* 28 March 1978.
4. *Sydney Morning Herald,* 16 September 1981.
5. D. Malouf, *An Imaginary Life,* Chatto & Windus, London, 1978, p. 135.
6. B. Brecht, 'Sonnet on Emigration', *Times Literary Supplement,* 16 January 1981.
7. S. Stedman, 'The Jewish Workers' Association in Brisbane', *The Bridge* VII, 1973, p. 27.
8. A. R. Chisholm, *Men were my milestones,* Melbourne University Press, Melbourne, 1958, pp. 119–20.
9. P. Goldhar, 'The Funeral', *Coast to Coast,* 1944, p. 20.
10. Chisholm, *Men were my milestones,* pp. 126–8; 132.
11. A. J. Sherman, *Island Refuge: Britain and refugees from the Third Reich,* University of California, Berkeley, 1973, pp. 105–6.
12. See generally D. Wyman, *Paper walls: America and the refugee crisis 1938–1941,* University of Massachusetts Press, Boston, 1968 p. 50; cf., B. Wasserstein, *Britain and the Jews of Europe 1939–1945,* Institute of Jewish Affairs, Clarendon Press, Oxford, 1979.
13. Wasserstein, *Britain and the Jews of Europe 1939–1945,* p. 46.
14. N. Angell and D. F. Buxton, *You and the refugee: the morals and economics of the problem,* Penguin, Harmondsworth, 1939, pp. 259–63.
15. R. Lemberg, 'The Problem of Refugee Immigration', *Australian Quarterly* XI, 3, 1939, p. 23.
16. I. N. Steinberg, *Australia – the unpromised land,* Gollancz London, 1948, especially pp. 21–2; 118–20; and W. D. Borrie, *Immigration: Australia's Problems and Prospects,* Angus & Robertson, 1949, Sydney, p. 89.
17. P. Y. Medding, The Melbourne Jewish community since 1945, MA thesis, University of Melbourne, 1962, p. 154.
18. Australian Archives (Melbourne), Dept. of the Army, MP 729/6, item 63/401/122, unsigned memorandum, 10 July 1940; ibid, item 63/401/141, W. P. Scott, O.C. 'Q Troops' to O.C. Prisoners of War, Information Bureau, Australian Forces, n.d.; ibid., Dept of the Army Minute Paper, November 1940. See also S. Encel, 'These Men are Dangerous', *Nation,* 18 September 1965; B. Patkin, *The Dunera Internees,* Cassell, Sydney, 1979; and, for a happier

account of the experience, K. G. Loewald, 'A Dunera internee at Hay 1940–1941', *Historical Studies* 17, 1977, pp. 512–21.

19.   J. and G. Kolko, *The Limits of Power, The World and United States Foreign Policy, 1945–1954*, Harper and Row, New York, 1972, p. 161.

20.   A. Kefala, *Thirsty Weather*, Outback, Collingwood, 1978, p. 13.

21.   ibid., p. 15.

22.   C. Kunrathy, *Impudent foreigner*, Edwards and Shaw, Sydney, n.d., p. 87.

23.   V. L. Borin, *The Uprooted Survive*, Heinemann, London, 1959, pp. 112–13.

24.   D. Chub, *So this is Australia*, Bayda Books, Melbourne, 1980, p. 25; and M. C. Cleggett, Migrants in the DLP, MA thesis, La Trobe University, 1971, p. 253.

25.   *H. Cartier-Bresson: Photographer*, Thames and Hudson, London, 1980, plate 68.

26.   J. Vernant, *The Refugee in the Post-war World*, George Allen & Unwin, London, 1953, p. 11.

27.   L. W. Holborn, *Refugees: The Problem of Our Time*, 2 vols, Scarecrow Press, Metuchen NJ, 1975, Vol. 1, p. 622 and Vol. 2, p. 1432.

28.   Department of Immigration and Ethnic Affairs, *Refugees and Australia. A perspective*, AGPS, Canberra, 1981, p. 6.

29.   E. Barcs, 'His Majesty's most loyal internees ...', *Quadrant* XII, 51, pp. 14–15; 18.

30.   M. L. Kovacs, Immigration and assimilation: an outline account of the IRO immigrants in Australia, MA thesis, University of Melbourne, 1955, pp. 424, 429; and L. Hawthorne (ed.), *Refugee: the Vietnamese experience*, Oxford University Press Melbourne, 1982, p. 70.

31.   I. Ehrenburg, *People and Life*, Macgibbon and Kee, London, 1961, p. 72.

32.   The source of the idea was the famous, if hurried and superficial, work by E. C. Banfield, *The moral basis of a backward society*, Free Press, New York, 1958.

33.   Z. Kruk, *The taste of hope*, Hutchinson, Melbourne, 1977, p. 172; cf., her war memoirs, *The taste of fear: a Polish childhood in Germany*, Hutchinson, London, 1973.

Chapter 4   Emigrants and their Odysseys.

1.   Y. Kemal, *Memed, my hawk*, Collins and Harvill, London, 1961, pp. 6; 24; 176.

2.   R. M. Bell, *Fate and Honor, Family and Village: demographic and cultural change in rural Italy since 1800*, Chicago University Press, Chicago, 1979, pp. 30–6.

3.   See, for example, V. Moberg, *The Emigrants*, Lannestock, London, 1956; M. Hong Kingston, *Woman Warrior*, Penguin, Harmondsworth, 1976, and her *China Men*, Picador, London, 1981; and A. V. Savona and M. L. Straniero (eds), *Canti dell'emigrazione*, Garzanti, Milan, 1976.

4. W. D. Borrie, *The growth and control of world population*, Weidenfeld and Nicolson, London, 1970, p. 89; J. Kirkpatrick, *Leader and vanguard in mass society: a study of Peronist Argentina*, MIT Press, Cambridge, Mass., 1971, pp. 17–19.

5. M. L. Hansen, *The immigrant in American history*, Harper and Row, New York, 1964, p. 6.

6. E. F. Kunz, *Blood and Gold*, Cheshire, Melbourne, 1969, pp. 61;70.

7. A. P. L. Stuer, *The French in Australia*, ANU Press, Canberra, 1982, p. 44.

8. L. Paszkowski, *Polacy w Australii i Oceanii 1790–1940*, B. Swiderski, London, 1962, p. 21.

9. P. Bosi, *Blood sweat and guts*, published by the author, Sydney, 1970, p. 12; I. Getzler, *Neither toleration nor favour*, Melbourne University Press, Melbourne, 1970, p. 14; and Stuer, *The French in Australia*, ANU Press, Canberra, 1982, p. 41.

10. A. Papageorgopoulos, *The Greeks in Australia – A home away from home*, Alpha Books, Sydney, 1981, pp. 40–2.

11. C. Y. Choi, *Chinese migration and settlement in Australia* , Sydney University Press, Sydney, 1975, pp. 19–20.

12. The fundamental study remains G. Mosse, *The nationalisation of the masses*, Howard Fertig, New York, 1975.

13. L. Avagliano (ed.), *L'emigrazione italiana*, Ferraro, Naples, 1976, pp. 112–13; A. Cornelisen, *Flight from Torregreca*, Macmillan, London, 1980, p. 132; P. Loizos, *The Greek gift: politics in a Cypriot village*, Blackwell, Oxford, 1975; E. Friedl, *Vasilika: a village in modern Greece*, Holt, Rinehart and Winston, New York, 1962.

14. See the beautiful film about Sardinia and the book on which it was based G. Ledda, *Padre padrone: the education of a shepherd*, Allen Lane, London, 1979; pp. 146, 170 refer to Sardinian migration to Australia.

15. D. Dolci, *Poverty in Sicily*, Penguin, Harmondsworth, 1966, p. 251.

16. Bell, *Fate and Honor, Family and Village*, p. 3.

17. For example, G. Capra, 'Il partito operaio in Australia: suo sforzo – suoi trionfi', *Critica Sociale* XIX, 1 May 1909; and J. Tampke, *Wunderbar Country*, Hale and Iremonger, Sydney, 1982, especially pp. 28–41.

18. M. C. Catalano, *L'era del Pacifico*, Fratelli Bocca, Milan, 1939, pp. 113–14; P. Zappa, *Singapore, porta del Pacifico*, Corbaccio, Milan, 1941, pp. 106–113.

19. W. K. Hancock, *Australia*, rev. edn, Jacaranda, Brisbane, 1961, p. 127.

20. P. A. Allum, *Politics and society in post-war Naples*, Cambridge University Press, Cambridge, 1973, p. 19.

21. J. and G. Kolko, *The Limits of Power, The World and United States Foreign Policy, 1945–1954*, Harper and Row, New York, 1972, pp. 161; 176–9; 185.

22. W. Petersen, *Some factors influencing post-war emigration from the Netherlands*, Martinus Nijhoff, The Hague, 1952, pp. 12–13.

23. Z. Ciuffoletti and M. Degl'Innocenti, *L'emigrazione nella storia d'Italia, 1868–1975*, Vallecchi, Florence, 1978, Vol. II, p. 232.

24. For these and many further details, see Department of Immigration and Ethnic Affairs, *Australian Immigration: consolidated statistics No. 12, 1981,* AGPS, Canberra, 1982, pp. 34–7. Characteristically, immigrants from the British Commonwealth are listed first, other countries come after, alphabetically, as in Victorian stamp albums.
25. J. Wilton and S. Rizzo, 'Limina: a Sicilian village and Australia', in G. Cresciani (ed.), *Australia, the Australians and the Italian Migration,* F. Angeli, Milan, 1983.
26. *International Migration* 1X, 3/4, 1971, p. 107.
27. Ciuffoletti and Degl'Innocenti, *L'emigrazione nella storia d'Italia,* Vol. I, pp. 51–2.
28. G. Are and L. Giusti, 'La scoperta dell'imperialismo nella cultura italiana del primo Novecento', *Nuova Rivista Storica* LIX, 1975, p. 108.
29. Avagliano (ed.), *L'emigrazione italiana,* p. 49.
30. Ciuffoletti and Degl'Innocenti, *L'emigrazione nella storia d'Italia,* Vol. I, pp. 99–100.
31. Avagliano (ed.), *L'emigrazione italiana,* p. 305.
32. P. V. Cannistraro and G. Rosoli, 'Fascist emigration policy in the 1920s, an interpretative framework', *International Migration Review* XIII, 1979, p. 687.
33. Ciuffoletti and Degl'Innocenti, *L'emigrazione nella storia d'Italia,* Vol. II, p. 252.
34. ibid., Vol. II, pp. 274; 296; 358.
35. ibid., Vol. II, pp. 337; 358.
36. For example, S. Fitzgerald, *China and the overseas Chinese,* Cambridge University Press, Cambridge, 1972; and A. T. Yarwood, *Asian Migration to Australia,* Melbourne University Press, Melbourne, 1967, pp. 104; 120–1.
37. Petersen, *Some factors influencing post-war emigration from the Netherlands,* p. 66.
38. 'Italian Emigration', *International Migration* IV, 2, 1966, pp. 125–6; J. Mendez and O. Moro, 'The Relation between Economic Policy and Economic Development and the Promotion of New Employment Possibilities for Returnees', *International Migration* IV, 1/2, 1976, p. 148.
39. G. Mottura and E. Pugliese, 'Observations on some characteristics of Italian emigration in the last fifteen years', *International Review of Community Development* 27/28, 1972, p. 19; U. B. Engelbrektsson, *The force of tradition. Turkish migrants at home and abroad,* Acta Universitatis Gothoburgensis, Göteborg 1978, pp. 62–74.
40. F. Piselli, *Parentela ed emigrazione: mutamente e continuità in una comunitá calabrese,* Einaudi, Turin, 1981, pp. xiv; 21; 41; 50; 181.
41. C. White, *Patrons and partisans: a study of politics in two Southern Italian 'comuni',* Cambridge University Press, Cambridge, 1980, p. 37.
42. Engelbrektsson, *The force of tradition,* pp. 74–5.
43. See J. Steinberg, *Why Switzerland?* Cambridge University Press, Cambridge, 1976.
44. C. Levi, *Christ stopped at Eboli,* Cassell, London, 1949, pp. 122–3.

45. F. Paisio, 'Homesickness' in R. H. Morrison (ed.), *Australia's Italian Poets,* Andor, Adelaide, 1976, p. 85.

46. For the full details on Italy see E. Sori, *L'emigrazione italiana dall'unità alla seconda guerra mondiale,* il Mulino, Bologna, 1979; B. M. Colakovic, *Yugoslav migrations to America,* R. and E. Research Associates, San Francisco, 1973, p. 65.

47. W. D. Borrie, 'The role of immigrants in population growth', *Australian Quarterly* XVI, 2, 1944, p. 32.

48. S. L. Thompson, *Australia through Italian eyes,* Oxford University Press, Melbourne, 1980, p. 231.

49. C. A. Price (ed.), *Greeks in Australia,* ANU Press, Canberra, 1975 pp. 15-16; T. P. Lianos, 'Flows of Greek out-migration and return migration', *International Migration* XIII, 3, 1975, pp. 122-3.

50. Australia. Senate Standing Committee on Foreign Affairs and Defence, *Australia and the refugee problem,* Parliamentary Paper No. 329, 1976, p. 118.

51. S. Harvey, 'Dutch return emigration', *La Trobe Sociology Papers* 4, n.d. p. 10.

52. Turiddu Chirico, 'Send Me' in Morrison (ed.), *Australia's Italian poets,* pp. 22-3.

53. Cornelisen, *Flight from Torregreca,* p. 301.

54. *Good Neighbour,* November 1955.

Chapter 5   Justification by Work

1. Department of Immigration, *Australia and your Future,* n.d. (1950?), p. 7; and *Your Introduction to Australia,* 1949, p. 3.

2. N. E. Botsas, 'Emigration and capital formation: the case of Greece', *Balkan Studies* 10, 1969, pp. 127-34.

3. J. Wilkes (ed.), *How many Australians?,* AIPS Summer School Papers, Sydney, 1971, pp. 4; 6; 8; 13; 83; 131-6; 155-6.

4. R. Birrell et al. (eds), *Refugees, resources, reunion: Australia's immigration dilemma,* VCTA Publishing, Melbourne, 1979, pp. 51-67; 93-6.

5. R. and T. Birrell, *An issue of people: population and Australian society,* Longman, Melbourne, 1981, pp. 67; 107.

6. *Sydney Morning Herald,* 18 February 1982.

7. ibid., 13 December 1982; cf., R. Birrell, 'How many migrants?', *Australian Society* 1, 22 October 1982, pp. 21-3.

8. *Sydney Morning Herald,* 14 December 1982.

9. *Sydney Morning Herald,* 16 February 1952.

10. D. Burrows, *Above the snowline,* Educational Press, Sydney, 1959.

11. Australia, House of Representatives, *Debates,* 1953, no. 221, p. 143. *Age,* 25 August 1956; and J. Zubrzycki, *Settlers of the Latrobe Valley,* ANU Press, Canberra, 1964, pp. 11-17.

12. N. R. Wills, 'The Iron and Steel industry and the Commonwealth Immigration programme', *Twentieth Century* VIII, 1953-4, pp. 5-19.

13. *Good Neighbour,* December 1950.

14. Department of Immigration, *These are yours,* Canberra, 1959.

15. G. Sherington, *Australia's immigrants 1788–1978,* George Allen & Unwin, Sydney, 1980, especially Ch. 5.

16. *Sun,* 2 August 1981.

17. *Sydney Morning Herald,* 3 January 1983.

18. *Good Neighbour,* March 1951.

19. E. Kunz, *The intruders. Refugee doctors in Australia,* ANU Press, Canberra, 1975, pp. 42–3.

20. *La Fiamma,* 8 July 1961.

21. Kunz, *The intruders,* pp. 113–14.

22. *Age,* 6 March 1978.

23. *Ethnos,* 17, February 1982; *Sydney Morning Herald,* 14 March 1981.

24. M. L. Kovacs, Immigration and assimilation: an outline account of the I.R.O. immigrants in Australia, MA thesis, University of Melbourne, 1955, p. 430.

25. J. Martin, *Refugee Settlers,* ANU Press, Canberra, 1965, p. 58.

26. Zubrzycki, *Settlers of the Latrobe Valley,* p. 162.

27. S. L. Thompson, *Australia through Italian eyes,* Oxford University Press, Melbourne, 1980, p. 72.

28. W. Lowenstein and M. Loh (eds), *The Immigrants,* Hyland House, Melbourne, 1977, pp. 112–13.

29. D. Sinclair in I. Burnley, R. Pryor and D. Rowland (eds), *Mobility and community change in Australia,* University of Queensland Press, St. Lucia, 1980, p. 143.

30. Lowenstein and Loh (eds), *The Immigrants,* p. 99.

31. C. Lever Tracy, Post-war Immigrants in Australia and Western Europe, in reserve or centre forward?, paper delivered to Ethnicity and Class Conference, Wollongong, 1981, p. 11; C. A. Price (ed.), *Australian immigration: A bibliography and digest* 4, supplement, Dept of Demography, ANU, Canberra, 1981, p. 31; and 'Migrant Workforce Fact Sheet', *Migration Action* VI, 2, 1982 (supplement).

32. Ethnic Affairs Commission of NSW, *Participation,* NSW Government Printer, 1979, p. 160.

33. A. Matheson *'Migrants in the Workforce'* in M. Bowen (ed.) *Australia 2000: the ethnic impact,* University of New England Press, Armidale, 1977, p. 195; R. and T. Birrell, *An issue of people,* Longman Cheshire, pp. 123–4; and A. Burbidge, J. Caputo and R. Rosenblatt, *'They said we'd get jobs',* CURA, Melbourne, 1982, pp. ii; 11.

34. E. Sori, *L'emigrazione italiana dall'Unità alla seconda guerra mondiale,* il Mulino, Bologna, 1979, p. 159.

35. Anne Deveson, *Australians at Risk,* Cassell, Sydney, 1973, pp. 369–70.

36. *Age,* 25 March 1948.

37. J. Hearn in D. Storer (ed.), *Ethnic Rights, Power and Participation,* CHOMI, Richmond, 1975, p. 67.

38. M. Quinlan, 'Australian Trade Unions and Post-war Immigration: Attitudes and Responses', *Journal of Industrial Relations* 2, 3, 1979, p. 269.
39. Thompson, *Australia through Italian eyes*, p. 78.
40. Kovacs, Immigration and assimilation, p. 276.
41. Quinlan, 'Australian Trade Unions ...' pp. 274; 268.
42. V. L. Borin, *The Uprooted Survive*, Heinemann, London, 1959, p. 157.
43. Thompson, *Australia through Italian eyes*, pp. 81–2.
44. P. Georgiou, 'Migrants, Unionism and Society', *Australian and New Zealand Journal of Sociology* 9, 1973, p. 39.
45. Department of Immigration and Ethnic Affairs, From the Ethnic Press 210, 1980.
46. N. Brennan (ed.), *The Migrant Worker: proceedings and papers of the Migrant Workers' Conference October 1973*, Melbourne, 1974.
47. R. Huber, *From Pasta to Pavlova*, University of Queensland Press, St Lucia, 1977, p. 76.
48. S. E. Teo, 'A Preliminary Study of the Chinese Community in Sydney: A Basis for the Study of Social Change', *The Australian Geographer* XI, 6, 1971, pp. 583–4.
49. C. Price, 'Southern Europeans in Australia: Problems of Assimilation', *International Migration Review* 2, 3, 1968, p. 8.

Chapter 6 Home, Health, and Happiness

1. P. Corte, 'Nel paese dei kanguroo e degli opossum', *Rivista d'Italia* VI, 1903, p. 1001.
2. P. Zappa, *Singapore, porta del Pacifico*, Corbaccio, Milan, 1941, pp. 110–12.
3. *Bulletin de l'Organisation Internationale pour les Réfugiés* 16, December 1949.
4. *Good Neighbour*, May 1953.
5. Department of Immigration, *Australia and your future*, Australian News and Information Bureau, London, 1951, p. 21.
6. A. Kondos and A. Messina, Migrants and the Australian Dream. A preliminary survey of migrant housing situations, unpublished report, University of NSW, 1980, p. 63.
7. I. Milutinovic, *Talk English Carn't Ya*, Hyland House, Melbourne, 1978, p. 1.
8. W. Lowenstein and M. Loh (eds), *The Immigrants*, Hyland House, Melbourne, 1977, pp. 90–1; 138.
9. R. Boyd, *The Australian Ugliness*, rev. edn, Penguin, Ringwood, 1980, pp. 65–6.
10. Australia. House of Representatives, *Debates*, 1945, no. 185, p. 6020 and 1951, no. 215, p. 1685.
11. Department of Immigration, *Reunion in Australia*, Australian News and Information Bureau, London, n.d. (1948?)
12. B. Patkin, *The Dunera Internees*, Cassell, Sydney, 1979, pp. 72–3; E. Barcs, 'His Majesty's Most Loyal Internees', *Quadrant* XII, 53, 1968, pp. 70–71; 75.

13. *Good Neighbour,* September 1950.

14. C. Kunrathy, *Impudent foreigner,* Edwards and Shaw, Sydney, n.d., p. 137.

15. D. Chub, *So this is Australia,* Bayda Books, Melbourne, 1980, p. 15; *Good Neighbour,* December 1952.

16. *Meie Kodu* 5, 16 September 1949.

17. A. Fitzgerald, *The Italian Farming Soldiers,* Melbourne University Press, Melbourne, 1981, pp. 153–63.

18. W.D. Borrie, *Immigration: Australia's Problems and Prospects,* Angus & Robertson, Sydney, 1949, p. 91.

19. Kondos and Messina, Migrants and the Australian Dream, p. 122.

20. Australia. House of Representatives, *Debates,* 1973, no. 86, p. 3113.

21. J. Vondra, *Paul Zwilling,* Wren Publishing, Melbourne, 1974, p. 14.

22. T. McBride, B. Rothberg, A. Arellaro and E. Rios, 'Hostels. Who are they for?', *Ekstasis* 13, 1975, p. 4.

23. L. Hawthorne (ed.), *Refugee: The Vietnamese Experience,* Oxford University Press, Melbourne, 1982, pp. 320–1; S. L. Thompson, *Australia through Italian eyes,* Oxford University Press, Melbourne, 1980, p. 100; *Australian,* 17 January 1978.

24. Kondos and Messina, Migrants and the Australian Dream, p. 121.

25. See, for example, J. V. Marshall, Sanctuary Down Under, unpublished manuscript, n.d. (1950?), pp. 95–109.

26. L. Berzins in M. Jurgensen (ed.), *Ethnic Australia,* Phoenix, Brisbane, 1981, pp. 194–200.

27. Senate Standing Committee on Foreign Affairs and Defence, *Australia and the Refugee Problem,* AGPS, Canberra, 1977, p. 134.

28. *La Fiamma,* 8 November 1982; *Il Globo,* 3 January 1983.

29. McBride et al., 'Hostels ...' p. 2.

30. Marshall, Sanctuary Down Under, pp. 73–82.

31. Report of the Committee appointed by the Minister for Immigration to investigate the grounds for the withholding of tariff payments by British migrants, p. 5; S. Johnston, *We Came to Australia,* Methuen, Sydney, 1980, p. 93.

32. *Australian,* 20 January 1978.

33. Kondos and Messina, Migrants and the Australian Dream, p. 123.

34. M. Loh (ed.), *With courage in their cases,* FILEF, Melbourne, 1980, pp. 46–7.

35. I. Kobal, *Men who built the Snowy,* Centre Books, Sydney, 1982, p. 26.

36. D. A. Sinclair in I. H. Burnley, R. J. Pryor and D. T. Rowland (eds), *Mobility and community change in Australia,* University of Queensland Press, St. Lucia, 1980, p. 147.

37. Kondos and Messina, Migrants and the Australian Dream, pp. 41–5.

38. D. Menghetti, *The Red North,* James Cook University of North Queensland Press, Townsville, 1981, p. 54.

39. *Sun-Herald,* 5 April 1981.

40. Thompson, *Australia through Italian eyes,* pp. 106–7; 114.

41. P. Skrzynecki, '10 Mary St' in P. Skrzynecki, *Immigrant Chronicle,* University of Queensland Press, St. Lucia, 1975, p. 17.

42. T. Aslanides, 'Open, Seven Days a Week', *Sydney Morning Herald,* 15 March 1982.

43. J. Wilton and S. Rizzo, 'Limina: a Sicilian village and Australia'; in G. Cresciani (ed.), *Australia, the Australians and the Italian Migration,* F. Angeli, Milan, 1983.

44. Kunrathy, *Impudent Foreigner,* p. 115.

45. P. Bosi, *Farewell Australia,* Kurunda Publications, Sydney, n.d., pp. 6; 18; 33; 71.

46. Vondra, *Paul Zwilling,* pp. 34; 78.

47. P. Bien, J. Rassias and C. Bien, *Demotic Greek,* University Press of New England, Hanover, New Hampshire, 1972.

48. V. Kalamaras 'Mademoiselle' in V. Kalamaras, *Other Earth: four Greek Australian stories,* Fremantle Arts Centre, Fremantle, 1977, pp. 35–44.

49. C. Price, P. Pyne, E. Baker, 'Immigrants in the vital statistics' in C. A. Price (ed.), *Australian Immigration: a bibliography and digest* 4, Supplement, Dept of Demography, ANU Canberra, 1981, pp. 35–6.

50. M. Friend and L. Sharpe in N. Parker (ed.), *Focus on migrants,* Australian Council of Social Services, Sydney, 1973, pp. 18–21.

51. H. E. R. Townsend, 'Towards a multicultural society', *Melbourne Studies in Education,* 1976, p. 34.

52. Ethnic Communities Council of New South Wales, *I'm an Australian too!,* The Consultancy, Sydney, 1981, p. 54.

53. A. Ata, 'The Lebanese in Melbourne: ethnicity, inter-ethnic activities and attitudes to Australia', *Australian Quarterly,* September 1979, p. 49.

54. D. Buckland, 'The Greek Family in Australia and the Process of Migration', *Polycom* 5, 1973, p. 21.

55. A. Richardson, *British immigrants and Australia,* ANU Press, Canberra, 1974, p. 20.

56. J. Martin, *The Migrant Presence,* George Allen & Unwin, Sydney, 1978, pp. 151–68. See also T. Dolk, Submission to the Inquiry into Health Services for the psychiatrically ill and developmentally disabled, Ethnic Affairs Commission of NSW, 1982.

57. J. O'Grady, *They're a weird mob,* Ure Smith, Sydney, 1957, p. 10.

58. *Sydney Morning Herald,* 24 January 1961.

59. ibid., 17 June 1981.

60. *Glebe,* 24 June 1981.

61. R. D. Francis, *Migrant Crime in Australia,* University of Queensland Press, St Lucia, 1981, pp. 141; 143.

62. *Good Neighbour,* October 1950.

63. *Sydney Morning Herald,* 4 February 1939.

64. Australian Archives (Canberra), Dept of the Interior, A434, item 48/3/5501, Secretary, ALP Port Kembla Branch to Calwell, 27 March 1948.

65.   Australia. House of Representatives, *Debates*, 1950, no. 210, p. 1874.
66.   *Sydney Morning Herald*, 13 February, 9 April 1981.
67.   I. H. Burnley, *Urbanization in Australia*, Cambridge University Press, Cambridge, 1974, pp. 169–75.
68.   ibid., p. 11; G. J. Hugo and B. J. Menzies in Burnley et al. *Mobility and community change*, pp. 175–6.
69.   G. Mikes, *Boomerang: Australia re-discovered*, Andre Deutsch, London, 1968, p. 82.

Chapter 7   Culture High and Low

1.   Department of Immigration and Information, *Your Introduction to Australia*, Federal Capital Press, Canberra, 1949 reprint, p. 3 and *Know Australia!*, Dept of Information, Melbourne, 1948 (8th ed.), p. 27.
2.   R. Johnston, *Future Australians*, ANU Press, Canberra, 1972, p. 145.
3.   J. Hearn, Migrant Political Attitudes, MA thesis, University of Melbourne, 1971, p. 133.
4.   L. Szymanski, *Living with the Weird Mob*, Trident International Books, Los Angeles, n.d. (1972?), p. 20.
5.   E. Barcs, 'His Majesty's most loyal internees ...', *Quadrant* XII, 55, 1968, p. 53.
6.   G. Serle, *From deserts the prophets come*, Heinemann, Melbourne, 1973, p. 225.
7.   D. Horne, 'An Australia without immigrants', *Bulletin* 93, 1 May 1971, p. 20.
8.   A. J. Grassby in J. Condous, J. Howlett and J. Skull (eds), *Arts in cultural diversity*, Holt, Rinehart and Winston, Sydney, 1980, p. 161.
9.   Serle, *From deserts the prophets come*, p. 56.
10.   APIC and AEAC, *Multi-culturalism and its implications for immigration policy*, AGPS Canberra, 1979, p. 3.
11.   W. A. Orchard, *The Distant View*, Currawong Publishing, Sydney, 1943, pp. 101–20; 203–10.
12.   D. Watson, *Brian Fitzpatrick*, Hale and Iremonger, Sydney, 1979, p. 68.
13.   M. Sagiova, *With Music to Eternity*, Hawthorne Press, Melbourne, 1972, p. 108.
14.   *Musica Viva Bulletin* 15, 4, August 1963.
15.   D. P. Mellor, *The Role of Science and Industry*, Australian War Memorial, Canberra, 1958, pp. 654–5.
16.   *Bulletin*, 10 July 1976, p. 32.
17.   N. Prychodko, *Good-Bye Siberia*, Simon and Schuster, Ontario, 1976.
18.   For a general discussion, see R. Bosworth and J. Wilton, 'Novels, poems and the study of Europeans in Australia' *Teaching History* 15, 1981, pp. 43–68.
19.   R. Brasch, *Australian Jews of Today*, Cassell Australia, Sydney, 1977, p. 134. N. Keesing, 'Where does a man belong?', *Overland* 63, 1976, pp. 10–15; A. A. Phillips, 'The writings of David Martin', *Meanjin* 20, 1, 1961.

20. J. Waten, 'My two literary careers', *Southerly* 31, 1971, pp. 87–8.

21. J. Waten, *Love and rebellion*, Macmillan, Melbourne, 1978, p. 99 cf., the neo-realism of *Season of Youth*, Gold Star, Melbourne, 1972.

22. J. A. Petrolias, Post-war Greek and Italian migrants in Melbourne, PhD thesis, University of Melbourne, 1959, p. 139

23. *Corriere della Sera*, 25–6 August 1982.

24. *Sydney Morning Herald*, 26 July 1982. See also *Bulletin*, 3 August 1982.

25. *Bulletin*, 10 August 1982.

26. *Digest*, 1952, p. 5

27. K. Milanov, 'Towards the assimilation of New Australians', *Australian Quarterly* XXIII, 2, 1951, p. 75.

28. *Sydney Morning Herald*, 26 September 1977.

29. J. Wilton and S. Rizzo, 'Limina: A Sicilian village and Australia' in G. Cresciani (ed.), *Australia, the Australians and the Italian Migration*, F. Angeli, Milan, 1983.

30. J. O'Grady, *They're a weird mob*, Ure Smith, Sydney, 1957, p. 74. See also F. Lewins, *The Myth of the Universal Church*, Canberra, 1978, pp. 7; 36.

31. F. Vecoli, 'Prelates and peasants: Italian immigrants and the Catholic Church', *Journal of Social History* 2, 1969, pp. 217–69.

32. M. G. Cleggett, Migrants in the DLP, MA thesis, La Trobe University, 1971, p. 61.

33. R. Huber, *From Pasta to Pavlova*, University of Queensland Press, St Lucia, 1977, pp. 92–3; Lewins, *The Myth of the Universal Church*, ANU Press, Canberra, 1978, p. 102.

34. ibid., pp. 108–15.

35. O'Grady, *They're a weird mob*, p. 164.

36. *Good Neighbour*, December 1950; June 1953.

37. *Sydney Morning Herald*, 22 November 1980.

38. V. De Grazia, *The culture of consent*, Cambridge University Press, Cambridge, 1981, pp. 169–76.

39. *National Times*, 8–14 November 1981.

40. Department of Immigration, *Employers! Want help? how you may obtain European migrant labour*, Canberra, 1949.

41. P. Weller and B. Lloyd (eds), *Federal Executive Minutes, 1915–1955*, Melbourne University Press, Melbourne, 1978, p. 486.

42. A. Richardson and R. Taft, 'Australian attitudes towards Immigrants: A Review of Social Survey Findings', *International Migration Review* 2, 3, 1968, pp. 51–2.

43. J. I. Martin, *The Migrant Presence*, George Allen & Unwin, Sydney, 1978, pp. 85 and 89.

44. J. I. Martin, *The Ethnic Dimension*, George Allen & Unwin, Sydney, 1981, p. 45.

45. E. Isaacs, *Greek Children in Sydney*, ANU Press, Canberra, 1976, pp. ix; 2; 75; 108.

46.   F. Lewins, 'Ethnic Schools and Multiculturalism in Australia', *Journal of Intercultural Studies* 1, 2, 1980, p. 31.

47.   M. P. Tsounis, *Greek ethnic schools in Australia,* ANU Press, Canberra, 1974; Father A. Mirzaian, *Armenians: A Pilgrim People in 'Tierra Australia',* published by the author, Sydney, 1975; and F. Lewins, 'Ethnic Schools and Multi-culturalism in Australia', *Journal of Intercultural Studies* 1, 2, 1980, pp. 30-9.

48.   A. J. Grassby, *Credo for a Nation,* AGPS, Canberra, 1974, p. 15.

49.   See also D. J. Whitton, 'Conformism as a function of survival', *Unicorn* 5, 1, 1979, pp. 24-5.

50.   M. Symons, *One Continuous Picnic,* Duck Press, Adelaide, 1982, pp. 222-4

Chapter 8   Immigrants and Old World Politics

1.   Catholic Bishops of Australia, *Australia's Bold Adventure,* (Pastoral Statement on Immigration), The Advocate Press, Melbourne, 1957, p. 14.

2.   Australia, House of Representatives, *Debates,* 1963, no. 40, p. 2010.

3.   *Sydney Morning Herald,* 2 May 1978; *Sun* 1 May 1978.

4.   J. Zubrzycki in *Australia's multicultural society,* (Meredith Memorial lectures), La Trobe University, Melbourne, 1978, p. 8.

5.   J. Jupp, *Arrivals and Departures,* Cheshire-Lansdowne, Melbourne, 1966, p. 91.

6.   P. Bosi, *Farewell Australia,* Kurunda Publications, Sydney, n.d., pp. 8; 42.

7.   Department of Immigration, *Your Introduction to Australia,* Federal Capital Press, Canberra, 1949, p. 20.

8.   *Good Neighbour,* July 1951; November 1954.

9.   P. R. Wilson, *Immigrants and politics,* ANU Press, Canberra, 1973, pp. 2; 22-3.

10.   Jupp, *Arrivals and Departures,* p. 91.

11.   Wilson, *Immigrants and politics,* p. 3.

12.   N. Mistilis, Explaining voting patterns among immigrant electors, unpublished paper delivered to ANU Ethnic Politics conference, 1981.

13.   J. Hearn, Migrant Political Attitudes, MA thesis, University of Melbourne, 1971, p. 14.

14.   Australia, House of Representatives, *Debates,* 1947, no. 192, p. 2651.

15.   ibid., 1947, no. 190, p. 1015.

16.   Australia. House of Representatives, *Debates,* 1950, no. 211, p. 3788; Australia Archives (Canberra), Dept of the Interior, A434, item 48/3/13193; *Tribune,* 31 July 1948; Australian Archives (Sydney), Commonwealth Investigation Service, CA912, ST 1604/1, item N48432/2.

17.   Australia. House of Representatives, *Debates,* 1950, no. 206, p. 399.

18.   ibid., 1952, no. 220, p. 4141.

19.   Australia. House of Representatives, *Debates,* 1975, no. 96, pp. 828-34, 1667-9.

20.   M. Gilson and J. Zubrzycki, *The foreign-language press in Australia, 1848–1964,* ANU Press, Canberra, 1967, pp. 4, 20–1; G. Kinne, 'Nazi Strategems and Their Effects on Germans in Australia up to 1945', *Journal of the Royal Australian Historical Society* 66, 1, 1980, pp. 1–19; and M. P. Tsounis, 'Greek Communities in Australia' in C. Price (ed.), *Greeks in Australia,* ANU Press, Canberra, 1975, pp. 44–45.

21.   Gilson and Zubrzycki, *The foreign-language press ...,* pp. 40–41.

22.   *La Fiamma,* 7 January 1961; 21 November 1961.

23.   Gilson and Zubrzycki, *The foreign-language press,* pp. 65–66; 147; 153; 161.

24.   C. Kunrathy, *Impudent foreigner,* Edwards and Shaw, Sydney, n.d., p. 80.

25.   E. Barcs, 'His Majesty's most loyal internees ...', *Quadrant* XII, 55, 1968, p. 60 and 'Backyard of Mars', *Quadrant* XX, 113, 1976, p. 65.

26.   On the formation of this group see *Magyar Elet,* 1 May 1980.

27.   S. K. Pavlowitch, 'The King who never was: an instance of Italian involvement in Croatia', *European Studies Review* 8, 1978, pp. 465–87. For some of his war papers which contain appalling evidence about the *Ustaša,* see G. N. Amoretti, *La vicenda italo-croata nei documenti di Aimone di Savoia (1941–3),* Rapallo, 1979, e.g., p. 72.

28.   C. Malaparte, *Kaputt,* Alvin Redman, London, 1948, p. 262.

29.   M. Djilas, *Wartime,* Secker and Warburg, London, 1977.

30.   Australia. House of Representatives, *Debates,* 1963, no. 40, pp. 1994–3; *Outlook* 7, 6, 1963; 'Ustasha's Ins and Outs', *Nation* 145, 1964, pp. 4–7; *Australian,* 6 April 1978; *Bulletin,* 20 November 1979; *Sydney Morning Herald,* 5 August 1981; and *Australian,* 10 October 1981.

31.   Australia, House of Representatives, *Debates,* 1964, no. 42, p. 1808.

32.   T. Voloschka, 'My Ukraine' in R. H. Morrison (ed.), *Australia's Ukrainian Poets,* Hawthorne Press, Melbourne, 1973, p. 50.

33.   *Sydney Morning Herald,* 23 April 1978; *National Times,* 6–12 February 1983.

34.   R. Unikoski, *Communal endeavours,* ANU Press, Canberra, 1978, pp. 20–40; 60–1; 116–17; 128–9.

35.   For a summary of the campaign, see E. Dunsdorf, *The Baltic dilemma,* Speller, New York, 1975; cf., D. Dunstan, *Felicia,* Macmillan, Melbourne, 1981, p. 266; and the descriptive account by a Liberal Senator, J. Knight 'The Baltic States: foreign policy and domestic responses, 1974–8', *Australian Journal of Politics and History* XXV, 1979.

36.   M. L. Kovacs, Immigration and assimilation: an outline account of the IRO immigrants in Australia, MA thesis, University of Melbourne, 1955, pp. 427–28 found that gardening followed closely by reading were the favourite pastimes of her early 1950s group of IRO refugees.

37.   J. Docker, *Australian Cultural Elites,* Angus and Robertson, Sydney, 1974, p. 135.

38.   Unikoski, *Communal endeavours,* p. 153.

39.   H. Richard, *Mary my hun*, H. Richard, Campsie, 1976, pp. 30; 37; 80; 111; 173; 176-7.

40.   J. Vondra, *Paul Zwilling*, Wren Publishing, Melbourne, 1974, pp. 38-9. For his comments on Australian politics, see pp. 48-9.

41.   See J. Boissevain, *Saints and fireworks: religion and politics in rural Malta*, Athlone Press, London, 1965.

42.   H. Opperman, *Pedals, politics and people*, Haldane Publishing, Melbourne, 1977, pp. 445; 480.

43.   G. Cresciani, *Fascism, Anti-Fascism and Italians in Australia 1922-45*, ANU Press, Canberra, 1980; and D. Menghetti, *The Red North*, James Cook University, 1981, p. 88.

44.   R. Huber, *Pasta to Pavlova*, University of Queensland Press, Brisbane, 1977, p. 76.

45.   M. P. Tsounis, Greek communities in Australia, PhD thesis, University of Adelaide, 1971, p. 334.

Chapter 9   Immigrants and Australian Political Structures

1.   B. A. Santamaria, *Point of View*, Hawthorne Press, Melbourne, 1969, pp. 220; 224; B. A. Santamaria, 'The future impact of migration upon Australia', *Twentieth Century* VII, 1952, pp. 33; 37.

2.   See, for example, V. L. Borin, 'Australia: Limited, Horrible and Unlimited', *Quadrant* IV, 1959-60; J. Playford, 'A chequered career', *Outlook* 13, 1969, and K. Milanov, 'Towards the assimilation of New Australians', *Australian Quarterly* XXIII, 2, 1951.

3.   *Sydney Morning Herald*, 19, 20, 21 July 1952.

4.   M. Loh (ed.), *With courage in their cases*, FILEF, Melbourne, 1980, p. 48.

5.   *Sun*, 18 July 1961; and *Sydney Morning Herald*, 19, 21 July 1961.

6.   ibid., 21 July 1961

7.   Loh (ed.), *With courage in their cases*, p. 48; O. Bonutto, *A Migrant's Story*, H. Pole, Brisbane, 1963, p. ix.

8.   Commonwealth Immigration Advisory Committee, *Report*, 27 February 1946, p. 31.

9.   J. Stone, 'Mass German immigration in Australia's future', *Australia Quarterly* XXIII, 1951, p. 23.

10.   *The New Citizen*, 15 February 1949.

11.   ibid., 15 March 1949, 15 December 1949.

12.   *Good Neighbour*, August 1950.

13.   ibid., July 1952.

14.   Good Neighbour Council of NSW, Report of the first area conference, Tamworth, 1958.

15.   *Good Neighbour*, December 1951.

16.   K. Milanov, 'Towards the assimilation of new Australians', p. 75.

17.   *Good Neighbour*, April 1952, April 1954, May 1954.

18.   ibid., November, December 1955, May 1957.

19. M. L. Kovacs, Immigration and Assimilation: An outline account of the IRO immigrants in Australia, MA thesis, University of Melbourne, 1955, p. 431.

20. Good Neighbour Council of NSW, Report of the first area conference.

21. *Good Neighbour*, April 1963, February 1965.

22. Cleggett, Migrants in the DLP, pp. 119; 139; 144.

23. *The Reflex,* Cooma, 1952, pp. 12–13.

24. *Sydney Morning Herald,* 17–18 April 1978; *The Australian,* 17–18 April 1978; *Sun,* 18 April 1978; *Sun-Herald,* 23 April 1978; *Sydney Morning Herald*, 28–29 August and 18 September 1979, 31 January and 29 March 1980.

25. D. Dunstan, *Felicia,* Macmillan, Melbourne, 1981, pp. 35–6.

26. R. Huber, *From Pasta to Pavlova,* University of Queensland Press, Brisbane, 1981, p. 186. See also J. Jupp, *Arrivals and Departures,* Cheshire-Lansdowne, 1966, pp. 86–9; Davies, 'Migrants in Politics', p. 126; I. McAllister, 'Migrants and Australian Politics', *Journal of Intercultural Studies* 2, 3, 1981, pp. 66–8; and L. Allan, 'Ethnic politics – migrant organisation and the Victorian ALP', *Ethnic Studies* 2, 1978, p. 24.

27. *Sydney Morning Herald,* 10, 11 November 1961.

28. I. McAllister and J. Kelly, Changes in the Ethnic Vote in Australia, 1967–79, Paper to Ethnic Politics Conference, Canberra, 1981, pp. 15–19; L. Allan, 'Ethnic politics—migrant organisations and the Victorian ALP', *Ethnic Studies* 2, 1978 and his 'The Ethnic Factor and Australian Politics', *Journal of HSC Politics* 9, 11, March 1981.

29. Ethnic Communities Council of NSW, Proceedings of the inaugural meeting held in the Sydney Town Hall, 27 July 1975, p. 2.

30. See, for example, the address by Bill Hayden, Proceedings of the First National Conference of Ethnic Communities Councils of Australia, Sydney, July 1979, p. 10.

31. Ethnic Affairs Commission of NSW, *Participation,* Government Printer, Sydney, 1979, p. 1.

32. K. Zervos, 'Son of an Englishman', χρονικο Μελβουρνη 1980–81, p. 32.

Chapter 10   Many Little Australias

1. See L. Hartz, 'A Theory of the development of the New Societies' and R. N. Rosecrance 'The radical culture of Australia' in L. Hartz (ed), *The Founding of New Societies,* Harcourt, Brace and World, New York, 1964, especially pp. 4 and 284.

Index

Aborigines, 7, 55, 92, 104
'Afghans', 2
Albanians, 15, 65, 66
Alcorso, Claudio, 59, 168
Alexander, Frederick, 48
Allen, Peter, 37
Alliance, Française, 137, 149
American blacks, 30, 31
Angell, Norman, 48
Anschluss, 46, 133
anti-Semitism
  in Australia, 3, 12, 30–1, 117, 154, 173
  in Europe, 3, 42, 46, 47, 158
Appleyard, Reginald T., 82
Archdale, Betty, 109
Arena, Franca, 181
Argentina, 61, 67, 169
Argentinians, 15
Armenians, 42, 44, 149, 170
army, Australian, 3, 20
Association of New Citizens, 173–4
Association of Refugees, 158, 173
Associations for Immigration Reform, 29
Assyrians, 44
Australia
  Aliens Classification and Advisory Committee, 20
  Commissioner for Community Relations, 34, 182
  Commonwealth Development and Migration Commission, 6
  Commonwealth Hostels Pty Ltd, 107, 113
  Commonwealth Immigration Advisory Council, 11–12, 156
  Commonwealth Investigation Service, 20
  Defence, Department of, 20

  Immigration and Ethnic Affairs, Department of, 17, 18–21, 26–7, 82, 113, 130, 174, 178
  Labour and National Service, Department of, 107
Australia Council, 138
Australian, 34
Australian Council of Trade Unions (ACTU), 48, 96, 98, 99
Australian Ethnic Affairs Council, 23
Australian Immigration Planning Council, 85
Australian Institute of Multicultural Affairs, 182
Australian Institute of Political Science (AIPS), 22, 81
Australian Institute of Public Affairs, 6
Australian Labour Party (ALP), 9, 151
  attitudes to immigrants and immigration, 9, 31, 127, 146, 157, 181
  immigrant participation in , 180
Australian Musicians Union, 133
Australian National University (ANU), 21–3
Australian War Memorial, 20
Australian Workers' Union, (AWU), 126
Austrians, 15, 122, 167

Baer, Werner, 132
Barcs, Emery, 158
Barnes, Charles E., 30
Barton Alexander, 59
Bathurst camp, 107–108, 113, 155–6
Berzins, Lucija, 111
Birrell, Robert, 82

209